Which? Way to
Save Tax
2000-1

Which? Way to
Save Tax
2000-1

CONSUMERS' ASSOCIATION

Which? Books are commissioned and researched by
Consumers' Association, and published by
Which? Ltd, 2 Marylebone Road, London NW1 4DF
Email address: books@which.net

Distributed by The Penguin Group:
Penguin Books Ltd, 27 Wrights Lane, London W8 5TZ

Editor: Anthony Bailey

Other contributors:
Jonquil Lowe, Jane Vass, Virginia Wallis

First edition August 1992
Second edition April 1994
Third edition April 1995
Fourth edition April 1996, reprinted May 1996
Fifth edition April 1997
Sixth edition September 1998
Seventh edition September 1999
Eighth edition September 2000

British Library Cataloguing-in-Publication Data
A catalogue record for this book is available from the
British Library

ISBN 0 85202 842 3

For a full list of Which? books, please write to Which? Books,
Castlemead, Gascoyne Way, Hertford X, SG14 1LH
or access our web site at www.which.net

Typographic design by Lee Riches
Cover design by Sarah Watson
Cover photography by Tony Stone Images/Peter Dazeley
Typeset by Saxon Graphics Ltd, Derby
Printed and bound in Great Britain by Clays Ltd, Bungay, Suffolk

Contents

Tax calendar

• first day of 2000–1 tax year	**6 April 2000**
• tax return for 1999–2000 sent out	**April 2000**
• last date for P60 (showing taxable pay and tax deducted for 1999–2000) to be given to employees and pensioners who come under the PAYE system	**31 May 2000**
• last date for P11D (showing taxable fringe benefits and expenses for tax year 1999–2000) to be given to employees and directors who receive fringe benefits and/or expenses	**6 July 2000**
• the second payment on account for 1999–2000 tax year*	**31 July 2000**
• send back 1999–2000 tax return if you want your tax office to work out your tax bill before payment deadline of 31 January 2001, and/or you want underpayments of tax of up to £1,000 to be collected by PAYE	**30 September 2000**
• last date to tell your tax office about any taxable income or capital gain in 1999–2000 which has not already been taxed in full, if you haven't received a tax return	**5 October 2000**
• last date for sending back 1999–2000 tax return if you want to avoid a penalty	**31 January 2001**
• remaining tax (if any) for 1999–2000, first payment on account for 2000–1*	
• capital gains tax for 1999–2000 due	
• PAYE Coding Notices for 2001–2 tax year sent out	**January/February 2001**
• Budget setting tax rates and allowances for 2001–2 tax year	**March 2001**
• last day of 2000–1 tax year	**5 April 2001**
• first day of 2001–2 tax year	**6 April 2001**
• tax return for 2000–1 sent out	**April 2001**
• last date for P60 (showing taxable pay and tax deducted for 2000–1) to be given to employees and pensioners who come under the PAYE system	**31 May 2001**
• last date for P11D (showing taxable fringe benefits and expenses for tax year 2000–1) to be given to employees and directors who receive fringe benefits and/or expenses	**6 July 2001**
• the second payment on account for 2000–1 tax year*	**31 July 2001**
• send back 2000–1 tax return if you want your tax office to work out your tax bill before payment deadline of 31 January 2002, and/or you want underpayments of tax of up to £1,000 to be collected by PAYE	**30 September 2001**
• last date to tell your tax office about any taxable income or capital gain in 2000–1 which has not already been taxed in full, if you haven't received a tax return	**5 October 2001**
• last date for sending back 2000–1 tax return if you want to avoid a penalty	**31 January 2002**
• remaining tax (if any) for 2000–1, first payment on account for 2001–2*	
• capital gains tax for 2000–1 due	

* Tax on account: profits from self-employment; freelance earnings; income from your job not yet taxed; investment income not taxed at source (including higher-rate tax); income from property; only one payment due (on 31 January following end of tax year) if less than £1,000 tax due

Key figures for the 2000–1 tax year

Allowances

Personal allowance	£4,385

Personal allowance (age 65–74)	£5,790
Personal allowance (age 75+)	£6,050
Married couple's allowance (age 65 by 5 April 2000)	£5,185*
Married couple's allowance (age 75+)	£5,255*
Married couple's allowance (minimum)	£2,000*
Income limit for age-related allowances	£17,000

Widow's bereavement allowance	£2,000*
Blind person's allowance	£1,400

*You save 10p in tax for every £1 of allowance.

Capital gains tax

annual exemption	£7,200

Income and capital gains tax rates

first	£1,520	10p	(maximum tax at 10p, £152)
next	£26,880	22p	(maximum tax at 22p, £5,913.60)
		20p	(savings interest and capital gains)
		10p	(shares and similar dividends)
over	£28,400	40p	(no maximum at 40p)
		32.5p	(shares and similar dividends)

National Insurance

Class 1	due on (monthly) earnings	over £329 up to £2,319
Class 2	due on (annual) earnings	over £3,825
Class 4	due on (annual) earnings	over £4,385 up to £27,820

Inheritance tax

exempt amount	£234,000

Pension contributions

earnings cap	£91,800

VAT

registration threshold	£52,000

Addresses and telephone numbers for those organisations marked with an asterisk (*) can be found in the address section on page 295.

Introduction

You cannot rely on the Inland Revenue to get your tax bill right – and that is one good reason for using a book like this. By the Inland Revenue's own admission, many tax bills based on self-assessment tax returns are wrong. And it is not only clerical errors you need to worry about. There is another problem – tax inspectors themselves not fully understanding the rules.

Here is an example. Half-way through the 1999–2000 tax year the Chancellor bowed to pressure and changed the rules on the new 10p tax rate he had introduced. Initially it had applied only to earned income. People on a low income and people with income from savings interest still had to pay 20p tax on the interest, even if the savings interest fell within the new 10p tax band. The Chancellor belatedly decided to extend the 10p rate to include investment income – and backdated the rule to the start of the 1999–2000 tax year. Unfortunately, even in the summer of 2000 taxpayers are still having trouble getting back half the 20p tax deducted on their savings interest because, it seems, confusion still reigns in tax offices.

Take another example. If you reach 65 at any time during the tax year you may be entitled to higher, age-related tax allowances from the start of the tax year. But while some tax inspectors give the allowance from the start of the tax year, others (wrongly) insist that you cannot get age-related allowances until you reach your 65th birthday.

This book sets out the basic tax rules. And at the end of each chapter we list relevant Inland Revenue leaflets and other literature. If you think that your tax office has misinterpreted the rules, you can often find them written in such leaflets – and can point your tax inspector to the relevant words when supporting your claim.

Enforcing your right to pay only 10p tax on savings interest or claiming a tax allowance involves relatively simple tax rules. But generations of Chancellors have contrived to make the tax system unnecessarily, and horrifically, complicated. This makes getting everything right – so that you pay neither too much nor too little tax – a daunting task.

That is where this book should help. And in addition to helping ensure your tax bill is correct, *Which? Way to Save Tax 2000–1* suggests ways in which you can legitimately use the tax rules to keep your tax bill down.

Introduction

Getting to grips with tax

Income tax takes up most of the book. It's by far the most important tax for the government, for which it brings in more money than anything else. Anyone with more than a very modest wage, salary or pension has to pay income tax. So do many people with no earnings but with money coming in from investments. The main aim of the book is to help you realise:

- what income tax is
- how it affects you
- how you can check your tax bill
- how you can make the most of the rules and pay less tax.

National Insurance
Although this is not called a tax, it is money that has to be paid to the government, and what you have to pay varies with your income. We explain how it works in Chapter 8, *National Insurance*.

Capital gains tax
You may have to pay capital gains tax if you sell some of your investments or possessions at a profit – or even if you give them away. The rules are complicated, and you're quite likely to find that there's no tax to pay. But it's as well to skim through our explanation in Chapter 14, *Capital gains tax*, to make sure that you're not at risk.

Inheritance tax
With inheritance tax there is no tax to pay on what you give away while you are still alive (with a few exceptions), as long as you live for at least seven years after making the gift. Even if you do die within seven years, there may be no tax to pay. Giving away

possessions and money while you are alive won't save *you* tax. Don't let the idea of saving your heirs tax threaten your own financial security. See Chapter 15, *Inheritance tax* for how inheritance tax works.

Value added tax (VAT)
We don't go into detail, but there is a brief summary of VAT rules in Chapter 6, *Working for yourself*.

How to use this book

Each chapter looks at tax from a different angle. So, for example, if you're not sure how your investments are taxed, go to Chapter 12, *Investments*, which looks at investments in general and includes details of schemes like individual savings accounts (ISAs), which have special tax perks.

Checking a specific point
Start with the *Index*, which should give you quick guidance to the right place.

Checking your tax bill over past years
If you're trying to adjust your tax bill from earlier years, see pages 16 and 18 for tax allowances and tax rates for the past six years.

Trouble with the Inland Revenue?
Chapter 2, *Dealing with the Revenue*, gives advice if you are in dispute with the Inland Revenue and gives details of the penalties you might face.

Tax tips

Making the most of the tax rules can reduce your tax bill.

Your family
- If you are a couple, does one of you own all the investments? Husbands and wives are taxed separately and there could be less tax to pay if you shared out the spoils differently – for instance if only one of you is a higher-rate taxpayer (p. 202).
- Does your child use his or her tax allowance? Any child, no matter how young, has a tax-free personal allowance (pp. 38 and 203).

In a job?
- Can you set any expenses against tax? See p. 64 onwards.
- Approaching retirement? It may be worthwhile making additional voluntary contributions (AVCS) to your employer's pension scheme (p. 164).
- Not in a pension scheme? You can get tax relief (at your top rate) on premiums paid into a personal pension (p. 165).
- A student? If you have holiday earnings, signing a form can save you the bother of paying tax now and claiming it back later (p. 76).
- Received a redundancy lump sum? Make sure you don't have too much tax deducted through the Pay-As-You-Earn (PAYE) system (p. 77).

In business?
- Self-employed? You may be able to save tax by employing your husband or wife (p. 126).
- Loans for your business? See if they qualify for tax relief (p. 41).
- Are you claiming all your expenses? See p. 112 onwards.
- Entitled to capital allowances? It may pay you to claim less than you're able to, and to roll on the balance to succeeding years (p. 117).
- Business losses? You can choose how to deal with them – and the choice you make can affect your tax bill and your cash-in-hand (p. 122).
- Losses in a new business? You can get tax relief by setting them against other income or capital gains (p. 122).
- Should you register for VAT? See p. 127 for the answer.

On a low income?
- Not a taxpayer? If you don't pay tax, and you've got money to invest, you should register as a non-taxpayer if you're putting it in a bank or building society account (p. 205).

When you are older
- Approaching 65? You may be able to claim a higher personal allowance for the whole of the tax year in which you reached 65: you don't have to wait for your 65th birthday (p. 44).
- Not getting full age-related allowances? Consider switching to investments where the return is tax-free (p. 204). Beware of cashing in a life insurance policy where the return is taxable (p. 221).
- Retiring from a business? You may be able to claim retirement relief from capital gains tax (p. 247).

- Coming up to retirement – and with a personal pension? You may be able to get yourself a larger pension and cut your recent tax bills (p. 164). If you haven't got a personal pension, see whether you should take one out.

Investments and life insurance

- Buying gilts? Is the income paid to you without tax being deducted? See p. 208 for how to arrange this.
- Have you made use of the annual capital gains tax exemption? Investing for capital gains, rather than income, may give you a better after-tax return (p. 234).
- A large amount to invest, and worried about inheritance tax? Consider investing in certain types of property (p. 278).
- Getting tax relief on a pre-March 1984 life insurance policy? Beware of extending the policy, or of altering it to increase the benefits. You may lose your tax relief (p. 225).
- Self-employed, or in a job but not in an employer's pension scheme? You can get tax relief on a life insurance policy (p. 226).
- Willing to take a risk? The enterprise investment scheme (EIS) gives you tax relief on your investments (p. 206).
- Life insurance for your family? Cut your inheritance tax bill by making sure the proceeds aren't added to your estate (p. 228).
- Made a loss when you sold some shares? Keep a record of any losses when you dispose of something. You may be able to use a loss to cut down any capital gains tax you have to pay (p. 239).

You and your home

- Buying a property? You could save £610, £5,030 or even £5,040 in stamp duty (p. 183).
- Letting a room in your home? The rent-a-room scheme can give you a tax-free income of up to £4,250 a year (p. 194).
- A home to let? If you're borrowing to buy the home, you can get tax relief on the interest you pay. For all the expenses you can claim, see p. 192.
- Selling your house and garden separately? Sell the garden first (p. 188).
- Working at home? See p. 114 for expenses you can claim.
- More than one home? Be careful about which home you choose as your 'main home' for capital gains tax purposes (p. 184).
- A home with your job and another which you own? Make sure that the home you own is free from capital gains tax (p. 185).

Passing your money on
- Can 'estate freezing' save you tax? See p. 281.
- Made a will yet? Make sure you word it correctly; otherwise, your spouse could be left short (p. 282).
- Married with valuable property which one of you owns exclusively? Sharing some of it between you can cut down your inheritance tax bill (p. 280).
- High income, and young children? Consider an accumulation and maintenance trust (p. 285).
- Inheritance tax to be paid by your beneficiaries when you die? Making regular gifts out of income can get rid of a lot of the value of your estate. And you can give away at least £3,000 a year tax-free (p. 273).
- A beneficiary under a will? You may be able to pay any inheritance tax by instalments (p. 291).

Charities
- Giving to charity? Your gift could be worth a lot more if you make use of the tax breaks (p. 42).
- Can you have your charitable donations deducted straight from your pay? If not, you should ask your employer to set up a payroll-giving scheme (p. 43).

Tax tip: keep in control

You have always been obliged to notify the Revenue if you have earnings or gains which should be taxed and which the Revenue does not already know about. If you are not sent a tax return, you must notify the Revenue within six months of the end of the tax year of any income or gains on which tax is due. For income or gains in the 2000–1 tax year, tell the Revenue by 5 October 2001. You will then be sent a tax return.

You are legally required to keep records in support of information you give on your tax return. Keep track of whom you worked for and what you were paid, and hold on to receipts for expenses or assets that you bought and sold. If you don't, you could face a penalty of up to £3,000 for each failure to keep an adequate record.

Tell the Revenue about changes in your personal circumstances. Otherwise you could be paying too much tax because you're not claiming an allowance that you're entitled to or because your income has dropped. If you don't get a tax return, it is up to you to keep the Revenue informed of any change in your circumstances which could affect your tax position, for example, if

- you become unemployed or retire
- you gain or lose a source of income
- you start or stop making a payment which qualifies for tax relief
- you change from being an employee to being self-employed.

Always check your tax. The Revenue will send out your tax code (if you're an employee or receiving a pension) and tell you how much tax it would like you to pay in advance (if, for example, you are self-employed). Whenever you get a tax statement, or a PAYE Coding Notice, make sure the figures are correct. Write to your tax office at once if you don't think they are.

Tax tip: act in time
Tax rules are hedged round with time limits. They can be as short as 30 days and as long as 6 years. You'll find details of the various time limits throughout this book.

Claiming for past tax years

You may have forgotten to claim personal allowances in past years. Or, more likely, you may have forgotten to claim some tax relief. Is it too late to make a claim? How far back can you go?

You can go back six tax years into the past, i.e. you can claim tax relief and allowances for the six tax years before the current tax year.

Tax years run from 6 April in one year to 5 April in the next. So if you act *before* 6 April 2001, you can go back six tax years before the 2000–1 tax year – which takes you to the 1994–5 tax year. See below for later tax years.

Note that the six-year rule has changed and from the 2002–3 tax year you will have two months less in which to act. See below for the precise time limits.

How much can you claim?
The *allowances* you can claim are the amounts which applied in the relevant tax year; the figures are on p. 17.

Together with any extra tax relief you can claim, these will (in normal cases) reduce your taxable income for the relevant tax year. Your tax bill for that tax year will be recalculated, using the tax rates that applied at the time; the rates are on p. 18.

The six-year rule
- Act before 6 April 2001 for the 1994–5 tax year.
- Act before 6 April 2002 for the 1995–6 tax year.
- Act before 31 January 2003 for the 1996–7 tax year.
- Act before 31 January 2004 for the 1997–8 tax year.
- Act before 31 January 2005 for the 1998–9 tax year.
- Act before 31 January 2006 for the 1999–2000 tax year.
- Act before 31 January 2007 for the 2000–1 tax year.

Allowances for the six tax years before 2000–1

	1999–2000	1998–9	1997–8
personal	£ 4,335	4,195	4,045
personal 65–74 [1]	£ 5,720	5,410	5,220
personal 75+ [1]	£ 5,980	5,600	5,400
married couple's [2]	£ 1,970	1,900	1,830
married couple's 65–74 [1][2]	£ 5,125	3,305	3,185
married couple's 75+ [1][2]	£ 5,195	3,345	3,225
additional personal [2]	£ 1,970	1,900	1,830
blind person's	£ 1,380	1,330	1,280
widow's bereavement [2]	£ 1,970	1,900	1,830
total income limit	£ 16,800	16,200	15,600
capital gains tax-free slice	£ 7,100	6,800	6,500

	1996–7	1995–6	1994–5
personal	£ 3,765	3,525	3,445
personal 65–74 [1]	£ 4,910	4,630	4,200
personal 75+ [1]	£ 5,090	4,800	4,370
married couple's [2]	£ 1,790	1,720	1,720
married couple's 65–74 [1][2]	£ 3,115	2,995	2,665
married couple's 75+ [1][2]	£ 3,155	3,035	2,705
additional personal [2]	£ 1,790	1,720	1,720
blind person's	£ 1,250	1,200	1,080
widow's bereavement [2]	£ 1,790	1,720	1,720
total income limit	£ 15,200	14,200	14,200
capital gains tax-free slice	£ 6,300	5,800	5,800

[1] Your age on the birthday falling within the tax year – husband or wife in the case of the married couple's allowance. Allowance is reduced if your income exceeds total income limit.
[2] Relief restricted to 20 per cent in 1994–5, 15 per cent from 1995–6 to 1998–9, 10 per cent from 1999–2000.

Rates of tax on income and gains for the six tax years before 2000–1

	starting rate band %		basic-rate band %		higher-rate band %	
1999–2000	10	£1,500	23*	£1,501–£28,000	40	£28,001
1998–9	20	£4,300	23*	£4,301–£27,100	40	£27,101
1997–8	20	£4,100	23*	£4,101–£26,100	40	£26,101
1996–7	20	£3,900	24*	£3,901–£25,500	40	£25,501
1995–6	20	£3,200	25	£3,201–£24,300	40	£24,301
1994–5	20	£3,000	25	£3,001–£23,700	40	£23,701

* 20 per cent basic-rate tax on most savings and investment income and capital gains, 10 per cent on savings and investments in 1999–2000 if within the starting-rate band – there will be further tax to pay on savings and investment income which falls into the higher-rate band.

Tax advice

No one person – and no one book – can answer every tax problem. In the following paragraphs, we suggest sources of advice which, depending on your circumstances, you might find useful.

Start with this book
It's the obvious starting place. With 300 pages of information and advice, it covers the great majority of tax problems.

Use Inland Revenue leaflets and helpsheets
These vary considerably in the amount of detail they give. Some are easy to read but quite sketchy. Others are labyrinthine. The majority provide relatively straightforward information, often with worked examples. Not all leaflets are up to date – though sometimes there are supplements, which should be given to you with the main leaflet. All leaflets are free, from tax offices and tax enquiry centres. Helpsheets may relate to a specific tax year. You can get these free helpsheets by phoning the Inland Revenue Orderline.*

Go to tax enquiry centres
These Inland Revenue advice centres may be nearer (and more convenient) than your own tax office. They should be able to sort out most problems.

Use the *Which? Tax Saving Guide*
This is the best short guide to the tax system, and takes you step by step through filling in your tax return. It's published early in the tax year.

Try *Simon's Taxes*
This is a nine-volume, loose-leaf tax encyclopaedia, certainly not worth buying unless you're a tax professional. But it's the best place to consult statutes. One of the problems for the ordinary person is that Finance Acts very often make changes to sections in earlier Acts, so you need to find a version of the earlier Acts which contains all the changes. *Simon's Taxes* (Volumes G and H) do just that. Your local library might have a copy; otherwise, try a reference library or university library.

Get professional help
Only if your tax affairs are complicated, or you're making a will, do you need a professional to handle your tax affairs. If you're setting up a trust, or engaging in detailed inheritance tax planning, you'll need a professional adviser – a tax consultant, accountant or solicitor. The level of competence and expertise varies enormously, and there's no easy way to find someone who's good. Try asking friends, or your employer.

Dealing with the Revenue

Around 730,000 taxpayers missed the deadline for sending back their 'self-assessment' tax returns in January 2000. They were hit with an automatic penalty of £100. So beware – learn the rules and follow them closely if you want to avoid interest, surcharges and penalties. If your affairs are straightforward and all the tax you owe is collected at source – e.g. through Pay-As-You-Earn (PAYE) or deducted from interest paid on a savings account – you may not be sent a tax return. But expect one if you are self-employed, in a business partnership, a company director, a higher-rate taxpayer or have several sources of income and/or capital gains.

Your obligations

Your obligations as a taxpayer are to be honest, to give accurate information, to keep records and – if you receive one – to file your tax return and pay your tax on time.

Even if you *don't* receive a tax return you are still required to notify the Revenue of income (including taxable benefits in kind – see Chapter 5) or capital gains (see Chapter 14) it doesn't know about within six months of the end of the tax year in which you make the income or gain. If you receive a P11D (which lists your taxable benefits) from your employer, you can assume the Revenue has been informed – provided you have no reason to believe that the P11D information has not been passed to the Revenue. Check with your employer.

All taxpayers are legally obliged to keep records of income, gains and tax paid. Keeping records is doubly important if you get a tax return because you must be able to support the figures you give on it. You may have to provide the paperwork if the Revenue launches an enquiry into your tax return – see p. 29. Failure to meet any of these obligations can result in penalties in the form of interest on tax paid late; surcharges for continued late payment; and penalties (some automatic) for not supplying information requested by the Revenue – for example, failing to file your tax return on time or to keep records.

Keeping the Revenue informed

If you need to tell the tax office about income that should be taxed, you'll need to find the right office.

- **Employees** As a general rule, your tax office will be the one which deals with the area where you work, or, more particularly, the place from which you are paid. But there are exceptions. PAYE for all employees in Scotland is handled by one office in Scotland. If you are a government employee – e.g. a civil servant – your affairs will be dealt with by one of the Public Department's offices in Cardiff. If you work for a large national organisation, or in a large city or town, your office may not be local. Your employer will be able to tell you the name and address of your tax office. If you change your job, your tax office may also change.
- **Self-employed** If you are in business on your own, or in partnership, your tax office is usually the one nearest your place of business. If you change from being an employee to being self-employed, you may need to change your tax office.
- **Income mainly from pensions or investments** If you are getting a pension from a former employer, your tax affairs may well be dealt with by the tax office dealing with the area in which the pension fund paying your pension has its office. But if the pension from your former employer is fairly small, or your only pension is a state pension, your affairs will be dealt with by the tax office for the area in which you live.
- **Unemployed** You stay with the tax office of your last employer.
- **Special cases** If you have to fill in a tax return in your capacity as trustee, the tax office will be one of the few that deal with the affairs of trusts and settlements.

General enquiries

If you just want to make a general enquiry or you want to get hold of one of the free Revenue leaflets, you don't need to go to your own tax office. Instead, you can phone any tax office or Inland Revenue enquiry centre. Find them in the phone book under *Inland Revenue*. Alternatively, if you just want a leaflet or form, phone the Inland

Revenue Orderline.* If your enquiry is specific to your particular tax affairs, it's always best to contact your own tax office.

Keeping records

You are legally obliged to keep records in support of the information you give on your tax return – for example, bank statements, tax credits for share dividends, business accounts. This applies to all taxpayers. Any taxpayer could find a tax return landing on his or her doormat, even if he or she has not received one in the past. If you choose to work out your own tax, you will also need to keep a copy of the *working sheets* of your calculations (which can either be part of the tax return guide or included in a helpsheet).

If you run a business you have to keep all records (not just your business records) for five years after the filing date for a particular tax year. If you don't run a business, records have to be kept for at least one year from the date you file your return, though it could be slightly longer if you filed your return late. If there is an enquiry, records have to be kept until the enquiry is complete.

Inadequate record-keeping

The Revenue can charge a penalty of up to £3,000 for each failure to keep adequate records in support of information provided on your tax return. In principle, this means that you should keep the originals of any documents. In practice, the Revenue will not charge a penalty if you can provide other documentary proof of tax deducted or tax paid *and* the Revenue accepts the proof.

The Revenue's obligations

The Revenue sets out what its obligations are in the Taxpayer's Charter. This states clearly what taxpayers are entitled to expect from the Inland Revenue.

To be fair The Revenue should treat everyone with equal fairness and impartiality and you should be expected to pay only what is due under the law.

To be helpful All Revenue staff should be courteous, and assist you in getting your taxes right, by providing clear information to help you understand your rights and obligations.

To be efficient The Revenue should be prompt, accurate, and keep your affairs confidential. Information obtained from you should be used only as allowed by the law. The Revenue should also strive to keep both your expenses and those of the tax office down.

To be accountable Standards, and how well the Revenue lives up to those standards, should be made public.

To be open to criticism Taxpayers should be told how to complain, and be able to have their tax affairs looked at again. An appeal can be made to an independent tribunal, or your MP can refer you to the Parliamentary Commissioner for Administration.

You the taxpayer have an obligation to be honest, to give the Revenue accurate information, and to pay your tax on time.

Copies of the charter are available from local tax and VAT offices. To back up the Taxpayer's Charter, the Revenue also publishes various codes of practice. These explain the standards the Revenue sets itself in particular aspects of its work. They also set out your rights as a taxpayer and what you should do if you feel you have been treated unfairly.

Overpaid and underpaid tax

If you have paid too much tax, the Revenue will repay it with interest – called a repayment supplement. The interest will be calculated from the date you made the overpayment to the date the repayment is made. However, no interest will be paid on overpayments of tax that you were not legally obliged to make.

If you have not paid enough tax because the Revenue failed to make use of the information you gave, you will not have to pay the tax (which is technically due) provided that:

• you could reasonably have believed that your tax affairs were in order
• you were told about the underpaid tax more than 12 months after the end of the tax year in which the Revenue received the information which indicated that tax was due
• you were notified of an over-repayment after the end of the tax year following the year in which the repayment was made.

In very exceptional cases, you won't have to pay underpaid tax you were told about less than 12 months after the end of the tax year in which the tax was due. However, this shorter time limit will apply only if the Revenue:

• failed more than once to make proper use of the facts you had given
• allowed underpaid tax to build up over two whole consecutive tax years by failing to make proper and timely use of the information you had given.

Revenue mistakes

The Revenue will reimburse additional costs that a taxpayer may have incurred as a direct result of serious errors and delays by the Revenue in dealing with the person's tax affairs. In addition – though only in exceptional circumstances – the Revenue will consider making a financial payment as consolation for worry and distress suffered as a direct result of an Inland Revenue mistake. Details are published in the Revenue's code of practice called *Mistakes by the Inland Revenue*.

Tax statements

To help you to keep track of how much tax you've paid and to remind you that tax is due, the Revenue will send statements of account. Interest you owe (or are owed) and any penalty payments will also be shown on these statements. If you ask the Revenue to calculate your tax bill, and you send back your tax return by 30 September, you will receive a statement a few weeks before the 31 January deadline for paying any tax you owe. If you calculate your own tax bill, your own calculations will provide the amounts you have to pay on 31 January. If you also have to make payments on account, you should receive a statement about one month before your second payment on account becomes due on 31 July. An example of a statement of account is given opposite.

PAYE **Coding Notice**

If you pay tax under PAYE – for example you are an employee, or you get a pension from a former employer – you may receive a PAYE Coding Notice. This is basically the Revenue's way of telling you which allowances and outgoings you're getting, and how much untaxed income it thinks you're receiving – i.e. what has gone into working out your tax code. It determines how much tax you pay under PAYE. See Chapter 4 for how your PAYE code is worked out.

The notice makes it easy to see which allowances you're getting since they are shown by their names. If an allowance you can claim doesn't appear on the notice you receive, you're not getting it and you should contact your tax office pointing this out.

You should also check that all your outgoings are included unless tax relief is given at source and the relief is restricted. Outgoings where relief is not restricted should appear on your notice if you are a higher-rate taxpayer, to take account of the extra tax relief due to you.

Revenue **Self Assessment - Statement of Account**

```
                              Statement consec no. 003
                              Tax Reference  YY 00 00 00 C

  384123 003253 AA 003253 935      Date      29 November 2000
                                   Issued by
  MR J SMITH                       Officer in Charge
  66 HIGH ROAD                     LONDON PROVINCIAL 22
  LONDON                           GRAYFIELD HOUSE
  SW25 2LS                         5 BANKHEAD AVENUE
                                   EDINBURGH
                                   EH11 4AE
                                   Telephone 0131 000 000
```

Interim Liabilities	£3242.76 due 31 JAN 2001		£3242.76 due 31 JUL 2001
Date	Transactions	Amount (£)	Balance (£)
		Current Balance	0.00

```
Amounts becoming due
     1st Interim Liability      31 JAN 2001       3242.76

     NOTICE TO PAY
     Your Liability has been calculated as shown above.
     Please make sure your payment reaches us by the due date.
```

This statement shows just your payments on account for 2000–1. It does not include any earlier tax you may owe.
➤ Please detach payment slip here when making payment direct to the Accounts Office or by Girobank ➤

Girobank Trans cash
Girobank plc Bootle Merseyside GIR 0AA

Revenue *Payslip*   **bank giro credit**

Reference	Credit account number	Amount due (no fee payable at PO counter)	By transfer from Alliance & Leicester Giro account number
000 000 000 0000	000 0000	£ 3242.76	
000 00		CHEQUE ACCEPTABLE	

MR J SMITH

Cashier's stamp and initials   Signature . . . .   Date . . . .

For official use only

```
              10-50-41        CASH
         BANK OF ENGLAND      CHEQUES
   HEAD OFFICE COLLECTION A/C TOTAL £
         INLAND REVENUE
```

SA300(Cumb)   ▼ Please do not fold this payslip or write or mark below this line ▼

If you think that any of the figures on your notice are wrong, contact your tax office telling it why. If you need more information on the notice you receive, and you haven't already got it, ask your tax office to send you leaflet P3(T) – *PAYE: Understanding your tax code.*

The tax return

You will be sent a tax return to fill in if the Revenue thinks that you have income and/or capital gains which should be taxed.

Tax returns are sent out each April to cover your taxable income and gains for the tax year just ended on 5 April. This book covers the rules for the 2000–1 tax year. Tax returns for the 2000–1 tax year will be sent out in April 2001.

The tax return is currently made up of an eight-page form that everyone who is sent one has to fill in, plus supplementary pages dealing with different types of income and gain. You will also get a tax return guide (giving guidance on what to put on your tax return) and a tax calculation guide showing how to calculate your own tax bill, if you want to do this yourself.

What to do when you get your tax return

Everybody who is sent a tax return will get the basic tax form but you may also need to fill in one or more supplementary pages. These deal with different types of income or gains. So if you have income from letting property, for example, you will need to fill in the basic tax form and the supplementary page dealing with land and property in the UK. It is your responsibility to make sure that you have all the bits you need.

You should receive only the supplementary pages appropriate to the particular type of income you receive or capital gains you make. But if you don't automatically get the supplementary pages you need, you must ask for them. The tax return guide will explain which supplementary pages deal with what. As well as checking that you have the right supplementary pages, it will be worth skimming through the tax form and the tax return guide to see if you want any helpsheets or Revenue leaflets. If there's anything you are not sure about, ask your tax office or phone the Inland Revenue Self-assessment helpline.*

Once you've got all the information you need from the Revenue and you've gathered together all your own records of your income, gains and outgoings, fill in the tax return.

Since April 2000, most people have been given the choice of sending back their tax return over the Internet (*e-filing*). If you e-file, you will receive a £10 discount and confirmation that the Revenue has received your tax return. To register, go to www.ir-efile.gov.uk

Working out the tax bill

The tax return includes full instructions on how to calculate the tax due. However, this is not compulsory. The Revenue will still do these calculations for you but you should make every effort to send back your return by 30 September. You can ask the Revenue to calculate your tax bills even if you send in your tax return after 30 September, but the Revenue won't guarantee to have worked out the amount of tax due by 31 January, the date by which tax has to be paid. As a result, you may have to pay interest and a surcharge for late payment of tax.

The deadline for sending back the return is 31 January. So, for the 1999–2000 tax return sent out in April 2000, the deadline is 31 January 2001 – but aim for 30 September 2000 if you want the Revenue to calculate your tax.

Late tax returns

If you miss the 31 January deadline for sending back your tax return, or if you send your tax return back incomplete – for example you do not fill in all the supplementary pages you need to – you will have to pay an automatic penalty of £100. A further £100 penalty will have to be paid if you haven't sent back your return within six months of the 31 January filing date. However, these automatic penalties cannot be more than the tax that is due for the year.

The Revenue can apply to the general or special commissioners to impose a daily penalty of up to £60 a day, but this is likely to happen only if it believes that you owe a substantial amount of tax.

Paying the tax

The 31 January *filing date* for tax returns is also the deadline for paying tax. Tax due will be income tax, capital gains tax and (if you are self-employed) Class 4 National Insurance not yet paid for the tax year ending in the previous April. In addition, some taxpayers will have to pay half the income tax and National Insurance for the current tax year *on account* (i.e. in advance) by the same date.

If you pay tax through PAYE and owe tax of £1,000 or less, and you want the amount to be collected through PAYE (rather than paying it in a lump sum), you must send your tax return back to your tax office by 30 September rather than the 31 January final deadline.

If you don't file a return, the Revenue will have to make an estimate of the tax it thinks you owe and the tax it thinks you should pay on account, and may issue a *determination*. This determination will be treated as the amount you have to pay until you send in your completed tax return. The figures you supply on your completed tax return will automatically replace the estimated figures in the determination.

Payments on account

Some people have to pay tax on account. The amount you have to pay will never be more than the previous year's bill for income tax and Class 4 National Insurance less tax deducted at source (for example through PAYE or tax credits on share dividends). So if your tax and

National Insurance bill for the 1999–2000 tax year was £9,150, and £2,095 of this tax was deducted at source, the amount you have to pay on account for the 2000–1 tax year will be £7,055 (i.e. £9,150 minus £2,095). Half of this *relevant amount* is payable on 31 January 2001 (the filing date for your 1999–2000 tax return), the rest on 31 July 2001.

If your tax bill for 2000–1 turns out to be more than what you paid on account, you make up the difference (or make a *balancing payment*) with your payment due on 31 January 2002. If your 2000–1 tax bill is less than the amount you paid on account, you can deduct the amount you have overpaid from the next payment on account.

Because your payments on account are based on your tax bill for the previous tax year, you may end up overpaying tax. If you know that your income has fallen, you can ask for your payments on account to be reduced. You can make a claim to reduce your payments on account in by completing form SA303 – *Claim to reduce payments on account*, by letter or on your tax return at any time.

Your written claim should give your reasons for believing that your payments on account will result in an overpayment of tax – for example you're going off travelling for six months and you won't be earning during that time. The claim should state that it is your belief that either you won't be liable to any or all of the tax due on account or your tax liability will be covered by tax deducted at source and that as a consequence the tax you end up owing will be less than the payments on account. A claim cannot be rejected but it's likely that the Revenue will look very carefully at your tax return to check that there isn't a significant difference between the amount of income tax due and the amount paid as reduced payments on account. Penalties exist to deter gross or persistent abuse.

Tax paid late

If you don't pay your tax on time, you will have to pay interest from the date the tax was due to the date you make payment. If the tax due on 31 January has not been paid by 28 February in the same year, you will have to pay a surcharge of 5 per cent of the tax due. If you still have not paid the tax you owe by 31 July, there will be another 5 per cent surcharge to pay – plus interest on the first surcharge.

Late payment of surcharges and penalties

Interest will also have to be paid on surcharges and penalties which are unpaid 30 days from the date of the written notice telling you that they are going to be imposed. You also have 30 days in which to appeal against the imposition of a surcharge or penalty.

Checking your self-assessment

Technically it's up to you to tell the Revenue how much tax you owe or are owed, but your completed tax return will be subject to two checks. The first check will simply ensure that your return is legible, that the sums are right (if you have worked out your own tax bill) and that the figures you have provided are correct in themselves. This first check will happen shortly after you send back your return. If there are any mistakes, your tax office will let you know and will ask you to correct your self-assessment.

The second check is a more in-depth one to make sure that the information you have provided on your return is complete and accurate and consistent with information from other sources – for example your employer or your bank. This second check may give rise to an *enquiry* into your tax return (see below).

Amending your assessment

You may need to *amend your assessment* if you send back your tax return and then discover that you have made a mistake. You may also be asked to amend your assessment by the Revenue as the result of an enquiry (see below). In the case of amendments you want to make yourself, you have 12 months from the 31 January filing date in which to do so.

The exception to the 12-month rule is where you realise that you have paid too much tax in the past because of a mistake you made on a tax return for an earlier tax year. In the 2000–1 tax year it is possible to ask for assessments back to the 1994–5 tax year to be corrected and the overpaid tax repaid to you. This might apply to you if, for example, you forgot to claim an allowance to which you were entitled.

Enquiries into your tax return

The Revenue has the right to make enquiries into the completeness and accuracy of any tax return. You cannot appeal against an enquiry being held, though you can appeal if you think it has gone on for too long or without good reason. Some enquiries will be made into tax returns selected at random. Others will be made where the Revenue suspects that something is wrong. Whatever the reason the enquiry process will be the same.

First you will receive a written notice that an enquiry is going to take place, together with a copy of the code of practice concerning enquiries. If you don't receive such a notice within a year of filing your return, you can assume that no enquiry will take place. Note that the time limits are longer if you file your tax return late or make an amendment to it: the time limit will be the quarter date (31 January, 30 April, 31 July, 31 October) after the anniversary of the date you file or amend your return – for example, if you send your tax return back on 28 February 2001, the Revenue will have until 30 April 2002 to enquire into it.

You may also receive a notice asking you to produce documents, accounts or other written particulars. You must produce whatever is asked for within 30 days of receiving the request. If you need more time or if the document requested doesn't exist, contact your tax office as soon as possible. The Revenue should request only information that is relevant to determining whether or not your return is complete or the information you have given is correct. If you don't think that the request is relevant to determining whether your return is complete and correct, you can appeal. You can also appeal if you haven't been given a minimum of 30 days in which to produce the papers requested.

Failure to produce records

If you fail to produce documents requested by the Revenue in the course of an enquiry, you will have to pay a fixed initial penalty of £50. If you still fail to produce the documents requested, a daily penalty of £30 can be imposed, though this could rise to £150 if formal penalty proceedings are held to determine the level of the penalty.

You cannot be penalised for failing to produce a document which does not exist – though you may have to pay a penalty for failing to keep adequate records.

Ending the enquiry

Once the enquiry is complete you should receive written notice that this is the case. If everything on your tax return is in order, that's the end of the matter. However, it may be that the Revenue believes that your return should be amended, in which case you will have 30 days in which to do so in the light of the Revenue's conclusions. If you fail to amend your return or if you amend it incorrectly, the Revenue then has 30 days in which to amend your return in the way that it concludes will make it correct. If you don't agree with what it has done you have 30 days in which to appeal.

If amendments made by the Revenue result in a higher tax bill, you will have 30 days from the date of the amendment to pay the additional tax you owe.

Unfairly treated?

When replying to any letters from your tax office, give the information requested if this is possible or explain why it's not possible.

If you are convinced that the Revenue is being unreasonable in a request for further information, a telephone conversation or meeting may succeed in sorting things out. A meeting should present no problem if your tax office is a local one. If it's not, you can arrange for your file to be passed to your local office for a short period so that you can discuss your affairs with a local tax inspector.

If you believe the person you are dealing with continues to be unreasonable, remind him or her of the requirements of the Taxpayer's Charter. If this step fails, you could write a personal letter to the district inspector, whose name will appear at the head of any letter you receive, on your tax return and on any tax statement. Ask for a review of all the correspondence; you should summarise the main points in your argument again. The district inspector should reply personally, and will either agree with you or set out fully the reasons why your argument is not accepted.

If you are still unable to get any satisfaction from your tax office, write to the regional director who deals with your tax office. Ask your tax office or the Inland Revenue Orderline* for leaflet IR120 – *You and the Inland Revenue* – which explains how to do this. Mark your letter for his or her personal attention, set out concisely and clearly your grounds for complaint against your tax office and ask for an investigation. If you still have no joy, you can refer your complaint to the Adjudicator's Office.* The Adjudicator will be able to look at your case impartially while still having access to all the files. Alternatively, you could try your MP, who may refer your case to the Independent Parliamentary Ombudsman (officially the Parliamentary Commissioner for Administration).

The Adjudicator will not look at complaints already referred to the Ombudsman, but the Ombudsman *can* look at complaints which have been investigated by the Adjudicator.

Discovery assessment

Occasionally the Revenue may issue *discovery assessments*. Unless you are guilty of serious negligence or fraud, it is unlikely that you will get one of these. If you do, you would be well advised to seek professional help.

Appeals

You should not need to appeal if you give honest and accurate information, keep records and pay your tax on time. To avoid creating problems, ask the Revenue for help *before* you send in your tax return.

There may still be occasions where you need to appeal because the Revenue has taken action which you don't agree with. You can appeal against:

- the imposition of surcharges and penalties
- a request for documents under an enquiry
- an enquiry that you think has gone on too long and hasn't got anywhere
- a Revenue amendment to your assessment if you don't agree with it.

If you want to appeal, your first stop should be your tax inspector, and you should have reasonable grounds for appealing. If, for example, you have been surcharged for late payment of tax, you have grounds for appeal if you can show that you actually paid your tax on time. The vast majority of appeals should be able to be settled after discussions with your tax office. However, if you can't reach agreement, you have a choice: you can either give up or ask for your appeal to be heard before the commissioners, who are independent of the Inland Revenue.

Appeals before the commissioners

You appeal to the *general commissioners* or the *special commissioners*. The special commissioners are tax experts. The general commissioners are unpaid local people who hear appeals in your area; they aren't usually tax experts, but have a paid clerk to advise them on legal matters.

In some cases you have no choice about whether to go to the general commissioners or the special commissioners. For example, the special commissioners must consider your appeal in certain specified (and usually complex) circumstances, or if you're claiming because you made a mistake filling in the income sections of your tax return and the inspector has refused your claim.

If, on the other hand, your appeal is about your PAYE code, or you're claiming tax back because you've failed to claim a personal allowance, the general commissioners must deal with it.

Other appeals normally go automatically to the general commissioners, too. But if your appeal depends on some fine point of law (as opposed to a matter of fact, or common sense) you can elect to have your appeal heard by the special commissioners.

At the commissioners' hearing

Taking an appeal before the commissioners will certainly be time-consuming, and may be expensive if you engage someone to appear on your behalf. You can appear on your own behalf, and the commissioners are required to hear any barrister, solicitor or qualified accountant who appears for you.

The preparation and presentation of your case before the commissioners is extremely important. As appellant, it is up to you to prove your case – not for the Revenue to disprove it. Although the proceedings before the commissioners are not as formal as in a court of law, the normal rules of evidence will apply.

You, as appellant, will open the proceedings and put your case. The inspector then responds by putting the view of the Revenue; you then have a final opportunity to stress the important points in your own case and deal with any points raised by the inspector which you had not previously covered. Any witnesses produced by either you or the inspector may be cross-examined; and the commissioners can summon anybody to appear before them.

Tips

- When preparing your case, bear in mind that the commissioners will know nothing about you or your affairs until the day of the appeal hearing. So introduce yourself, and the facts of the matter under dispute, as clearly and briefly as you can.
- If you want to show documents in support of your case, make sure you have enough copies for the commissioners (there are usually three of them at a general commissioners' hearing) and the clerk. The inspector will probably have copies already, but have extra copies just in case.
- You may want to refer to previously decided tax cases: the clerk will almost certainly have copies of these available, but it would be as well to take copies of these, too.
- It may be possible, before the hearing and in conjunction with the inspector, to prepare an agreed statement of facts, supported by appropriate documents, which can be presented to the commissioners. This will save time on the day of the hearing. However, it will still be necessary to explain the facts to the commissioners and provide the commissioners and clerk with a copy of the agreed statement of facts and documents.
- It is a good idea to have your own presentation typed out in full, with copies for the commissioners and clerk.
- Take the commissioners carefully through the arguments, both for and against your case.

- Do not ignore the points you know the inspector will make. If you deal with these points at the same time as you deal with your own, you are likely to strengthen your own case while at the same time reducing the impact of what the inspector will say later. You will also give the impression of being a reasonable person – there will almost certainly be something in the inspector's argument, and it is just as well if you are seen to recognise this.

If, in spite of all your efforts, the commissioners decide in favour of the inspector, and you don't agree, you must immediately register your dissatisfaction with the decision. If you don't do this immediately, you lose the right to take the case further. Do this verbally at the end of the hearing or (if the decision is communicated by letter) by an immediate written reply. You may then, by giving notice in writing to the clerk within 30 days, require the commissioners to state and sign a case for the opinion of the High Court (see below). You must also pay the fee of £25.

After the commissioners' hearing

The tax payable as a result of the decision of the commissioners must be paid, regardless of any request for the opinion of the High Court.

The decision of the commissioners on a question of fact (for example, what your business takings were) is final and can be overturned only if the decision was one that no reasonable body of commissioners could have reached on hearing the evidence.

Otherwise, an appeal against the decision of the commissioners can be made only on a point of law. The appeal is normally to the High Court, then to the Court of Appeal and ultimately to the House of Lords. But certain appeals against the decision of the special commissioners may be referred direct to the Court of Appeal, missing out the High Court. Some appeals may skip even the Court of Appeal and go straight to the House of Lords. In Scotland, the equivalent of the High Court is the Court of Session, and an appeal from the Court of Session is direct to the House of Lords.

Taking an appeal through the procedure outlined above can be very expensive. At the commissioners' hearing each party pays its own costs. However, if you or the Revenue are found to have behaved unreasonably in pursuing your case, costs can be awarded. In the later stages of appeal it is usual for the costs of *both* sides to be awarded against the side that loses. You could be faced with a bill running to many thousands of pounds, so think very carefully before you start on this road. If you feel that your case has been mishandled

– that you've suffered maladministration, bias, or delay, for example
– your MP can refer your case to the Parliamentary Commissioner for Administration, also known as the Independent Parliamentary Ombudsman.

Useful Inland Revenue reading

You can ring the Inland Revenue Orderline* for leaflets and notes.

Leaflets and notes

IR167	Charter for Inland Revenue taxpayers
CA47	Charter for National Insurance contributors
AO1	How to complain about the Inland Revenue and the Valuation Office Agency
IR160	Inland Revenue enquiries under self-assessment
IR162	A better approach to local office enquiry work under self-assessment
IR72	Investigations – the examination of business accounts
IR73	Inland Revenue investigations – how settlements are negotiated
IR37	Appeals against tax, National Insurance contributions, statutory sick pay and statutory maternity pay
IR131	Inland Revenue Statements of Practice
IR120	You and the Inland Revenue – tax, collection, National Insurance contributions and Accounts Office
IR120	You and the Inland Revenue – Enforcement Office
IR120	You and the Inland Revenue – FICO
IR120	You and the Inland Revenue – Capital Taxes Office
IR120	You and the Inland Revenue – Special Compliance Office
IR120	You and the Inland Revenue – Tax Credit Office (working families and disabled person's tax credit)
IR141	Open government
SA/BK3	Self assessment – a guide to keeping records for the self-employed
SA/BK4	Self assessment – a general guide to keeping records
SA/BK6	Self assessment – penalties for late tax returns
SA/BK7	Self assessment – surcharges for late payment of tax
SA/BK8	Self assessment – your guide
WFTC/AP	If you think a tax credit decision is wrong
WFTC/APNI	If you think a tax credit decision is wrong (Northern Ireland)

Codes of practice

COP1   Mistakes by the Inland Revenue
COP2   Investigations
COP6   Collection of tax
COP8   Special Compliance Office investigations – cases other than suspected serious fraud
COP9   Special Compliance Office investigations – cases of suspected serious fraud
COP10 Information and advice
COP11 Enquiries into tax returns by local tax offices
COP17 Enquiries into applications for working families' tax credit or disabled person's tax credit

Concessions

Extra-statutory concessions let you off paying tax that is technically due. Booklet IR1 gives details of each concession.

A19   Arrears of tax arising through official error

Working out your tax bill

This chapter helps you work out how much income tax and capital gains tax you should pay and gives guidance on:

- calculating in advance how much money you are likely to need when you get a tax bill (or *assessment*)
- checking a tax bill once you have received one
- checking whether you have had the right tax deducted through the Pay-As-You-Earn (PAYE) system and from savings and investments taxed at source
- working out whether you are due a rebate.

You'll need to read the relevant chapters in this book to work out what part of the money you receive is actually taxable, for example what capital gains or rental income is taxable. This chapter looks at how taxable income and taxable capital gains are taxed, taking account of outgoings (i.e. payments that qualify for tax relief), allowances, different tax bands and different tax rates within the same tax band.

Income tax and capital gains tax are both annual taxes. For the purposes of working out your final tax bill, you can think of them as a single annual tax.

What you have to pay tax on, and the amount of tax you have to pay, varies from year to year, depending on changes announced in the Budget. Your annual tax bill is generally based on the income and capital gains you receive in a *tax year* and calculated according to the rules (and rates) which apply to that tax year.

A tax year runs from 6 April in one year to 5 April in the next. This book describes the tax rules for the tax year running from 6 April 2000 to 5 April 2001 – in other words, the 2000–1 tax year. If you want to check your tax bill for a different tax year, see pp. 17 and 18 for a summary of tax rates and allowances for the last six years.

Everyone, from the youngest baby to the oldest person in the country, is potentially a taxpayer. If your child is a non-taxpayer because all of his or her income falls within the personal allowance, you can claim back tax deducted at source – e.g. from interest on a building society account. To get it paid without deduction of tax, see p. 205.

A child can make his or her own claim for a tax rebate if the tax was deducted from income 'within his or her control', e.g. if tax was deducted from the child's earnings from a holiday job. If your child's tax affairs are complicated, you can ask your tax office for a tax return to complete on your child's behalf. As parent or guardian you are responsible for paying any tax your child owes, out of your own income if the tax isn't paid from the child's income.

A husband and wife are taxed on their own income, can claim their own allowances, set their income against their own tax bands and are responsible for their own tax affairs, such as dealing with the Revenue, filling in their own tax return, paying their own tax and claiming any tax rebate due.

Your income for tax purposes

Not all of the money you have coming in counts as income for the purposes of working out your income tax bill (though some money may be subject to inheritance tax and capital gains tax). Some income is tax-free, and can also be disregarded.

Items which aren't income
- gifts and presents
- money you borrow
- money you inherit, though there may be inheritance tax
- gains (i.e. profits) you make when you sell something for more than you bought it though you may have to pay capital gains tax, unless you did this as a business venture or as part of your business
- betting winnings, unless you bet (e.g. on horses) for a living
- lottery winnings
- premium bond prizes.

Items which are tax-free
- some investment income – see p. 204
- many social security and local authority benefits – see p. 154

- most grants (and parental contributions), scholarships and awards for education, including postgraduate grants from one of the research councils – but check with your tax office if you're not sure
- money paid to you to cover the time you spend at college or while you are on a sandwich course, if you are being sponsored by a company or one of the armed forces – but not money paid to you for the time spent at work
- some items from your employer, including certain benefits in kind (see p. 87) such as the first 15p a day of luncheon vouchers, lump-sum payments from abroad (see p. 137), redundancy pay of up to £30,000 (see p. 77), and gifts which are genuine personal gifts – and not given because you're an employee
- maintenance payments
- income from a covenant
- money from an insurance policy excluding sick pay insurance where your employer pays the premiums (and some insurance pay-outs could result in a capital gains tax bill – see p. 259)
- interest from a delayed settlement of damages for personal injury or death
- strike and unemployment pay from a trade union
- interest on a tax rebate
- compensation for mis-sold personal pensions paid into a tax-approved pension scheme
- cash lump sums awarded by a court or out-of-court settlements in respect of mis-sold personal pensions
- damages for personal injury
- cashbacks, discounts or refunded commission you receive when buying goods or services as an ordinary customer
- compensation paid by banks on dormant accounts opened by victims of the Holocaust.

Income which is taxable

Once you have disregarded money which doesn't count as income for tax purposes and income which is tax-free, you are left with income which *is* taxable. But remember that you still won't pay tax on all of this because of outgoings and allowances (see below). The main sources of taxable income are:

- earnings (and some benefits in kind such as a company car) from your job with an employer
- any spare-time earnings
- profits you make from running a business

- earnings and fees for freelance and self-employed work
- some social security benefits
- pensions (including the state pension)
- rent from letting property
- interest from bank, building society and other savings accounts
- dividends from shares
- distributions from unit trusts and open-ended investment companies.

Outgoings

From a tax point of view, your outgoings are the amounts of money that you spend on which you get tax relief. Tax relief is given at your highest rate of tax. These outgoings can be deducted from your income for tax purposes. However, some outgoings can be deducted only from specific income. For example, expenses are outgoings which can be deducted only from the income to which they relate. If, say, you run a business, you deduct your business expenses only from the money the business made, and not from any other source of income. And payments towards a pension can be deducted only from *net relevant earnings* – see Chapter 10.

Some tax relief is given at source. You get tax relief by making lower payments. If you don't get tax relief at source, you will have to claim relief by giving details on your annual tax return. If you pay tax through PAYE the Revenue may alter your tax code to take your outgoings into account.

Below are some common outgoings on which you get tax relief. Unless stated otherwise, you will need to claim the relief on these outgoings by filling in a tax return.

Interest on loans for property you let

Any amount of loans to buy or improve a property to let count for full tax relief. The interest can be deducted as an allowable business expense from your letting income. See p. 192.

Interest on a loan to buy an annuity

You get tax relief of 23 per cent on the interest on up to £30,000 of loans to buy an annuity, provided you are 65 or over, the loan is secured against your only or main home, and you had a written offer from your lender before 9 March 1999. Relief is given at source: you make lower payments to the lender.

Interest on loans to pay inheritance tax

You get tax relief for up to 12 months on the interest you pay on a loan to pay inheritance tax when someone dies, provided you actually pay the tax before probate is granted or letters of administration are received.

Interest on other loans

You can get tax relief on the interest you pay on loans for a variety of purposes connected with business:

- contributing capital to, or buying a stake in, a partnership (but not a limited one)
- buying a stake in, or lending to, a 'close' company (e.g. a family business)
- buying a stake in an employee-controlled company or industrial co-operative which employs you more or less full-time
- buying machinery or plant (e.g. a car) for use in your job or in your partnership, provided capital allowances can be claimed for it. There's no relief on interest payable more than three years after the end of the tax year in which you took out the loan.

You must use the money borrowed for one of these purposes within a 'reasonable' time (usually six months) before or after taking out the loan. The loan must not have to be paid back within 12 months of being taken out, unless the interest is paid in the UK to a bank, stockbroker or discount house. You will lose relief on this type of loan if you recover capital from the business (for example, you sell some shares) without using the proceeds to pay off your loan. Overdrafts and credit cards don't qualify.

These outgoings apply to individuals: *businesses* (including the self-employed and partnerships) can claim interest paid on loans, overdrafts and credit-card debts for most business purposes as an allowable expense. See p. 112 for more information on allowable business expenses.

Expenses in your employment

You get tax relief on money you spend *wholly, exclusively and necessarily* in carrying out the duties of your employment. This is interpreted very strictly. See p. 64.

Maintenance payments

You get tax relief, restricted to 10 per cent of £2,000 in the 2000–1 tax year, on maintenance payments you're legally obliged to make if you were 65 or over on 5 April 2000. All other relief for maintenance payments ceased to be available from 6 April 2000.

Pension payments

You get tax relief on contributions to employers' pensions, personal pensions, and additional voluntary contributions (AVCs) to either an employer's scheme or a separate free-standing scheme.

There are limits on the amounts of contributions that qualify for relief in any one year – between 15 per cent and 40 per cent of your earnings or profits depending on the type of pension you pay into and your age. But you may be able to claim tax relief on extra contributions if you didn't pay the maximum allowed in previous years.

With employers' pensions (including AVCs) you get the relief automatically by paying less tax through PAYE.

With free-standing AVCs (FSAVCs), or personal pensions taken out by employees after 1 July 1988, you get basic-rate relief at source by making lower payments. The government pays the basic-rate tax relief direct to the pension provider. You get this tax relief even if you don't pay basic-rate tax. If you pay higher-rate tax, you'll need to claim your extra relief by filling in a tax return.

With personal pensions taken out by the self-employed (or employees before 1 July 1988) you do not get tax relief at source. Instead, you pay your pension contribution in full and will need to claim tax relief on your tax return. See Chapter 10.

Gift aid

From 6 April 2000, the previous minimum of £250 for a gift to charity to qualify for gift aid tax relief has been abolished, and any donation, however small, now qualifies. The relief applies to genuine gifts; you cannot claim relief if you get any significant benefits in return. A well-run charity should know the limits. People who are not resident in the UK for tax purposes can make gift aid donations if they pay income or capital gains tax in the UK against which they can claim relief.

The basic rate of tax of 22 per cent goes straight to the charity. So for taxpayers who pay no more than 22 per cent tax, tax relief is a way of increasing the value of a gift and there are no direct benefits to the person making the gift.

Here's how it works. You make a donation from your after-tax income. The charity can reclaim the tax you paid on that income assuming you paid the basic rate of 22 per cent on it – regardless of what rate of tax you actually pay.

You need to give the charity a gift aid declaration in writing, or by fax, by Internet or simply over the phone. The declaration can cover one donation or a number of donations. You can ask for all further donations to a charity to count as gift aid until further notice.

You can work out the tax a charity reclaims by *grossing up* (see p. 48). Simply divide your donation by 0.78. Let's say you give £39; £39 divided by 0.78 comes to £50. So the charity gets an extra £11. But you must have paid at least £11 in income tax or capital gains tax. It doesn't matter if your top rate of tax is only 10 per cent, provided you have paid enough tax to cover the tax reclaimed by the charity. If you haven't paid enough tax, the Inland Revenue can bill you for the tax it pays to the charity.

Higher-rate taxpayers can benefit directly by claiming higher-rate tax relief to reduce their tax bill. You can claim higher-rate relief through your tax return. The higher-rate relief works out as roughly equivalent to 23.08 per cent of your net gift. Again, consider a gift of £39; 23.08 per cent of £39 is £9. The higher-rate tax relief is worth £9, so the gift costs the higher-rate taxpayer only £30 once the extra relief has been claimed through the tax return. In addition, the charity can reclaim basic-rate tax making the gift worth £50. So a gift worth £50 to a charity costs a higher-rate taxpayer only £30. Likewise, a gift of £78 would be worth £100 to the charity but cost a higher-rate taxpayer only £60 once higher-rate tax relief has been claimed. (If the only higher-rate tax you have paid is on dividend income, the higher-rate relief will be less, because higher-rate tax on dividend income is only 32.5 per cent.)

Covenants
From 6 April 2000, gifts to charity by covenant will come under gift aid (see above). If you already had a covenant to charity in place before that date, the deed of covenant counts as your gift aid declaration so you need take no action. Enter details of payments on the gift aid section of the tax return.

Payroll giving
You can give to charity through payroll giving and get tax relief if your employer runs a payroll-giving scheme. From 6 April 2000 there is no limit on the amount you can give under payroll giving. And for three years from this date the government will pay a 10 per cent supplement to charities for all payroll-giving donations they receive. You get the tax relief at your highest rate of tax automatically because your donations are deducted from your gross pay before tax under the PAYE system is worked out.

Shares and securities – gifts to charity

From 6 April 2000 you can get tax relief on gifts to charity of certain shares and securities. Qualifying investments include shares and securities listed on any recognised stock exchange, unit trusts, open-ended investment companies (OEICs) and holdings in certain foreign collective investment schemes. Contact the Financial Intermediaries and Claims Office (FICO)* if you're not sure whether an investment qualifies.

The value of the gift is the market value of the shares on the day of disposal, plus any incidental costs of disposal: for example, you may pay a broker to transfer the shares from a nominee account. The relief reduces your income tax bill. In addition, the gift does not count as a disposal for capital gains tax and so can be excluded from your calculations when you work out what, if any, capital gains you have made during the tax year.

What applies to a gift of shares applies also to shares sold to a charity at less than market value. You can claim tax relief for the difference between what you received and the actual market value on the day of the sale, and can exclude that difference from your capital gains tax calculations.

Settlor-interested trusts – gifts to charity

From 6 April 2000, the settlor (including non-UK residents) of a settlor-interested trust can get income tax relief where a trust's beneficiaries include a charity (including non-UK residents). You can claim relief on the income paid by the trust to a charity. Settlor-interested trusts are those where the settlor retains an interest in the trust and so has to pay income tax on the trust's income.

Allowances

Subtracting allowances from your income is the last step in arriving at your taxable income. Everyone gets a basic personal allowance. Other allowances depend on your individual circumstances.

Full allowances for the 2000–1 tax year

Full allowances give you tax relief at your highest rate of tax. Provided you are entitled to them, you can deduct them from your income to arrive at your taxable income.

- **Personal allowance – £4,385** Everyone, including children, gets the basic allowance.
- **Higher personal allowance, age 65 to 74 – £5,790** Depending on your *net statutory income* (see p. 47) you can claim a higher

personal allowance if you reach the age of at least 65 by the end of the tax year on 5 April 2001.
* **Higher personal allowance, age 75 and over – £6,050**
Depending on your net statutory income (see p. 47) you can claim a higher personal allowance if you reach the age of at least 75 by the end of the tax year on 5 April 2001.
* **Blind person's allowance – £1,400** This allowance is given to people who are registered as blind with a local authority in England and Wales. In Scotland and Northern Ireland there is no register. A person must be unable to perform any work for which eyesight is essential. A concession means that you may get the allowance backdated by a year when you first claim.

You can transfer the blind person's allowance between husband and wife (and *vice versa*) if the person who gets the allowance is unable to make use of some or all of it. The Revenue will send you form 575 to complete and will then estimate the amount of allowance to be transferred. This will be given to the other spouse on a provisional basis but will be reassessed.

After the end of the tax year, the Revenue will check its estimate (or you can do this through your tax return). If it was too low, a rebate of tax already paid will be sent to the spouse to whom the allowance was transferred. If the estimate was too high, that spouse will owe some tax which will be collected the following year through the PAYE code or by altering the tax assessment.

Fixed-relief allowances for the 2000–1 tax year
Fixed-relief allowances give the same tax saving to all taxpayers, regardless of income. You save 10p for every pound of allowance. On 6 April 2000, several fixed-relief allowances were abolished:

* **married couple's allowance** for those who had not reached 65 by 5 April 2000 – people who reach the age of 65 after that date will never be able to claim married couple's allowance
* **additional personal allowance** (similar to the married couple's allowance but for non-married couples with children)
* **maintenance deduction**, except for those who had reached 65 by 5 April 2000
* **widow's bereavement allowance** – but see below.

A new fixed-relief allowance called children's tax credit, which will replace married couple's and additional personal allowances, is planned for the 2001–2 tax year.

The following fixed-relief allowances remain.

- **Married couple's allowance – 10 per cent of £2,000** You can claim the married couple's allowance if either partner had reached the age of 65 by 5 April 2000. The maximum tax saving is £200. In the year that you get married your allowance will be reduced by one-twelfth for each complete month after 6 April you remain single. So you can claim the full allowance only if you marry before 6 May.

A husband and wife who separate will each get the same amount of married couple's allowance they were receiving at the time of separation. But you cannot claim the allowance in tax years following your separation, regardless of whether you actually divorce. An exception applies to men who separated before 6 April 1990 and who have been wholly maintaining a wife by making voluntary maintenance payments. The man can claim the allowance if either he or his estranged wife was 65 by 5 April 2000.

A husband can claim the allowance for the whole of the tax year in which his wife dies, less any part that his wife used against her income. A wife can claim any married couple's allowance her husband had not used in the tax year within which he dies.

- **Higher married couple's allowance – 10 per cent of £5,185** Depending on your net statutory income (see p. 47) you can claim a higher married couple's allowance (provided either partner had reached the age of 65 by 5 April 2000). The maximum tax saving is £518.50.
- **Higher married couple's allowance, age 75 and over – 10 per cent of £5,255** Depending on your net statutory income (see p. 47) you can claim a higher married couple's allowance if either partner reaches 75 by 5 April 2001. The maximum tax saving is £525.50.
- **Widow's bereavement allowance – 10 per cent of £2,000** This can be claimed if your husband died during the 1999–2000 tax year, provided you did not remarry before 6 April 2000. The allowance has been abolished for women who are widowed during the 2000–1 tax year or later. Prior to abolition, the allowance could be claimed for the tax year within which a husband died and the following tax year. The maximum tax saving in 2000–1 is £200 (£197 in 1999–2000).
- **Maintenance deduction – 10 per cent of £2,000** Maintenance payments are regular payments made out of your income to

maintain a spouse from whom you are divorced or separated. You can claim for enforceable payments – those you are legally obliged to make, for example under a legally binding written agreement or a court order, or as assessed by the Child Support Agency – if either you or your ex-partner had reached 65 by 5 April 2000. You cannot claim for payments made under most foreign court orders or agreements, though you can claim for payments made under a European Union (EU) country (plus Liechtenstein and Norway) order or agreement. You cannot claim for capital payments or lump sums, even if they are paid in instalments, or for voluntary payments, i.e. those you cannot be forced to make. The maximum tax saving is £200.

Net statutory income and age-related allowances

The higher age-related personal allowance and higher married couple's allowances are reduced if your net statutory income is over £17,000 per year. Your allowances are reduced by half the amount of income over the limit. So if your income is £600 over the limit, you will lose £300 of the extra allowances.

When working out your net statutory income you must include the *gross* amount of any income from which tax has been deducted. So, for example, you may need to gross up (see p. 48) interest from a building society account. With dividends and distributions from shares and share-based investments such as unit trusts you add on the 10 per cent tax credit to get the gross amount. You must include the whole of any *taxable* gain on a life insurance policy even if you can claim top-slicing relief (see p. 48). But you can ignore tax-free income, such as income paid from a tax-free individual savings account (ISA) and capital gains. Deduct from your income the gross amount of outgoings (see p. 40) such as payments to a pension on which you get tax relief.

If you are over the income limit, consider whether you would be better off switching any investments to tax-free investments (e.g. Savings Certificates from National Savings or investments held within an ISA) or to your husband or wife. Tax-free income does not count towards net statutory income. Once you are over the limit, it is your higher personal allowance that is reduced first. Once that has been reduced to the level of the basic personal allowance your higher married couple's allowance will be reduced, depending on by how much you are over the limit.

The age-related part of the married couple's allowance always goes initially to the husband but it can be transferred to the wife at the end of the tax year if the husband has insufficient taxable income to make use of it. Any reduction in the age-related part of the married couple's allowance is based on the husband's income, even if he qualifies for the allowance because of his wife's age, or all of the basic allowance has been transferred to his wife, and even if her total income exceeds the income limit.

Gross and net income

Throughout this book, you'll come across references to *gross payments* and *net payments*, and to *gross income* and *net income*.

A gross payment, outgoing or deduction is the full amount. A net payment, outgoing or deduction is what you pay after tax relief has been taken into account – i.e. what you pay if tax relief is claimed at source. For example, an employee could pay a net contribution to a personal pension plan of £78. The gross premium would be £100 once the plan provider has reclaimed basic-rate tax relief and paid it into the plan.

Similarly, gross income is income before tax has been deducted, and net income is income after tax has been deducted. As an example, consider a share dividend of £9 which comes with a tax credit of £1. The gross income is £10 – the full amount of the share dividend once you've added back the tax deducted at source. The net income is £9 – what you actually receive after tax.

If you know the net amount and want to work out the gross amount, *divide* the net amount by:

- 0.9 for 10 per cent
- 0.8 for 20 per cent
- 0.78 for 22 per cent
- 0.77 for 23 per cent
- 0.76 for 24 per cent
- 0.75 for 25 per cent
- 0.675 for 32.5 per cent
- 0.6 for 40 per cent.

Alternatively, if you know the gross amount and want to work out the net amount, *multiply* the gross amount by the relevant figure from those given above.

EXAMPLE 1

Bert has invested £30,000 in a fixed-rate account paying 7 per cent interest. He'll get £2,100 interest in a year. But as he's a higher-rate taxpayer, he knows that the net return won't look as attractive once he's deducted the 40 per cent tax that he'll have to pay. To calculate the net (after-tax) return, he multiplies the gross (or before-tax) return of £2,100 by 0.6, which gives him £1,260. So tax will be £840. Half of that (20 per cent tax) will be deducted at source. So Bert knows he'll have to set aside £420 (£840 ÷ 2) to pay the extra higher-rate tax.

EXAMPLE 2

Percy turned 65 this tax year and wants to work out his net statutory income to find out how much age-related personal allowance he'll get. To do this he needs to calculate the gross amounts of his income and outgoings.

Percy knows what the gross amount of his pension is, but he needs to add the interest he gets from his building society account. His passbook shows only the net amount of interest he has received – i.e. the amount after deducting tax at 20 per cent. The net amount is £160 so he divides this by 0.8 to give the gross amount of £200.

How your tax bill is worked out in 2000–1

Here's a guide to working out (or checking) your tax bill. It will give the correct answer for many, but not all, taxpayers. Bear in mind that the tax calculation guide sent out with tax returns is 29 pages long, and there can be complications, for example if you have made business losses. Check for specific details elsewhere in this book.

Step 1 List all the money you received during the year Include the gross amount of all income where tax has been deducted at source, i.e. include your before tax pay and savings interest including the tax deducted at source. You may also need to include some income that you did not receive. For example you'll have to give details of rental income that you should have received during the year, even if you did not receive it.

Step 2 Take away deductions Deductions (sometimes called outgoings or expenses) reduce your tax bill. For example, you can deduct allowable business expenses before arriving at the figure for your taxable profits. Most deductions can be taken only from specific income – for example, the expenses of letting a UK property can be deducted only from the rental income you receive from UK property. If you do not have enough of this particular type of income because your deductions add up to more than the income received, you won't be able to deduct these from any other form of income. Check for details elsewhere in this book. A few deductions such as a gift of shares to charity (see p. 44) can be deducted from any taxable income.

Employees who pay into a personal pension plan or free-standing additional voluntary contribution (FSAVC) plan, and those who make gift aid donations to charity, should deduct these payments at Step 8 and not at this point.

Step 3 Cross off things that don't count as income and things that are tax-free This might include a gift of money or betting winnings, or the non-taxable part of an *asset disposal*, e.g. the non-taxable proceeds from a sale of unit trusts, or tax-free income from an ISA.

Step 4 List taxable items in the order they are to be taxed Your income and capital gains are allocated to different tax bands according to the following order:

- non-savings income (excluding taxable redundancy and lump-sum compensation payments and any taxable part of life insurance proceeds)
- savings income
- dividend income
- taxable redundancy and lump-sum compensation payments
- any taxable part of life insurance proceeds
- capital gains.

Step 5 Take away your personal allowance and any blind person's allowance If you are eligible for higher age-related allowances you'll first need to work out your net statutory income to find out what personal allowance you are entitled to (see p. 47).

Your tax office should allocate your allowances and any deductions which are not specific to particular income in a way that is most beneficial to you. For example, it would be normal for a basic-rate taxpayer to set the personal allowance against, say, employment income which is taxed at 22 per cent, rather than against savings income where tax is lower at just 20 per cent. You do not have to set your allowances against income in the order in Step 4.

You cannot set unused personal, blind person's (or married couple's) allowances against capital gains. They can be set only against taxable income. This means that you cannot use any unused allowances to reduce capital gains tax. Anyone who has taxable capital gains can claim the £7,200 exemption (see p. 234). But you always have to pay tax on any taxable gains over £7,200. Now skip to Step 6, unless you have a zero or minus figure after Step 5 (in which case see below).

If you are on a low income you could have a zero or minus figure once you have set your allowances against your taxable income. If this is the case you are a non-taxpayer (though if you have capital gains to take into account, follow Step 6.) A minus figure means you have not made full use of your personal or blind person's allowances.

If you have a zero or minus figure, you may be able to claim a refund of tax already paid. For example, if tax has already been deducted at source from savings interest you'll be able to reclaim the tax deducted. You may have shares or share-based investments such as unit trusts. These are paid with a 10 per cent tax credit but no one can claim back any tax even if they have unused allowances.

Step 6 Allocate the different tax rates according to the order in Step 4 The order is important because there are three tax rates in the basic-rate band and two tax rates in the higher-rate band. The order determines what (if anything) falls into the basic-rate band and what (if anything) falls into the higher-rate band:

- the *starting-rate band* (up to £1,520) – you pay tax of 10 per cent
- the *basic-rate band* (from £1,501 to £28,400 – i.e. the next £26,880) – you pay tax of 22 per cent on non-savings income, 20 per cent on savings income and capital gains, 10 per cent on share dividends and share-based investment income
- the *higher-rate band* (anything over £28,400) – you pay 32.5 per cent on share dividends and share-based investment income, 40 per cent on everything else.

If your income (and gains) do not go above the starting-rate band of 10 per cent, you'll be able to claim back half the 20 per cent tax deducted from any savings interest you have (as well as any other overpayment if, for example, too much tax has been deducted under PAYE). And even if your income (and gains) take you over the 10 per cent band, you'll still be able to reclaim half the tax deducted at source from any savings interest that falls within the 10 per cent band.

Step 7 Take away the tax you save by claiming a fixed-relief allowance Note that you cannot use married couple's or widow's bereavement (or personal or blind person's) allowances to reclaim tax on dividend income from shares or share-based investments. Nor can you use them to reduce capital gains tax (see Step 5 above).

Step 8 Deduct higher-rate tax relief if it is available Two items are most likely to apply here: employees' payments to personal pensions or FSAVC plans and gift aid donations to charities. You get basic-rate tax relief at source on both. The Revenue gives higher-rate relief by widening your basic-rate tax band by £100 (the gross payment) for every £78 you pay.

For example, George (see Example 3) gives £156 to charity. This is a gross gift of £200, including the 22 per cent basic-rate tax claimed by the charity (see p. 42). The Revenue would increase George's basic-rate band by £200 from the normal £26,800 to £27,000. Each £100 kept out of the higher-rate band saves £18 in tax, i.e. £200 would save £36. In George's case this would make no difference since his income and gains are already well within the basic-rate band. But if he were a higher-rate taxpayer, he could work out the approximate amount of tax to deduct under Step 8 by taking 23.08 per cent of his net payment. So 23.08 per cent of £156 comes to a fraction over the £36 he would actually save.

Pension payments can be deducted only from *pensionable earnings* (see p. 164) that fall into the higher-rate tax band. Gift aid payments can reduce any higher-rate tax, including higher-rate capital gains tax.

Does your calculation produce a different figure from the tax you have paid or been billed for the year? Small differences can result from the way certain figures are rounded up or down, especially in the PAYE system.

However, you will be able to claim some tax back if you have overpaid. For example, if you were being taxed under PAYE and stopped work during the year you may not have received all your allowances. Alternatively, you may owe some tax if, for example, your tax office does not know about an item of income or capital gain.

EXAMPLE 3

George is 63. He received £35,600 in 2000–1 but only £11,095 of this amount is taxable and he can reduce the tax bill on that money with the married couple's allowance.

Step 1 List all the money you received during the year
George draws up a list of the money he received in 2000–1.

- £20,000 came from the sale of shares but only £8,000 is taxable and he can claim an exemption on the first £7,200, so only £800 is taxable.
- £13,580 (before deduction of tax) came from an employer's pension.
- £700 came from a taxable savings account (that's the gross interest including the 20 per cent tax deducted at source).
- £500 he inherited.
- £420 came from an investment in a tax-free ISA.
- £400 came from share dividends (including the 10 per cent tax credit).

Step 2 Take away deductions
George has no deductions to take from any of his income.

Step 3 Cross off things that don't count as income and things that are tax-free
George crosses off £19,200 from the share sale, £500 he inherited and £420 income from his ISA. He is left with:

- £800 taxable gain on shares
- £13,580 (gross) employer's pension
- £700 (gross) from a taxable savings account
- £400 (gross) from share dividends.

Step 4 List taxable items in the order they are to be taxed

gross pension £13,580
gross savings interest £700
gross share dividends £400
share sale £800
total £15,480

Step 5 Take away your personal allowance and any blind person's allowance

George takes away his personal allowance of £4,385 from £15,480 to leave:

gross pension £9,195
gross savings interest £700
gross share dividends £400
share sale £800
total £11,095

Step 6 Allocate the tax rates
starting-rate band up to £1,520
£1,520 of pension at 10 per cent tax = £152
basic-rate band, the next £26,880
£7,675 of pension at 22 per cent tax = £1,688.50
£700 of savings interest at 20 per cent = £140
£400 of share dividends at 10 per cent = £40
£800 from share sale at 20 per cent = £160
total £2,180.50

Step 7 Take away the tax you save by claiming a fixed-relief allowance

George is married to Carol who was born before 6 April 1935, so he can claim the married couple's allowance (see p. 45). He works out his net statutory income (see p. 47) to see whether he can claim a higher married couple's allowance. His total income is £13,580 plus £700 (his savings interest) plus £400 (his share dividends) which comes to £14,680. (Note that capital gains from, for example, sales of shares, do not count towards net statutory income.) From this George can take away a £200 gross gift aid payment to charity. (He actually donated £156, which grosses up to £200 – see p. 42.) George is left with £14,480, well under the £17,000 total income limit, and can therefore claim a higher married couple's allowance of £5,185. He can deduct 10 per cent of £5,185, which comes to £518.50. This can then be deducted from the £2,180.50 total in Step 6 leaving £1,662.
total £1,662

Step 8 Deduct higher-rate tax relief if it is available

George is not a higher-rate taxpayer so he will not get a reduction in his tax bill for his gift aid donation to charity.
George's final tax bill is £1,662

Tax Schedules

Tax Schedules go back to the earliest days of income tax and are a way of dividing income up into different types. For example, earnings from your job are taxed under Schedule E, earnings from being self-employed under Schedule D.

Why are Schedules important?
Schedules affect the *expenses* you can deduct from your income before tax is worked out and also when the tax has to be paid. They also distinguish investment income from earned income. The distinction can be important. For example, when working out how much you can pay in pension contributions (which qualify for tax relief), you can take into account only earned income and *not* any income you receive from investments.

Cases
Some of the Schedules are divided up into Cases. Traditionally, Cases are given Roman numerals – Case I, Case II, Case III, Case IV, Case V and Case VI.

Rules about expenses can differ from Case to Case. For example, Schedule D Case I income has fairly generous rules, whereas Schedule D Case III is the meanest.

Working through the Schedules
Schedule A
Schedule A deals with the rules for taxing investment income, including all income from land and property.

Expenses you can claim Although income from property is taxed as investment income, you will pay tax as though the income is profits from a business. You will be able to deduct expenses incurred in the business of letting property. For the expenses you can claim when running a business, see pages 113 onwards.

Schedule D Case I, Schedule D Case II
Case I and Case II of Schedule D deal with the tax rules for earned income from self-employment. If the profits are from a trade (for example window-cleaner, shopkeeper, manufacturer), you're taxed under Case I. If the profits are from a profession (for example barrister, architect, accountant), you're taxed under Case II. The tax rules in each case are virtually identical.

Expenses you can claim You can claim any expense incurred *wholly and exclusively* for your trade or business. This definition is more generous than for people who are employed.

Schedule D Case III

Case III income is investment income. The main items are interest (for example interest from National Savings accounts, interest from loans), income from annuities and income from gilts. Other things taxed under this Case are annual payments (for example maintenance payments).

Expenses you can claim There are no expenses you can claim. Case III income is often referred to as *pure profit income* – i.e. it's assumed that you don't have any expenses.

Schedule D Case IV, Schedule D Case V

Case IV and Case V income is investment income (unless it comes from carrying on a business). These are both concerned with income from abroad. Case IV covers income from foreign securities. Case V covers most other types of income from abroad – for example rents, dividends, pensions, trading profits, maintenance payments. Broadly speaking, if you're not domiciled in the UK, or (for UK or Irish citizens) you're not ordinarily resident in the UK, you're taxed only on money which comes into the UK. Otherwise, you're taxed on the lot – whether or not it reaches the UK. If the money comes from a pension, one-tenth of the income normally escapes UK tax.

Expenses you can claim If the money comes from a trade or profession, tax is charged on your taxable profits – so you can subtract the usual expenses in working these out. Otherwise, there are normally none.

Schedule D Case VI

Case VI income is investment income (and *post-cessation* receipts). Case VI is a rag-bag of odd bits of income which don't fit in anywhere else. Examples are income from occasional freelance work; post-cessation receipts – i.e. after a business or partnership ends; income from investing in plays – unless you do this for a living.

Expenses you can claim There's nothing in the tax Acts about exactly what you can claim, but you have to pay tax on 'profits or gains'. So expenses necessarily incurred in making those profits are deducted when working out how much income is taxed. Losses can be set against other Case VI income for the same (or a following) tax year, but not against income from other Schedules or Cases.

Schedule E

Schedule E income is earned income and it covers:

- income from your employment – e.g. wages, expense allowances, tips, fringe benefits (if they're taxable)
- pensions from employers
- taxable social security benefits
- freelance earnings under a contract of employment – this can be a grey area, but if, for example, you're a teacher, and receive some money for marking examination scripts the Revenue will normally tax this extra income under Schedule E.

Schedule E is divided into three cases, of which Case I is by far the most important. Broadly, Case I catches income from employment if the employee is resident and ordinarily resident in the UK. Case II applies to people who normally live and work abroad, but who have some earnings arising in the UK. Case III applies to income remitted to the UK (by people resident in the UK) earned in employment abroad.

Expenses you can claim The rules are stricter than those for self-employed people: you can claim only expenses which are *wholly, exclusively and necessarily* incurred in the performance of the duties of your employment. For example, you could spend money on something which was entirely for use in your job, but unless it was *necessary* you wouldn't be able to claim it against tax.

Schedule F

Schedule F income is investment income in the form of dividends from companies resident in the UK and distributions from unit trusts and open-ended investment companies resident in the UK.

Expenses you can claim There are no expenses you can claim.

Useful Inland Revenue reading

You can ring the Inland Revenue Orderline* for leaflets and notes.

Leaflets and notes

SA/BK4	Self assessment – a general guide to keeping records
IR171	Income tax – a guide for people with children
IR139	Income from abroad? A guide to UK tax on overseas income
IR153	Tax exemption for sickness or unemployment insurance payments
IR65	Giving to charity. How individuals get tax relief

IR75	Gift aid – a guide for donors and charities
IR90	Tax allowances and reliefs
IR170	Blind person's allowance
IR93	Separation, divorce and maintenance payments
SA151	Tax calculation guide
SA152	Tax calculation guide – capital gains
SA153	Tax calculation guide – lump sums etc.
SA154	Tax calculation guide – capital gains and lump sums etc.
SA951	Tax calculation guide for trusts and estates
IR120	You and the Inland Revenue. Tax Credit Office (working families and disabled person's tax credit)
WFTC/BK1	Your guide to working families' tax credit
WFTC/FS1	Working families' tax credit
CTC/BK1	Working families' tax credit and disabled person's tax credit
CTC/FS1	Working families' tax credit, disabled person's tax credit and childcare
DPTC/FS1	Disabled person's tax credit
DPTC/BK1	Your guide to disabled person's tax credit
WFTC/AP	If you think a tax credit decision is wrong
WFTC/APNI	If you think a tax credit decision is wrong (Northern Ireland)
IR45	What to do when someone dies

Concessions

Extra-statutory concessions let you off paying tax that is technically due. Booklet IR1 gives details of each concession.

A16	Annual payments (other than interest) paid out of untaxed income
A17	Death of a taxpayer before due date for payment of tax
A30	Interest on damages for personal injuries (foreign court awards)
A40	Adoption allowances in Scotland
A43	Interest relief – partnerships, co-operatives, close companies and employee-controlled companies
A44	Education allowances under Overseas Service Aid Scheme
A81	Legal costs paid when you sue employer for loss of job
A84	Allowances to experts seconded to European Commission
A86	Blind person's allowance

4

Pay-As-You-Earn (PAYE)

For people who work for an employer, tax on wages or salaries is collected under the Pay-As-You-Earn (PAYE) system. Your earnings are taxed in the way described in this chapter if you are employed under a *contract of service* and are paid a wage or salary on a regular basis. See Chapter 5 for detailed rules about tax on perks at work, and Chapter 7 if your job involves working abroad for some or all of the time.

If you are employed under a *contract* (or contracts) *for services*, and are paid when you send in a bill or invoice, you are likely to count as self-employed. Earnings from employment are taxed under the rules of Schedule E, earnings from self-employment under Schedule D. Details of how self-employed people are taxed are given in Chapter 6.

If you work through an agency, for example as a temp, you will be treated as an employee (normally of the agency) and taxed under PAYE. But there are exceptions to this rule: you may be able to work through an agency and be treated as *self-employed* if you're an entertainer, model, sub-contractor in the building industry, or if all your work is done at or from your own home.

If you work for an employer, you pay tax on the pay you get from your job as you receive it during the tax year. The PAYE system collects tax on earnings, sometimes on regular freelance earnings and also on pensions. PAYE is also often used to collect tax on investment income. You may be paying tax on the investment income sooner than you need to. You can ask to pay it later.

> **Sub-contractors in the building industry**
> Even though you may regard yourself as self-employed, basic-rate tax will be deducted from all your earnings unless you hold a sub-contractor's tax certificate. Holding a certificate is not necessarily proof that you are self-employed. See Inland Revenue leaflet IR40 for more details.

Understanding your payslip

Your payslip will show a large gap between your earnings before any deductions – *gross pay* – and your take-home pay – *net pay*. Below is an example of a payslip. Your payslip may be laid out differently, but the same type of information should appear on it.

Typical deductions are for income tax, National Insurance contributions, pension contributions, season ticket loans, trade union subscriptions and gifts to charity under a payroll-giving scheme.

How the figures match up
On the example payslip, there's a large difference between £2,000.00 (the figure for gross pay) and £1,384.50 (the figure for net pay). Here's how you get from one to the other.

1. Gross pay   £2,000.00

EMPLOYEE NAME					EMPLOYEE NO		DEPT
GEORGE WATKINS		DELCO LTD			676		51
BASIC	OVERTIME ETC	HOLIDAYS	BONUS/OTHER PAY	ADJUSTMENT	TAX-FREE ALLOWANCE	PERIOD	DATE
2000.00						3	30/6/00
E/E NI	E/E NI TO DATE	DED 1	DED 2	TAX CODE	GROSS TO DATE	TAX TO DATE	TAX THIS PERIOD
167.07	501.21	49.50		438L	6000	986.79	328.93
E/R NI	GROSS PAY	CUMULATIVE PENSION	PENSION DEDN	PRE-TAX B	PRE-TAX C	TOTAL DEDUCTIONS	NET PAY
199.59	2000.00	210.00	70.00			615.50	1384.50

a   b   c   d

e f   g h   i j   k   l m   n   o p   q r

Deductions

2. Pension
   contributions [1]   £70.00

3. Tax   £328.93

4. National Insurance [1]   £167.07

5. Other deductions (in this case,
   for season ticket loan)   £49.50

6. Total deductions   £615.50

1 *minus* 6   = £1,384.50

[1] What you pay (not your employer's contributions).

A quick check on tax

If you're a basic-rate taxpayer, you can use a calculator to check that
the tax on your payslip is broadly correct for 2000–1.

Gross pay   A
                                                           _____

Pension contributions [2] plus payroll giving   B
                                                           _____

Free-of-tax pay. To find this, take your current PAYE code,
add the figure 9 to the end. For example, if your PAYE code
is 438 (ignoring any letters), make this 4389. Then divide by
12 if paid monthly or 52 if paid weekly.   C
                                                           _____

Add B to C and subtract the total from A   D
                                                           _____

Multiply D by 0.22   E
                                                           _____

Then, to take account of the 10 per cent band, deduct
£15.20 if you are paid monthly, £3.50 if you are paid weekly.
                                                             F
                                                           _____

F should be roughly equivalent to the tax deducted for the month or
week, and will be the correct deduction *if* you have the right PAYE code.

[2] Don't include if your employer's pension scheme is not an 'approved' or
'statutory' one.

Key to payslip entries

a **Basic**   Pay before additions for things like overtime or bonus.

b **Holidays**   Depends on company policy. May include your pay while you're on holiday, or only exceptional payments (e.g. pay in lieu of holiday).

c **Adjustment**   On this payslip, statutory sick pay and pay from company's own sick pay scheme (less any amount attributable to contributions you've made to the scheme) or statutory maternity pay are entered here.

d **Tax-free allowance**   Depends on company policy. Non-taxable payments (e.g. the mileage allowance you receive within the fixed-profit car scheme) paid with your salary may be entered here.

e **EE NI**   Employee's National Insurance contributions for the month.

f **ER NI**   Employer's National Insurance contributions for the employee.

g **EE NI *to date***   Employee's National Insurance contributions since the beginning of the tax year.

h **Gross pay**   This is the month's salary before deductions, including (possibly) amounts for overtime and bonus if these were paid.

i **Ded.1/Ded.2**   Deductions – such as repayment of company loan, an advance on salary, your contributions to your employer's private medical bills scheme, a payment under a payroll-giving scheme – would be entered in these boxes. In the example, Ded.1 is the monthly repayment of a season ticket loan.

j **Cumulative pension**   Employee's contributions to employer's pension scheme that have been made since the beginning of the tax year.

k **Pension dedn**   Employee's contributions to the employer's pension scheme for the period covered by the payslip. If it is a 'statutory' or 'approved' employer's scheme you get tax relief on contributions you pay (within certain limits) so they will be deducted before tax is worked out on the rest of your pay. 'Statutory' employers' schemes are for civil servants, employees of state-owned businesses, etc.; other schemes have to be approved by the Revenue.

l **Tax code**   PAYE code number. For how this is worked out see p. 70.

which are, and aren't, allowable. If an expense is allowable, the answer to both questions is yes. If it's not allowable:

- you get no tax relief on what you pay yourself
- you're taxed on what your employer pays, *less* anything you pay towards the cost.

For an expense to be allowable, the money must be spent *wholly, exclusively and necessarily in the performance of the duties of your employment*. So if you get a fixed expense allowance and don't spend all of it on allowable expenses, you are taxed on the difference. Note that *necessarily* means necessary within the context of your job, and not simply necessary to you. So if working late means that you'll have to stay in a hotel overnight because your home is a long distance away, the hotel bill won't be allowable if the job could be done by someone else living closer to your workplace. However, small differences in individual circumstances (or in a tax inspector's assessment of them) may mean that an expense disallowed for one person is allowable for someone else. Allowable expenses can be set off only against earnings from your job and not, for example, against investment income.

Expenses paid out of your own pocket

In trades where it's customary to provide your own tools or clothing (e.g. plumbing) many trade unions have agreed a *fixed deduction* for cleaning and maintaining special clothing and tools where employers do not provide help with these things. The amount of fixed deduction varies from £45 to £110 a year depending on the type of work you do. Full details are available in the Inland Revenue leaflet IR1. A special form is available to healthcare workers to enable them to claim this deduction for up to six years before the 1998–9 tax year. Ask your tax office for details. You can claim the whole fixed deduction as an allowable expense even if you don't spend it all. And if you spend more, you can claim more.

Expenses your employer pays for

If an expense *isn't* allowable, it counts as part of your pay and you're taxed on it – either under PAYE or through your tax return. If an expense *is* allowable, how it's dealt with varies.

- Has your employer got a *dispensation* for the expense? If so, your employer doesn't have to give the Revenue details of expenses paid to you and you don't have to declare them on your tax return.

- Is the expense covered by a PAYE settlement agreement with the Revenue? If so, your employer voluntarily agrees to pay any tax due on it and you do not need to put it on your tax return.
- Your employer has to tell the Revenue at the end of the tax year about all expenses paid to you (or for you) for which there isn't a dispensation or PAYE settlement agreement (except in the case of some low earners – see next point). This is done at the end of the tax year on form P11D. You'll have to put all these expenses on your tax return, and you'll be taxed on any which aren't allowable. Allowable expenses have to be entered twice on a tax return – as income and as deductions. Entering them as deductions means that you don't pay tax on them.
- If you count as a low earner (see p. 86), allowable expenses, including 'scale payments' (for example, a mileage allowance) agreed between your employer and the Revenue are ignored. Other expenses, if they're not allowable, haven't been taxed as part of your pay and total more than £25 a year, are declared by your employer on form P9D, and any tax due is normally collected under PAYE in a later tax year.

Expenses in your job

To get a job
• **normally allowed** cost of retraining provided by employer to acquire new work skills, if you have left or are about to leave your job; this includes fees, books, travelling and extra living costs for the course
• **not allowed** agency fees; expenses of interview

Training
• **normally allowed** cost of fees and essential books met by your employer for a full-time external training course lasting from four weeks to one year; possibly, extra cost of living away from home and extra travelling expenses, if away for under two years
• **not allowed** books you buy yourself and fees, even if they are for a course you are required to take by your employer; examination fees; re-sit courses or examinations

Fees and subscriptions to professional bodies
• **normally allowed** subscriptions to professional bodies provided membership is relevant to your job; fee for keeping your name on a professional register approved by the Revenue – if this is a condition of your employment

Clothes
• **normally allowed** cost of replacing, cleaning and repairing protective clothing (for example overalls, boots) and functional clothing (for example uniform) necessary for your job and which you are required to provide; cost of cleaning protective clothing or functional clothing provided by your employer, if cleaning facilities are not provided
• **not allowed** ordinary clothes you wear for work (e.g. a suit) which you could wear outside work – even if you'd never choose to

Tools, instruments
• **normally allowed** cost of maintaining and repairing factory or workshop tools and musical instruments you are required to provide; cost of replacing instruments and tools, less any amount from sale of old, provided new ones not inherently better than old; often, fixed amounts agreed with trade unions
• **not allowed** initial cost of tools and instruments, but may be able to claim *capital allowances*

Books and stationery
• **normally allowed** cost of reference books necessary for your job which you have to provide (for example actuarial tables, government regulations). If the book's useful life is more than two years you may have to claim *capital allowances* instead. Cost of stationery used strictly for your job (for example business notepaper if you are a sales rep). Possibly, cost of books essential for a full-time training course
• **not allowed** cost of other books; subscriptions to journals to keep up with developments, general stationery (for example pens, notepaper, etc.)

Use of home for work
• **normally allowed** proportion of heating and lighting costs and, possibly, proportion of telephone, cleaning and insurance costs. If part of home is used *exclusively* for business, you may be able to claim a proportion of rent and council tax. But these expenses are allowed only if it is necessary that you carry out some of your duties at or from home (i.e. if it is an express or implied condition of your employment)

Interest
• **normally allowed** interest on loans to buy equipment (for example car, typewriter) necessary for your job
• **not allowed** interest on overdraft or credit card

Legal expenses
• **normally allowed** costs and expenses if held liable for some wrongful act as an employee; cost of insurance to cover such expenses
• **not allowed** cost of suing your employer for pay

Travelling
• **normally allowed** expenses incurred strictly in the course of carrying out job. *Running costs of own car*: whole of cost if used wholly and necessarily in carrying out your job, proportion of cost if used privately as well. Work out what proportion your business mileage bears to your total mileage, and claim corresponding proportion of cost. Alternatively, use the fixed-profit car scheme – see below. *Company car*: if you pay for running costs (for example petrol, repairs, maintenance), claim proportion of cost of business mileage. Occasional late-night journeys home or extra travel costs if public transport disrupted by industrial action. The cost of travelling to a temporary place of work, see p. 69
• **not allowed** travel to and from your normal place of work (but if you travel to or from a job abroad, see p. 136). Cost of buying a car and depreciation – you may be able to claim a *capital allowance* if the car is necessary for you to carry on your job and it is necessary for you to provide one

Spouses travelling together
• **normally allowed** if paid by (or for) employer, and if spouse has, and uses, practical qualifications associated with trip, or if their presence is necessary for essential business entertaining of overseas trade customers, or if your health is so poor that it is unreasonable to travel alone. Often only a proportion of cost is allowed

Entertaining
• **normally allowed** expenses of entertaining customers (but only if you can claim these expenses back from your employer, or pay them out of an expense allowance given specifically for entertaining). Employees of non-trading organisations like schools, local authorities and trade unions can claim all entertaining expenses, but only if spent *wholly, exclusively and necessarily in the performance of your job*
• **not allowed** any other entertaining expenses

Hotel and meal expenses
• **normally allowed** reasonable hotel and meal expenses when travelling in the course of your job, see p. 69
• **not allowed** laundry, phone calls (though these may be tax-free benefits in kind – see Chapter 5)

Allowances for business mileage

If you use your own car, motorcycle or bike for business, your employer may pay you a mileage allowance. This allowance could come to more or less than the actual costs you incur doing business mileage. If your employer pays you an allowance based on Inland Revenue authorised mileage rates (also known as the fixed-profit car scheme for car mileage), the Revenue ignores any profit you make and the whole allowance is tax-free. If the allowance is less than your actual costs, you can claim the excess as an allowable expense.

You can use authorised mileage rates to work out what, if any, tax or tax relief is due, even if your employer does not use them – see table below. For example, if you do 3,500 business miles a year in a 1,300cc car, your tax-free allowable motoring costs are 3,500 x 35p = £1,225 a year. If your employer pays you less than this in mileage allowance, you can claim the difference as an allowable expense; if your employer pays no allowance, you claim the whole tax-free amount; if your employer pays you more, you must pay tax on the excess. The advantage of using the scheme is that you do not have to keep detailed records of all your motoring or cycling costs. You simply need to note your annual business mileage.

Authorised mileage rates

	Rate on first 4,000 business miles in a tax year	Rate on each mile over 4,000 business miles in a tax year
Cars – engine size		
up to 1,000cc	28p	17p
1,001cc to 1,500cc	35p	20p
1,501cc to 2,000cc	45p	25p
over 2,000cc	63p	36p
Motorcycles	24p	24p
Pedal cycles	12p	12p

Working away from home

You can claim travel, hotel and meal expenses when working away from home as long as you can show that the journey is not ordinary commuting or private travel. Ordinary commuting is travel between your home (or anywhere else which does not count as your workplace) and your 'permanent workplace'. Your permanent workplace – in tax terms – is one at which you expect to work for more than 24 months (or the whole of your period of employment, if less than 24 months).

However, even if you work somewhere for more than 24 months, you may still be able to claim tax relief if you spend less than 40 per cent of your working time there. So if, for example, you live in Brighton but are working on a three-year project in Wrexham one day a week, you have breached the 24-month rule but you can still claim tax relief for the cost of getting to Wrexham and back (with meal and hotel expenses en route) because you spend less than 40 per cent of your time there.

Much depends on exactly what your contract of employment requires in the way of attendance, and there are special rules for foreign travel. Inland Revenue leaflet IR161 summarises tax relief on business travel, but if you need more details see the Inland Revenue booklet *Employee Travel: A Tax and NICs Guide for Employers*.

Pay-As-You-Earn (PAYE)

Principles

PAYE is a way of collecting tax as you are paid. The Revenue gives you a PAYE code which indicates an estimate of the amount of free-of-tax pay you're entitled to over the tax year. Any excess over this free-of-tax amount will be taxed. For how the free-of-tax amount is worked out, see the illustrated PAYE Coding Notice on pp. 78–9. Each pay-day, you'll be allowed $\frac{1}{52}$ or $\frac{1}{12}$ (depending on whether you're paid weekly or monthly) of the free-of-tax amount.

How it works

The PAYE Coding Notice will show you how your PAYE code is calculated; your employer is just told what your code is. Your employer then uses your code, and *tax tables* supplied by the Revenue, to deduct the right amount of tax from your pay.

The *pay adjustment tables* allow your employer to work out how much of each month's or week's pay is free of tax. For example, if your code is 438L, this gives you up to £4,389 free-of-tax pay for the tax year (for precisely how the £4,389 figure is reached see p. 75). On monthly pay, you'll get $\frac{1}{12}$ of £4,389 (£365.75) of your pay free of tax each month. If you're paid weekly, you'll get $\frac{1}{52}$ of £4,389 (£84.41) of your pay free of tax each week. Any excess, after deducting pension contributions to 'statutory' or 'approved' employers' pension schemes and payments to charity under a payroll-giving scheme, is taxable. The *taxable-pay tables* tell your employer how much tax to deduct.

As the tax tables work on a cumulative basis, this makes dealing with a change to your PAYE code part-way through a tax year comparatively simple.

PAYE code changes during the tax year

If your code number goes up (except for 'K' codes – see p. 75) you get more free-of-tax pay and so pay less tax. Because the PAYE system works cumulatively, you will have been given too little free-of-tax pay since the start of the tax year. So the first time your new code is used you'll pay less tax than in subsequent months (or weeks) to make up for the time you were paying too much; you may even pay no tax and get a rebate.

If your code number goes down (except for 'K' codes – see p. 75) you will have been given too much free-of-tax pay since the start of the tax year and so paid too little tax. If the amount of underpaid tax is large and would mean a sharp drop in your take-home pay the first time the code is used, the Revenue will tell your employer to apply your new code on a *week 1* or *month 1* basis. For the rest of the tax year you'll get $\frac{1}{52}$ or $\frac{1}{12}$ of your new tax-free pay (depending on whether you're paid weekly or monthly) each pay-day. So on each pay-day, you pay the amount of tax you would have paid if your tax code had been correct at the beginning of the tax year.

But you will still owe the underpaid tax from the pay-days before your code was changed. This will be shown as a deduction on next year's PAYE Coding Notice so that the unpaid tax will be collected over the whole of the following year. If, however, you owe a substantial amount of underpaid tax, you'll be sent a bill for the tax due.

EXAMPLE 1

Boris's code was 438L. This meant that he could earn £4,389 a year (£365.75 a month) free of tax.

Boris discovers he can claim a mileage allowance for the 5,000 miles he drives for his employer. He can claim £1,200 (see p. 68). In August, Boris put in his claim and got a revised code of 558L. This meant that he was entitled to free-of-tax pay of £5,589 (£4,389 + £1,200) for the whole tax year, £465.75 a month. That's £100 extra free-of-tax pay a month, saving £22 basic-rate tax every month.

In addition to this regular monthly saving of £22, Boris got an extra £110 in his pay when his employer first used the new code in September. This was a rebate of tax for the first five months of the tax year when he paid too much tax. So Boris's total extra pay in his September pay packet was £132.

PAYE Coding Notice

Not everyone gets a coding notice each tax year. You're likely to get one if, for example, you're a higher-rate taxpayer, you are 65 or over, if certain of your outgoings this year look like being more (or less) than last year, you receive taxable benefits in kind, you claim expenses in your job, you owe tax from a previous year, or if there are any other 'complications'. You won't normally get a coding notice if there are no complications, you are a starting-rate or basic-rate taxpayer and your only allowance is the basic personal allowance for those under 65. Most notices are sent out in January or February each year and apply for the tax year starting on the following 6 April.

Allowances for the coming tax year may well be changed in the spring Budget, after the PAYE Coding Notices have been sent out. If the only allowance you receive is the basic personal allowance, you won't be sent a new coding notice but you will be given the new personal allowance automatically if it is changed in the Budget.

You get a separate PAYE code for each job in which your earnings are taxed under PAYE and each private pension taxed under PAYE. You may also receive a separate coding notice for each source of PAYE income. If possible, all your outgoings and allowances are included in the code for your main job or private pension.

You should always check that a notice is correct. If you think there's a mistake, tell the Revenue at once. The same applies if your circumstances change during the tax year – for example, if you get rid of your company car or find that you can claim an allowable expense.

If your PAYE code is not correct at the end of the tax year you'll have paid the wrong amount of tax under PAYE. You'll have to claim a rebate, or pay more tax in a later year. To get your code changed, phone or write to your tax office and give details of why your code is wrong, quoting your tax reference number or National Insurance number.

How to read a PAYE Coding Notice

An example of a PAYE Coding Notice is given on pp. 78–9, and below we explain the sort of things you might find on your notice.

Your tax allowances

Here you'll find details of the personal allowances you are entitled to and the Revenue's estimate of any deductions you can claim on which tax relief isn't given at source.

Allowances   Details of the allowances you're entitled to will be included here. If you are entitled to one of the higher levels of allowance because of your age, this may be reduced if your income is above a certain amount. An estimate of your income for the tax year will be shown under the heading **Estimated income £ . . .**

Job expenses   An estimate of allowable expenses in your job which qualify for tax relief. If you're counted as earning at a rate of £8,500 a year or more, for example, it will include expenses for which your employer does not have a *dispensation* or PAYE *settlement agreement*.

Professional subscriptions   Subscriptions to professional bodies which qualify for tax relief.

Retirement annuity payments   Payments into personal pensions (called 'retirement annuity contracts') taken out before 1 July 1988.

Personal pension relief   Payments to a personal pension taken out since 1 July 1988 or a free-standing additional voluntary contribution (FSAVC) scheme made by a higher-rate taxpayer. There'll be no entry for basic-rate tax payers: you get tax relief by making net payments to the pension provider.

Maintenance payments   The amount of maintenance you pay which qualifies for tax relief will be shown here. Since 6 April 2000, this has been a maximum of £2,000 and it is available only where either party to the former marriage was born on or before 5 April, 1935.

Taxed annual payment   Extra tax relief for higher-rate taxpayers on qualifying payments to charity will be shown here.

Amounts taken away from your total allowances

In this section you'll find details of income you get which is taxable but is paid without any tax being deducted, e.g. taxable perks from your job, etc. The tax owed on this income will be collected through the PAYE scheme by deducting the total from your total allowances.

State pension/state benefits   Includes state pensions and benefits the Inland Revenue believes you are entitled to and which are not taxed before you get them.

Benefits and expenses provided by your employer   Perks from your job which count as taxable income (see Chapter 5).

Taxable expenses payments   Payments from your employer to cover expenses in your job.

Part-time earnings/tips/commission/other emoluments   Extra income from your main job and freelance or part-time earnings on which you don't pay tax under PAYE.

Jobseeker's allowance   Includes taxable benefits you have claimed because of unemployment (see Chapter 9).

Untaxed interest   Interest received without tax being deducted (e.g. from taxable National Savings).

Property income   The amount of any income you receive from letting property.

Tax underpaid £ . . .   If you owe tax for an earlier year (or years) the amount owed will be included here. A deduction from your allowances will be made to collect this tax. If you pay basic-rate tax, the tax owed is divided by 0.22 and the figure you get (less any fraction) is a deduction – see Coding Notice illustration on pp. 78–9; for higher-rate taxpayers, the deduction is the amount of tax owed divided by 0.4.

Higher-rate tax adjustment   If you pay tax at the higher rate and have investment income already taxed at the 20 per cent rate, there may be an adjustment here to collect the extra tax owed.

Allowance restriction   If you claim one of the fixed-relief allowances, there will be an adjustment here to restrict the relief you get. Under the **Allowances** column of the notice, you will see the full amount of the married couple's allowance or widow's bereavement allowance (available only to women who were widowed in the 1999–2000 tax year or an earlier tax year – see p. 46). You will also see an entry called **Allowance restriction** in the other column. This is an adjustment to ensure that the relief you get is restricted to 10 per cent (so there is no need for a restriction if your top rate of tax is 10 per cent).

You can multiply your allowance by 10 per cent to get a figure for the tax the allowance saves you. To check that the allowance restriction produces the correct tax saving, deduct the allowance restriction from the allowance you are entitled to and multiply by your highest rate of tax. This should give the correct tax saving, except where you are only a little over the basic- or higher-rate threshold. See Example 2.

EXAMPLE 2

Bert is a 66-year-old married man and a basic-rate taxpayer. He is entitled to a married couple's allowance of £5,185. Relief is restricted to 10 per cent so is worth £518.50. The allowance restriction on his coding notice is £2,828. Bert deducts £2,828 from the full allowance of £5,185 to get £2,357. He then multiplies £2,357 by 22 per cent (his top rate of tax) to get £518.54, the same figure (apart from rounding adjustments) as the fixed-rate relief of 10 per cent. So the restriction is correct.

Total deductions
This is the total figure for all deductions and adjustments.

Your tax-free amount for the year
This figure is reached by subtracting your total deductions from your total allowances and determines your PAYE code.

The number in your code
This is arrived at by knocking the last figure off the figure in **Your tax-free amount for the year**. So if this figure is 950 your code number is 95. Because of the way rounding works, this code entitles you to tax-free pay of £959 instead – an extra £9 of tax-free pay. If it's zero, you have no free-of-tax amount to be deducted.

The letter in your code
L if you get the *basic* personal allowance.

P if you get the *full* personal allowance for someone aged 65 to 74.

Y if you get the *full* personal allowance for someone aged 75 and over.

V if you get the *full* personal allowance for someone aged 65 to 74 plus the *full* married couple's allowance for someone aged 65 to 74 and are likely to pay basic-rate tax.

H if you get the *basic* personal allowance plus the *basic* married couple's allowance and are likely to pay basic-rate tax.

A if you get the *basic* personal allowance plus the *basic* married couple's allowance and are likely to pay higher-rate tax.

K if the total deductions shown on your notice come to more than your total allowances; the Revenue will have to collect tax under PAYE at a higher-than-normal rate.

BR if all your allowances have been given elsewhere and all your earnings will be taxed at the basic rate. You're most likely to get this if it is a code for a second job.

T in all other cases – e.g. if you get a reduced amount of age-related personal allowance because your income is above a certain level. You can ask to be given a T code if you don't want your employer to know about your age or marital status.

PAYE queries

If you pay tax under PAYE, it's possible that your tax office is a long distance away. This may make resolving any tax problems you have more difficult. Check to see if there's a local tax office or tax enquiry centre – look in the phone book under *Inland Revenue*. If necessary, details of your tax affairs can be sent to the local office so that the people there can discuss your problems with you, give you advice and chase up matters (e.g. a long overdue tax rebate) for you.

Starting work

If you've started work for the first time after full-time education or are returning to work after a break, for example to bring up children (and haven't claimed jobseeker's allowance or income support) your employer will ask you to complete form P46. You will also be asked to complete P46 if you have changed jobs and have no P45 (see below) to give your new employer. You will be given an emergency code – 438L in 2000–1 – which assumes that you're entitled only to the basic personal allowance. This code gives you £365.75 of tax-free pay each month (£84.41 each week) – i.e. $\frac{1}{12}$ (or $\frac{1}{52}$) of £4,389 (the personal allowance of £4,385 rounded up to £4,389).

Tax won't be deducted until the free-of-tax pay since the beginning of the tax year has been used up. So, for example, if your first monthly pay-day is in the fourth month of the tax year (July), you are entitled to four months of free-of-tax pay on code 438L, i.e. £365.75 × 4 = £1,463. So on your first pay-day tax will be deducted only on any excess over £1,463. If your total pay for the month is less than this amount, the balance of the free-of-tax pay owing to you will be given to you on subsequent pay-days until it runs out. Note that if you don't complete form P46, the emergency code will be operated on a *week 1* (or *month 1*) basis (see p. 70).

When your proper code has been worked out, you will be sent a PAYE Coding Notice and your employer will be told your new code. This new code may allow you a higher amount of free-of-tax pay than the emergency one. If so, any over-paid tax will be refunded to you.

Changing jobs

When you change jobs, your old employer should give you a form P45. This shows your PAYE code and details of the tax deducted from your total pay for the year to date. Give this to your new employer on your first day so that the correct amount of tax can be deducted from your pay.

If you don't do this, your employer will follow the procedure described in *Starting work* (above), and you may pay too much tax for a while.

Students working in the holidays

A student who gets a holiday job can avoid paying tax on weekly or monthly earnings above the usual tax-free threshold. His or her earnings and other taxable income for the whole year must not exceed the personal allowance of £4,385.

Both the student and the employer have to complete form P38(S) to get this exemption.

Interrupting work
Off sick

Statutory sick pay paid by your employer and sick pay you get from your employer's own sick pay scheme are taxable under PAYE. But if the amount you get is lower than the amount of free-of-tax pay you are entitled to, your employer will refund some of the tax you've already paid, in each pay packet. You get statutory sick pay only for a limited period; then you may get state incapacity benefit which is taxable (see Chapter 9).

Some employers have *sick pay insurance schemes* which pay out income when you're off sick. Tax will normally be deducted from payments you receive from these schemes. But if you contribute towards the insurance premiums, you'll be taxed only on the part of the payment attributable to your employer's contributions. If you've taken out your own sick pay insurance policy, income from it is not taxable.

Maternity

Statutory maternity pay and any extra maternity pay paid by your employer is taxable under PAYE. If either statutory maternity pay or other maternity pay is paid when (or before) you stop working, the tax deducted will depend on your PAYE code. If it's paid *after* you've stopped working, i.e. after you have received a P45, tax is deducted at

Inland Revenue

Mr A Green
100 Acacia Avenue
New Town
Midshire

MD9 1AB

222

Please quote your Tax reference
and National Insurance number
if you contact us

Your tax code for the year shown above is   457L

**This tax code is used to deduct tax payable on your income
from**   ANYOLD BUSINESS LTD

If you move to another job, your new employer will normally
continue to use this tax code.
The tax code is made up as follows:

See note	Your tax allowances	£	Amounts taken away from your total allowances	£

PAYE Coding Notice

This form shows your
tax code for the tax year   2000–2001

> *Please keep all your coding notices. You may need
> to refer to them if you have to fill in a Tax Return.*

Mrs Z Black
HM Inspector of Taxes
Midshire 1
Crown Buildings
New Town
Midshire   MD9 9BC

Date of issue
30 SEP 2000

Tax Office telephone ☎
01122 334455

National Insurance number
AB 12 34 56 Z

Tax reference
222/A900

The '*See note*' columns below refer to the numbered notes
in the guidance leaflet P3 *Understanding Your Tax Code*.
Leaflet P3 also tells you about the letter part of your
tax code.

Check that the details are correct. If you think they are
wrong, or you have any queries, contact your Tax Office
(details above).

This coding notice replaces any previous notice for the
year. You should pass it to your agent if you have one.

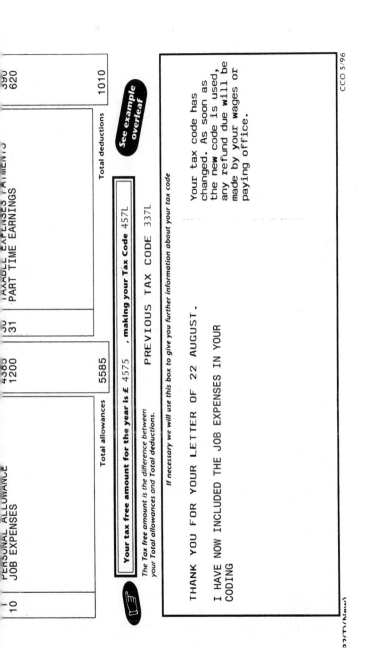

PERSONAL ALLOWANCE
JOB EXPENSES

	390
10	620

TAXABLE EXPENSES PAYMENTS
PART TIME EARNINGS

4365	
1200	31

Total allowances 5585

Total deductions 1010

Your tax free amount for the year is £ 4575 , making your Tax Code 457L

*The Tax free amount is the difference between
your Total allowances and Total deductions.*

PREVIOUS TAX CODE 337L

See example overleaf

If necessary we will use this box to give you further information about your tax code

THANK YOU FOR YOUR LETTER OF 22 AUGUST.

I HAVE NOW INCLUDED THE JOB EXPENSES IN YOUR
CODING

Your tax code has
changed. As soon as
the new code is used,
any refund due will be
made by your wages or
paying office.

CCO 5/96

P2(T)(New)

the basic rate. This could mean too much tax is deducted. If so, claim a rebate. State maternity allowance isn't taxable.

Laid off, on short-time, on strike
If you have been laid off or put on short-time, too much tax may have been deducted from your pay since the beginning of the tax year. Tax refunds due will be given on your normal pay-days by your employer. If you've paid too much tax because you are on strike or involved in a strike, you will have to wait until you return to work (or the end of the tax year if sooner) for a tax refund.

Stopping work
Redundancy
If you're made redundant, earnings your employer owes you and which are paid when you leave your job, are taxed in the normal way under PAYE, for example normal wages, pay in lieu of holiday, pay for working your notice period. But the following payments are tax-free:

- any lump sum for any injury or disability which meant you couldn't carry on your job
- compensation for loss of a job done entirely or substantially outside the UK
- terminal grants or gratuities you receive when you leave the armed forces
- certain lump-sum benefits from employers' pension schemes
- money your employer pays into a retirement benefit scheme or uses to buy you an annuity (if certain conditions are met)
- outplacement counselling services paid for by your employer for employees who are or become redundant, to help them find new work.

Other payments are also tax-free if, when added together, they total less than £30,000. These are:

- redundancy payments made under the government's redundancy payments scheme or a scheme 'approved' by the Revenue
- pay in lieu of notice, in most circumstances, provided your conditions of service don't say you're entitled to it
- other payments made to you, as long as they are not payments for work done, not part of your conditions of service, and, technically at least, unexpected: this would normally cover redundancy payments over and above the government minimum.

Anything more than £30,000 is added to the rest of your income and taxed in the normal way.

Your employer has to deduct tax under PAYE on the excess over £30,000 before paying it to you. Unless a special, reduced tax payment is negotiated with your tax office, too much tax will be deducted because the tax tables don't allow for these special rules, and you'll have to claim a rebate.

Sometimes your employer may carry on giving you some payment or benefit after you have left your job – for example, allowing you to keep your company car for a period. If so, the payment or benefit will be taxed as pay in the year it is received.

Employer going bust

Pay in lieu of notice is normally tax-free. But if you lose your job because your employer goes bust, and get pay in lieu of notice from the liquidator (or trustee in bankruptcy), basic-rate tax will be deducted from the whole amount. You can't claim a full rebate, but if this tax is more than the tax that would have been deducted if you'd received it as normal pay, you can get a refund of the difference. You get the refund from your local Redundancy Payments Office.

Refunded pension contributions

If you leave an employer's pension scheme within two years, you may be offered a refund of your contributions, but 20 per cent tax will have been deducted. This can't be reclaimed.

Dismissal

Earnings your employer owes you will be taxed under PAYE. In most circumstances pay in lieu of notice, together with any other payments (provided they are not payments for work done, not part of your conditions of service and, technically, unexpected), totalling less than £30,000 are tax-free. Anything over £30,000 is taxed in the normal way.

If you are awarded compensation for unfair dismissal by an industrial tribunal, the amount you get for loss of wages will be paid after deduction of basic-rate tax, though any compensation for loss of your job would not be taxed. As with pay in lieu of notice paid by a liquidator (see above), the only tax rebate you can get is the difference between the amount actually deducted and any (smaller) amount that would have been deducted if you'd received the money as normal pay.

Spare-time income

Many people who have jobs in their spare time don't realise that they almost certainly need to tell the Revenue about the income they get. Below are some common examples of how you might get spare-time income.

- You have a second job in the evenings, or at weekends (for example working behind the bar at your local pub), completely different from your main job.
- You're someone with a skill (for example an electrician, plumber, carpenter, motor mechanic) and you normally work full-time for an employer, but you get spare-time income doing work for other people, often for cash.
- You're a professional person (for example a schoolteacher, architect) using your professional skills and knowledge to get spare-time income (for example, if you're a teacher, you may give private tuition).
- You have some extra income (such as commissions from running mail-order catalogues).
- You own a second home or a caravan which you let out, or you let rooms in your house.

How the Revenue finds out about your activities

- If you are employed, your employer should tell the Revenue that you have started work, and ask for a PAYE code for you to be able to work out how much tax to deduct from your pay.
- If your activities consist of a trade or business, or the letting of property, and you advertise in local or national papers, the Revenue has a department which monitors these ads and checks to see that the income has been declared.
- The Revenue has wide powers to compel employers to send details of payments they make to freelance staff, consultants, caterers, etc. – in short, any people who do work for them.
- The Revenue also gets a number of letters from informants – some of them anonymous, and a few of them paid by the Revenue. What they say may or may not be taken seriously, but it may tie in with suspicions the Revenue already has, or it may alert it to taking an interest in your affairs.

Since the Revenue can get to know of your income without your telling it, it makes it more important for you to report your income yourself. If the Revenue starts an enquiry into your affairs as a result of information received you're more likely to be charged penalties in addition to the tax due than if you disclose your income voluntarily.

Telling the Revenue
If you get a tax return

If you get a tax return it should be 'specific' to your particular income circumstances. The return consists of a standard eight-page return (which everybody gets) and then 'supplementary pages' for specific types of income. You will need to make sure you have the correct supplementary pages for your type (or types) of income.

If you have more than one employer, you will need to complete an 'employment' supplementary page for each one. If you receive different types of income from your employer (such as tips or commission, as well as salary), the employment supplementary page has specific headings for this.

If you do freelance work, or have spare-time income from a trade or business as well as being employed, you will need to complete both the employment and self-employment supplementary pages. However, if the freelance income is one-off, you can put it under 'any other income' on the main part of the tax return.

If you don't get a tax return

If you *don't* get a tax return and you receive income the Revenue does not already know about, you must declare it within six months of the end of the tax year in which the income arose – for example income earned in August 2000 must be reported to the Revenue by 5 October 2001 at the latest – so that the Revenue can send out a tax return. If you fail to do this you can be charged a penalty when you eventually tell the Revenue about the income, or the Revenue finds out about it from other sources. You will also be charged interest from the date on which the tax ought to have been paid to the date on which it was actually paid.

How will your income be taxed?

Income from spare-time activities can be taxed in a number of ways:

- under Schedule E if your income is from an employment
- under Schedule D Case I or II if it amounts to a trade or business
- under Schedule A if your income is from the letting of property
- under Schedule D Case VI if the income doesn't fit in anywhere else, or arises from activities which do not amount to a trade or business and are not an employment, for example a casual commission: income under this Case will almost always be taxed as investment income.

Why bother about the Schedules?

The type and level of expenses which you can claim and the treatment of any losses differ from Schedule to Schedule. The rules for allowable expenses under Schedule E are more stringent than the rules under Schedule D Cases I and II. For example, the cost of travelling between your home and your place of work is not allowable under Schedule E. But if you're in business and work from your home, the cost of travelling to see your clients or customers is allowable under Schedule D Cases I and II.

Useful Inland Revenue reading

You can ring the Inland Revenue Orderline* for helpsheets, leaflets and notes.

Leaflets and notes

IR34	Pay As You Earn
IR56	Employed or self-employed? A guide for tax and National Insurance
IR33	Income tax and school leavers
IR60	Income tax and students
IR122	Volunteer drivers
IR125	Using your own car for work
IR161	Tax relief for employees business travel
480	Expenses and benefits – a tax guide
CIS FACT 5	The new construction industry scheme – a handy guide
IR164	Advice to subcontractors going on to deduction under the construction industry scheme
SA150	Tax return guide
SA151	Tax calculation guide – capital gains
SA152	Tax calculation guide – lump sums
SA154	Tax calculation guide including capital gains and lump sums
SA951	Tax calculation guide for trusts and estates

Helpsheets

When you receive a helpsheet, make sure it relates to the tax year for which you want information.

IR204	Lump sums and compensation payments
IR206	Capital allowances for employees
IR207	Non-taxable payments or benefits for employees
IR208	Payslips and coding notices
IR209	Mobile phones

Concessions

Extra-statutory concessions let you off paying tax that is technically due. Booklet IR1 gives details of each concession.

A1	Flat rate allowances for cost of tools and special clothing

Tax on perks at work

If your employer lets you use a company car, gives you luncheon vouchers, or pays for private medical bills insurance, *benefits in kind* are a part of your life. The tax system can treat some benefits favourably compared with a rise in salary. But there are disadvantages:

- no choice – you may find that benefits in kind aren't the things you'd choose to spend your money on
- lower pension, life insurance and redundancy money – all these are often linked to your pay in cash, *excluding* the value of the non-cash benefits you get.

A benefit – or an expense?

Some payments which you might get from your employer are on the borderline between a benefit, which is generally taxable, and an allowable expense, which isn't. These include mileage allowance, removal expenses and overnight allowances, and are normally regarded as expenses because your employer is reimbursing you for money you have to spend in the course of your job. They are all tax-free as long as they count as *allowable expenses* – see p. 64.

Your employer may have what's called a *dispensation* for certain expenses and benefits you get, such as a mileage or subsistence allowance. You don't have to pay tax on these expenses and benefits or declare them on your tax return. Your employer can tell you which, if any, benefits have a dispensation. If you get expenses and benefits for which there is no dispensation, your employer will give details to both you and your tax office on form P11D if you earn more than a certain amount.

Tax-free benefits

There are many benefits in kind which you can get without having to pay any tax, provided certain conditions are met. Some of the more common ones include pension contributions from your employer, free life insurance and sick-pay insurance, cheap or free drinks and meals.

Taxable benefits

With these benefits, you pay tax on the *taxable value* of the benefit. This is also the amount you have to put on your tax return if you get one. The taxable value will be the amount the benefits cost your employer to provide, less anything you pay towards the cost (but see p. 87 onwards for exceptions) *if you count as earning £8,500 or more a year*. If you don't, the taxable value will be the *second-hand value* of the benefits. The taxable value of benefits which don't have a second-hand value (for example, free hairdressing at work) is nil.

Do you count as earning £8,500 or more?

You count as earning £8,500 or more a year if you're paid *at a rate of* £8,500 or more a year. *At a rate of* means you'd be caught if, say, you were paid £4,250 for six months' work. If you are paid at a lower rate than £8,500 a year, you will still count if the total of the following comes to more than £8,500:

- your earnings from your job
- your benefits in kind *valued as though you did earn £8,500 or more*
- any expenses reimbursed to you by your employer for which there is no dispensation (see p. 85), even if these count as allowable expenses.

EXAMPLE 1

Joseph is paid a salary of £7,800. His employer lets him use a two-year-old car in which he drives over 18,000 miles on business. The list price of the car when registered was £12,000. To find out if he counts as earning £8,500 or more, Joseph adds the taxable value of the car, assuming he does fall into this category, to his salary. This is £1,800, which takes him over the limit of £8,500. So Joseph counts as earning £8,500 or more.

If you have more than one job with the same (or an associated) employer and your total earnings and expenses from these jobs come to £8,500 or more, you'll also be caught. This also applies to directors.

Directors

A director is normally treated as earning £8,500 or more whatever he or she earns. An exception is a director earning at a rate of less than £8,500 a year who:

- owns or controls 5 per cent or less of the shares in the company (together with close family and certain other associates), *and*
- is a full-time working director of the company, *or* works for a charity or non-profit making company, *and*
- is not a director of an associated company.

Swapping pay – a warning

No matter how much (or little) you earn, if you can swap some of your pay for a perk (or *vice versa*) the Inland Revenue may tax you on the amount of pay you give up if this is more than the taxable value of the perk under the normal tax rules. However, if you have a choice of having a company car or being paid more cash, you will be taxed on the taxable value of the car if you choose the car, or the cash if you choose the cash. And there are measures to stop job-related accommodation being valued at an artificially low cash alternative.

How each benefit in kind is taxed

(*indicates tax-free if you don't count as earning £8,500 or more)

certain clothes needed for work, for example overalls   tax-free

*company car, including private use of the car   you pay tax on the taxable value of car – see p. 91

*company van available to you for your private use   you pay tax on a standard amount of £500 if the van is less than four years old or £350 if the van is more than four years old. A *pro rata* amount will be calculated if you share the van with other employees or if you had use of the van for only part of the year. Vans over 3.5 tonnes are tax-free

crèche or day-nursery provided by employer   tax-free – but childcare cash payments or vouchers are taxable

credit cards, charge cards   you pay tax on what employer pays out, *less* anything you pay towards employer's costs and *less* allowable expenses

discounts on goods and services, if employers sell their own products   tax-free, as long as employer doesn't end up out of pocket

employees' outings, including Christmas party   normally tax-free (up to £75 per head per year)

fees and subscriptions to professional bodies and learned societies   tax-free if organisation approved by the Revenue and relevant to employment; if not, taxed on cost to employer

food and drink – free or cheap meals, tea, coffee, etc.   tax-free, if provided for all employees – even if separate facilities are provided on the employer's premises for different groups of employees

gifts – wedding or retirement gifts, etc. (not gift of money on retirement)   tax-free

gifts of things (not cash) from someone other than your employer   tax-free, provided they cost £150 or less

gifts of something previously lent, for example furniture, TV you pay tax on taxable value – see p. 96 (the second-hand value if you don't count as earning £8,500 or more)

*hairdressing at work   you pay tax on cost to your employer

liability insurance, for example professional indemnity insurance paid by employer   tax-free

life insurance – cost of providing this under a Revenue-approved scheme   tax-free

living accommodation, for example rent-free or low-rent home sometimes tax-free – see p. 95

*loans of money   tax free if the loan is a *qualifying* one or if the total of other loans is less than £5,000, but there may be tax to pay if other loans are more than £5,000 – see p. 94

*loans of things, for example furniture   loans of computers worth up to £2,500 and bikes lent for work are tax-free, on other things you pay tax on taxable value – see p. 96

long-service awards, for example gifts of things or shares (but not a gift of money)   tax-free, if given for service of 20 years or more with the same employer; the cost must not be more than £20 for each year of service, and you must not have had such an award within the past ten years

luncheon vouchers   15p each working day is tax-free

*****medical bills insurance**   you pay tax on the cost to your employer (tax-free if insurance is to cover working abroad)

mobile phones   tax-free

mortgage – low-interest or interest-free   you pay tax on the taxable value – see p. 94

pension contributions employer pays to 'approved' or 'statutory' pension   tax-free

*****petrol or diesel – if you get any for private use in company car** you pay tax on taxable value – see p. 93

relocation allowances towards extra expenses in higher-cost housing areas   tax-free (within limits)

removal expenses   normally tax-free up to a limit of £8,000, if you have to move to take a new job or are transferred by your employer. Expenses must be reasonable and can include solicitor's, surveyor's and estate agent's fees, stamp duty, removal costs, an allowance for carpets and curtains, temporary subsistence allowance, rent while you're looking for a new home and, in certain circumstances, the interest on a bridging loan

scholarship and apprenticeship schemes awarded to you by your employer   tax-free if you are enrolled for at least one academic year and attend full-time for an average of at least 20 weeks a year; the rate of payment (including lodging, subsistence and travelling allowances but excluding tuition fees) must not be above £7,000 or the amount of a grant from a public body such as a research council, if higher – otherwise taxable in full; payments for time at work are taxable in normal way

*****scholarships awarded by your employer to your children** normally you pay tax on the amount of scholarship; special rules apply if scholarship comes from a trust fund

*****season ticket loans**   tax-free if the total of the cheap loans from your employer is £5,000 or less – see p. 94

shares in employer's company through employee share scheme approved by the Inland Revenue   usually tax-free – but see p. 97

sick-pay insurance – cost of insurance paid for you by employer
the cost of insurance met by employer is tax-free if the scheme meets the Revenue's conditions; income from scheme normally taxed as part of your earnings; if you pay some of the premiums, only the income provided by the employer's contributions is taxable

*social and sports facilities   tax-free if provided for staff use generally; facilities for limited groups of staff may be taxable

staff suggestion schemes – awards from schemes   tax-free up to an overall maximum of £5,000

training, for example attending a course or studying on normal pay; tuition fees   pay is taxed in the normal way; genuine training (*not* holidays, rewards or asset transfers disguised as training) paid for by your employer are tax-free, as are costs associated with the training – for example books, course materials, travel and subsistence expenses; similar expenses for retraining in new work skills if you are leaving or have left your job are also tax-free. Once individual learning accounts (ILAs) are up and running (expected to be late 2000), employers' contributions to the cost of education or training of an ILA holder will be tax-free if the education or training qualifies for a grant or discount from the Department for Education and Employment (DfEE)

transport between home and work   tax-free if for disabled employees who can't use public transport

travel costs, for example for taxi, hire car for late-night journeys from work   tax-free, provided you have to work to 9pm or later, it doesn't happen regularly or frequently and public transport would be difficult

travelling and subsistence allowance   tax-free when public transport is disrupted by industrial action

vouchers   this includes things like a travel voucher (for example rail season ticket) or any other voucher exchangeable for goods or services (for example a letter to a tailor ordering you a new suit) or for cash (for example a cheque); you pay tax on amount your employer pays out less anything you pay towards the cost; if you work for a transport organisation, any transport voucher under a scheme in operation on 25 March 1982 is tax-free.

Company cars

The government has announced a change in the way company cars are to be taxed, which will take account of the level of a car's carbon dioxide emissions. However, the changes are not scheduled to take effect until the 2002–3 tax year.

In 2000–1 the taxable value of a company car that you have for private use is:

- 35 per cent of the car's list price (including extras) at the time it was first registered, or
- 25 per cent of the car's list price if you drive between 2,500 and 17,999 business miles in the tax year, or
- 15 per cent of the car's list price if you drive 18,000 or more business miles in the tax year.

But from this figure you can deduct:

- one-quarter of the value if the car is four or more years old at the end of the tax year
- anything you pay to your employer for private use of your company car.

If you are disabled and your car has been converted to suit your special requirements, the taxable value will not include the costs of supplying and fitting accessories designed specifically for disabled people.

If you have had use of the car for only part of the year, the taxable value is reduced in line with the amount of time the car was available to you.

There is no tax on a company car if you do not count as earning £8,500 or more a year, but see Example 1 on p. 86.

EXAMPLE 2

The list price (including extras) of Jonathan's company car was £12,000 when it was first registered. Jonathan travels more than 18,000 business miles so the taxable value is 15 per cent of £12,000 – i.e. £1,800. The car is four years old at the end of the tax year, so the value is reduced by one-quarter of £1,800 (£450) to £1,350.

Jonathan is a higher-rate taxpayer, so will pay tax of 40 per cent of £1,350, which comes to £540.

Second cars

A second company car provided for you or a member of your family is taxed in the same way as the first car, but with one important difference. The taxable value is 35 per cent of the list price unless you drive 18,000 or more business miles. If so, the taxable value is 25 per cent of the list price.

Special rules for old and valuable cars
The Revenue will use the open-market value to work out the basic taxable value of cars for which there is no list price. The open-market value will also be used if the car is over 15 years old, its open-market value is over £15,000, and the car's list price is lower than the open-market value.

Tax on company cars in the last six tax years

For the tax years 1994–5 to 1998–9, the taxable value of a company car was

- 35 per cent of the list price (as described above)
- less one-third of the full taxable value if you drove between 2,500 and 17,999 business miles in a tax year
- less two-thirds of the full taxable value if you drove 18,000 or more business miles in a tax year.

You could reduce the figure for taxable value based on mileage by one-third if the car was four or more years old by the end of the tax year. And if you paid your employer anything for private use of the car, the taxable value was reduced by what you paid your employer. If you had use of the car for only part of the year, the taxable value was reduced in line with the amount of time the car was available to you. The full taxable value of a second company car could be reduced if you drove 18,000 or more business miles, but by one-third only.

In 1999–2000, the rules for taxing company cars were the same as for the 2000–1 tax year – see p. 91.

Motoring costs for a company car paid by your employer

If your employer pays certain costs, such as repairs, business petrol, insurance, direct (for example settling a company account), it doesn't affect your tax position. But if *you* pay them, claim the business part of what you pay as *allowable expenses* in your tax return, i.e. the proportion attributable to your business mileage. And if your employer reimburses you in full or in part (for example by a mileage allowance), put what you get under *expense allowances* (unless your employer has a dispensation, see p. 85).

If your company car has a telephone, you have to pay extra tax. And if your employer provides you with a telephone for your own private car, there'll be tax to pay on private use unless you reimburse your employer.

A free car-parking space provided at or near your place of work isn't taxable. And there will be no tax to pay if your employer pays for a parking space (or reimburses the cost).

Pool cars

A pool car doesn't count as a benefit in kind and there is no tax to pay by the people who use it. To qualify as a pool car, the car must be made available to (and used by) more than one employee, and it must not normally be kept overnight at, or near, an employee's home. Any private use of the car must be incidental to business use – for example occasional travel between home and office as part of genuine business trips.

Car fuel

Fuel you get from your employer for private use is taxable. If you count as earning £8,500 or more a year, fixed taxable values (based on engine size and shown in the table below) apply if you get *any* petrol for private use from your employer which you don't pay for in full – no matter how much or how little. It might be worth considering paying for any private mileage yourself. If you don't count as earning £8,500 or more, car fuel is tax-free.

Size of engine	Charge for petrol	Charge for diesel
1,400cc or less	£1,700	£2,170
1,401 to 2,000cc	£2,170	£2,170
over 2,000cc or no cylinder capacity	£3,200	£3,200

Tax on car fuel benefit in the last six tax years

	Petrol: engine cc			Diesel: engine cc	
	up to 1,400	1,401 to 2,000+	*2,001+	up to 2,000	2,001+
1999–2000	£1,210	£1,540	£2,270	£1,540	£2,270
1998–9	£1,010	£1,280	£1,890	£1,280	£1,890
1997–8	£800	£1,010	£1,490	£740	£940
1996–7	£710	£890	£1,320	£640	£820
1995–6	£670	£850	£1,260	£605	£780
1994–5	£640	£810	£1,200	£580	£750

*or no cylinder capacity

Cheap loans

If your employer lets you have a loan on which you pay little or no interest, there may be tax to pay if you count as earning £8,500 or more (see p. 86).

Since 6 April 2000, *qualifying* loans have been tax-free. Broadly, these are loans where you can claim tax relief on the interest. They include a loan that you use to buy plant or machinery, such as a computer or car, that you must have for your job. Other loans, for a season ticket for example, are tax-free provided the total amount of other loans comes to less than £5,000.

If the total of these other (non-qualifying) loans is over the £5,000 limit, you'll pay tax on the difference between the interest you actually pay and the interest you would have paid if you had been charged the official rate of interest *on the total of all your loans* – i.e. *not* your total loans less £5,000. In 2000–1, the official rate of interest is 6.25 per cent. It applies for the whole of the tax year. So to avoid paying tax on your cheap or interest-free loans, don't borrow more than £5,000 from your employer.

EXAMPLE 3

Brenda has a £10,000 home-improvement loan from her employer. She paid interest of 3 per cent in the 2000–1 tax year. Because the loan is over the £5,000 limit for tax-free loans, she will have to pay tax. The difference between the official rate of interest of 6.25 per cent and the 3 per cent she pays her employer is 3.25 per cent. Interest of 3.25 per cent on £10,000 is £325. So £325 is the taxable value of the loan. Brenda pays tax at the higher rate of 40 per cent. Tax at 40 per cent on £325 comes to £130.

Living accommodation

A rent-free or low-rent home can be a tax-free benefit if one of the following applies:

- it is necessary to live in the home to do your job properly (for example you are a caretaker)
- living in the home enables you to do your job better, and it is customary for people doing your sort of job to live in such a home (for example you run a pub)
- there is a special threat to your security, and you live in the home as part of special security arrangements.

A home provided for a company director for either of the first two reasons above qualifies as a tax-free benefit only if he or she owns 5 per cent or less of the shares in the company, *and* is a full-time working director *or* the company is non-profit-making or a charitable body.

There are special rules for free or cheap accommodation abroad – see p. 137.

Even if the home does count as a tax-free benefit, if you count as earning £8,500 or more you will have to pay some tax on what your employer pays for heating, lighting, cleaning, decorating or furnishing (but the value put on these by your tax inspector cannot be more than 10 per cent of your earnings not including these benefits).

If a rent-free or low-rent home doesn't count as a tax-free benefit, the Revenue values the benefit at either the *gross value* of the home (the figure the rateable value used to be based on, but with an adjustment in Scotland) or the rent your employer pays if greater, less any rent you pay. For properties which don't have a gross value (such as property built since the abolition of rates) your employer will estimate what the gross value would have been and agree a figure with the Revenue. This method of valuing the benefit applies whether or not you count as earning £8,500 or more.

If you share the right to use a property with other employees, the total tax bill for all the users cannot come to more than the amount that one person with sole use of the property would pay. The Revenue will decide how much each user pays according to the relevant facts.

If the home costs your employer more than £75,000 to provide, there could be an extra tax bill. The extra tax bill is worked out by finding how much the accommodation cost to buy and set up and deducting £75,000. You then multiply this figure by the *official rate of interest* on loans – 6.25 per cent in 2000–1. But you can deduct any rent paid in excess of the *gross value*. If the taxable value of the home is based on the full market rent, the extra tax bill will not apply.

Agricultural workers whose employers give them free board and lodging may be able to take higher wages and arrange their own accommodation instead. That would normally make the value of their board and lodging taxable. But, by a concession, agricultural workers who don't count as earning £8,500 or more will generally avoid the tax.

Workplace nurseries

The cost of workplace nurseries provided by employers is not taxable. The exemption applies to nurseries run by the employer at the workplace or elsewhere and to nurseries set up jointly with other employers, voluntary bodies or local authorities (provided the employer participates in the cost and management of the scheme). Facilities provided for older children after school or during school holidays are also tax-free.

Any cash payments or vouchers provided by an employer to cover child care (for example childminders or private nurseries) are taxable for all employees. Any childcare places bought by an employer in other companies' schemes where the employer is not involved in the management are also taxable.

Loans of items/gifts of items loaned

If your employer lends you a computer worth up to £2,500 or a bicycle which you use for work, there is no tax to pay. If you count as earning £8,500 or more and your employer lends you something like furniture or a television, you are taxed on 20 per cent of the market value at the time your employer first loaned the item out, *less* anything you pay for the use of it. For items first loaned out before 6 April 1980, the 20 per cent figure becomes 10 per cent. Anything your employer pays for servicing (or any other costs) is added to the taxable value.

If your employer gives you something previously lent to you, your tax inspector will value it at the market value at the time your employer first loaned it out, *less* anything you've paid towards it, and *less* any amount you've already paid tax on (for example under the 20 per cent rule). But if this value is lower than the market value when the item is given to you, you'll be taxed on the higher (market) value, *less* anything you've paid towards it. And if the item was first loaned out before 6 April 1980, its value is taken as the market value when the item was given to you (*less* anything you've paid towards it).

If you count as earning £8,500 or more and you use something for which your employer pays rent (such as a flat or a television) your tax inspector can value the benefit at the amount your employer pays in rent, running costs, etc., *less* anything you pay, if this comes to more than the value using the normal method.

If you don't count as earning £8,500 or more, there's no tax on a loan and you're taxed on the *second-hand value* of a gift.

Employee share schemes

The following sorts of schemes have considerable tax advantages if they are *approved* by the Revenue:

- profit-sharing schemes
- company share option plans
- share option schemes you joined before 17 July 1995
- savings-related share option schemes
- all-employee share ownership plans.

Profit-sharing schemes
Under a scheme approved by the Revenue you can get shares in your employer's firm free of tax – up to £3,000 worth of shares, or 10 per cent of your earnings, if higher, with an overall limit of £8,000-worth of shares a year. The scheme must meet various conditions. For example, the shares must be held in trust for you. They can't normally be handed over to you from the trust for at least two years (unless you reach retirement age, are made redundant, or stop work through injury or disablement). If you withdraw your shares within three years of getting them, there will normally be some income tax to pay (unless the shares are withdrawn because you die).

If you sell the shares for more than their value at the time you were given them, you make a capital gain, and there may be capital gains tax to pay (see Chapter 14). Any dividends you get count as part of your income for the tax year in which you get them.

Company share option plans
A share option plan gives you the right (or *option*) to buy shares in your employer's company at some future date, but at today's market price. There is no income tax to pay on any gain you make when you exercise your option if the scheme is an *approved* one and you exercise the option at least three years and no more than ten years after you received it. Instead, any gain you make when you sell (or give away) the shares will count as a chargeable capital gain.

Any capital gains tax will be based on the difference between the price you paid to buy the shares and the price when you sell (or give away) the shares. To get approval, the scheme must meet certain conditions. For example, the shares must not be issued at a discount (i.e. at an option price below the current market value), and the value of any other approved options held by the employee (apart from under savings-related schemes) must not exceed £30,000.

Executive share option schemes were the forerunner of company share option plans. On 29 April 1996, all existing approved executive share option schemes automatically became approved company share option plans (see above). However, if you received your option under an approved executive share option scheme before 29 April 1996, special tax rules may apply.

If your rights were granted on or after 17 July 1995, or you are in a share option scheme which is *not approved*, and the value of the shares covered by the option exceeds £30,000, you will pay income tax. Income tax is levied on the difference between the market value when you exercise your option and the cost to you of the shares, including any amount paid for the option. You might have to pay capital gains tax when you sell (or give away) your shares, based on the difference between their market value when you exercise your option and their value when you dispose of them.

Share option schemes joined before 17 July 1995
If your share option was granted before 17 July 1995 you will not have to pay tax when you use this option to buy shares if you use it:

- at a time when the scheme is still an approved scheme, *and*
- at least three and no more than ten years after you received it, *and*
- more than three years after the date on which you last used an option under any approved share option scheme (except a savings-related scheme) for which income tax relief was given.

Savings-related share option schemes
Your company can run a savings scheme giving you the option to buy its shares some years in the future at a price fixed now. The maximum saving is £250 a month and the minimum is generally around £5. Provided the scheme is approved by the Revenue and you buy the shares with the proceeds of a save-as-you-earn scheme – which normally runs for three, five or seven years – there will usually be no income tax to pay when the option is given to you, nor on the

difference between the value of the shares when you buy them and the price you pay for them (which must not be less than 80 per cent of their market value at the time the option is given). But if you sell (or give away) the shares, there could be capital gains tax to pay based on the difference between the price you buy at and the market value when you sell or give them away.

All-employee share ownership plans
From 6 April 2000, you can receive up to £3,000 worth of free shares in your employer's company. In addition, you can buy up to £1,500 worth of shares each tax year from your before-tax income. For each share you buy, your employer can give you a further one or two shares.

Company takeovers and share option schemes
It is possible for employees in a company which is taken over to exchange their existing share options under an approved share option plan (including savings-related schemes) for options to buy shares in the company which takes over. The replacement options can be granted only if certain conditions are met to ensure that the employees concerned will be no better or worse off than if the takeover had not happened.

Individual savings accounts
You can transfer any shares you get from an employee share scheme into a 'stocks and shares' individual savings account (ISA). You will not be liable to capital gains tax when you do so. The value of the shares at the date of transfer counts towards your annual ISA investment limit.

Useful Inland Revenue reading

You can ring the Inland Revenue Orderline* for helpsheets, leaflets and notes.

Leaflets and notes
IR134	Income tax and relocation packages
IR133	Income tax and company cars from April 1994
IR136	Income tax and company vans. A guide for employees
IR145	Low interest loans provided by employers
IR115	Tax and childcare

IR95   Approved profit sharing schemes. An outline for employees

IR97   Approved save as you earn share option schemes. An outline for employees

IR101   Approved company share option plans. An outline for employees

SA102   Notes on share schemes

Helpsheets

When you receive a helpsheet, make sure it relates to the tax year for which you want information.

IR201   Vouchers and credit cards

IR202   Living accommodation

IR203   Car benefits and car fuel payments

IR207   Non-taxable payments or benefits for employees

IR210   Assets provided for private use

IR213   Payments in kind – assets transferred

IR214   Service rights connected with job-related accommodation

IR216   Shares as benefits

IR217   Shares acquired – post acquisition charges

IR218   Shares acquired – operation of PAYE

IR287   Employee share schemes and capital gains tax

Concessions

Extra-statutory concessions let you off paying tax that is technically due. Booklet IR1 gives details of each concession.

A2   Meal vouchers

A4   Travelling expenses

A6   Miners – free coal and allowances in lieu

A22   Long service awards

A56   Accommodation in Scotland provided for employees

A57   Suggestions schemes

A58   Travelling and subsistence allowance when public transport disrupted

A59   Home to work travel of severely disabled employees

A60   Agricultural workers' board and lodgings

A61   Clergymen's heating and lighting

A65   Workers on offshore oil and gas rigs or platforms – free transfers from or to the mainland

A66   Employees' late night journeys home

A70   Small gifts to employees by third parties and staff Christmas parties

Working for yourself

Being self-employed includes all sorts of occupations – owning a shop, being a wholesaler, working as a doctor, barrister or writer, and so on. Most of this chapter is for people in business on their own ('sole traders', in the jargon), but it also includes some information about partnerships (see p. 128). You may be taxed as if you're a business, even if you don't think you are, if your tax inspector says you are *trading*. You might be said to be trading if, among other points:

- you frequently buy and sell similar items
- you sell items which you haven't owned for very long
- you alter the items so that you can sell them for more
- your motive in buying and selling is to make a profit.

Casual earnings are dealt with in Chapter 4 on p. 81.

The advantages of setting up a company

In general, the taxation of companies is outside the scope of this book. However, when starting a business, you should consider whether a company or self-employment would be the most suitable form for your business. And you should review the position from time to time. There is a wide range of factors to take into account, one of which is tax.

If you are self-employed, your business does not have a separate identity from you. Profits from the business are simply added to any other income you have and tax is worked out in the normal way. Depending on your income, allowances and other deductions, you might be a non-taxpayer or a starting-rate, basic-rate or higher-rate taxpayer.

If your business is set up as a company, it has a separate legal identity from you. The company must pay corporation tax on any profits. From 1 April 2000, companies with taxable profits of £10,000 pay corporation tax at the starting rate of 10 per cent. Between £10,000 and £50,000 the average rate gradually increases until it reaches 20 per cent. The small companies rate of 20 per cent is payable by companies whose profits are in the range between £50,000 and £300,000. Between £300,000 and £1.5 million, the average rate again increases gradually until it reaches 30 per cent, which is the main corporation tax rate paid by companies with profits of £1.5 million or more.

You personally may have to pay income tax on money you take out of your company, either in the form of earnings (see Chapter 4) or as share dividends (see p. 213). If you take out money as earnings, both the company as employer and you as employee may have to pay National Insurance contributions (see Chapter 8). Traditionally, this has amounted to considerably more than the National Insurance contributions which you pay as a self-employed person, but changes to National Insurance from April 2000 have narrowed this gap.

Although a company does not benefit from the personal and any other allowances which a self-employed person can claim, overall profits may be taxed less heavily if you run your business as a company rather than as a self-employed person. You should get expert advice from an accountant.

Employed or self-employed?

To be treated as self-employed, you must convince the Inland Revenue that you are genuinely in business on your own account. If you own a shop or offer a car mechanic service, say, provide all your own equipment and find all your own customers, there is little doubt that you are self-employed. But there can be circumstances in which, though you may regard yourself as self-employed, the Revenue says you are not.

In general, you are on dangerous ground if all (or nearly all) your work comes from just one source – from one company you have a contract with, say – and you are paid on a regular basis without having to send in an invoice, or you must keep set hours or you use your client's equipment, or your client dictates what work you will do and can switch you from one task to another. The Revenue may decide you are an employee with a *contract of service* rather than a self-employed person with a *contract for services*. If the Revenue says you have a contract of service, you may be taxed under Schedule E as an employee and the company will have to deduct income tax and National Insurance from your pay under the Pay-As-You-Earn (PAYE) system. This is particularly likely to happen if all the work you do is carried out on the company's premises.

You are also unlikely to count as self-employed if you find contracts or clients through an agency – in general, the agency will be treated as your employer.

With some professions, the Inland Revenue has agreed to treat you as self-employed for income tax purposes, even though you pay National Insurance contributions as if you were an employee. This has the advantage that you qualify for more social security benefits than a self-employed person. This dual status applies to most actors, some teachers and ministers of religion among others.

Each Revenue and Contributions Agency local office has someone responsible for saying whether or not you will be treated as self-employed, and who will confirm decisions in writing if you wish. Also, see Inland Revenue leaflet IR56.

If you are a director of a company, no matter how small, you are an employed person, not self-employed.

IR35 – an end to your self-employed status?

In the past, you may have set yourself up as a contractor or consultant by establishing a service company or partnership. You would then hire your own services out to clients. This practice has been common in industries such as engineering and information technology, and has had tax and National Insurance advantages because, for example, you could claim more expenses. Also, you could pay yourself through dividends taken from your company. There is no National Insurance on dividends and they may be taxed less heavily than earnings had you been employed directly by the client. From 6 April 2000, the law has changed to crack down on these arrangements – the new approach has been dubbed 'IR35' after the number of the Budget 1999 press release that first announced the change.

Under the new rules, the Inland Revenue will look at what the position would have been if you had been engaged directly by the client instead of through your company or partnership (called an 'intermediary' in the legislation). Your income from the client will be taxed as if you were an employee if it appears you would have been engaged as an employee rather than a self-employed person using the usual criteria (see above). The Inland Revenue has published detailed guidance on which contracts will be affected in its February 2000 Tax Bulletin.* It has also set up an IR35 Service* to which you can send copies of contracts for an official opinion on whether they are affected by the new rules.

Starting a business

- Decide whether to register for value added tax (VAT) – see p. 126.
- Inform your local tax office so that you can pay the correct income tax and National Insurance contributions. You can do this using the forms in the back of leaflet CWL1 – *Starting your own business?*
- Make a list of fixed assets, e.g. office equipment, car.
- Get cash books to show cash paid into (and taken out of) the bank, and a book for petty cash.
- Set up an accounting system (e.g. in a book or on a computer) to show details of sales and purchases and sort the purchases into different types, e.g. stationery, travel, heating and lighting.
- If you need stocks of raw materials and other goods, keep records of what you've bought, what you've sold, and what has gone from stock.
- Get written receipts and file them in date order.
- Get a notebook or petty cash vouchers to record items for which there's no receipt.
- Plan how you are going to pay your tax bill – e.g. by putting money aside each month.
- If a car is used partly for your business, keep a record of business mileage, petrol, and all running costs.
- If you are going to use in your business items you already own, e.g. a car, computer, include them in your accounts. You will be able to claim capital allowances on them (and you may be able to recover the VAT).
- Choose your accounting year-end – see below.
- Consider employing your spouse or making your spouse a partner – see p.126.
- Ask for any expenditure before you start your business to count as pre-trading expenses – see p. 113.
- If you make a loss in the first year, remember you can set it off against other income – see p. 122.
- Make sure you have adequate life insurance and pension cover. Think about permanent health insurance in case you're ever too ill to work.

Your accounting year

Tax is not deducted from the earnings of the self-employed before they are paid, as it is for employees. This is because they are taxed under the rules for Schedule D Case I or Case II, rather than as employees, who are taxed under Schedule E. Your tax bill is based on profits for the accounting period which ends in the tax year.

If you choose your accounting year to coincide with the tax year – called *fiscal accounting* – working out your tax is very straightforward, because you are taxed simply on what you have earned during each tax year. To operate fiscal accounting, your year-end does not have to be exactly 5 April – it can be a day or two earlier or later – and the Revenue will accept a year-end of 31 March as fiscal accounting, if you ask.

Although very straightforward, fiscal accounting has a major drawback. You must account to your tax office fairly soon after the end of your accounting year, which does not give you much time to get your books sorted out. You would have until 30 September (6 months) to prepare your accounts if you want the Inland Revenue to work out your tax bill, or until 31 January (10 months) if you are happy to calculate your own tax.

If you choose a different year-end, there is a longer delay – for example, if your year-end is 30 April, your 2000–1 tax bill will be based on profits for the accounting year ending on 30 April 2000. You will need to send your accounts to your tax office by 30 September 2001 (a delay of 17 months) or 31 January 2002 (a delay of 21 months).

Rules for new businesses
With fiscal accounting, there are no special rules when you first start in business. You immediately start to be taxed year-by-year on the profits you make each tax year.

If you don't choose fiscal accounting, your tax affairs will be more complicated in the opening years. To find out which profits are taxed in the first two or three years of business, you need to work through the following steps.

- Find the first tax year that includes the end of an accounting period falling at least 12 months after the date you started in business. Tax is based on profits for the 12 months up to the end of that accounting period.
- Tax for the next and subsequent tax years is based on profits for the accounting year ending in that tax year – i.e. normal rules apply.
- There will be one or two opening tax years falling before the one you identified in the first step. For the first of these you are taxed on your actual profits for the tax year – i.e. from the date you start in business until the following 5 April.
- If there is a second opening year and the end of an accounting period falls during that year, you are taxed on your profits for the

first 12 months of business. If no accounting period ends during the year, you are taxed on your actual profits for the tax year – see Example 1, below.

EXAMPLE 1

Peter started in business on 1 October 1998. He wants his year-end to be 31 December and opts to end his first accounting period on 31 December 1999. His profits for the first two accounting periods are as follows:

1 October 1998 – 31 December 1999 (15 months) £15,000
1 January 2000 – 31 December 2000 (12 months) £16,000

Peter finds the first tax year in which an accounting period ends more than 12 months after the start of business. This is 1999–2000. Tax for that year is based on profits for the 12 months to 31 December 1999 – i.e. £15,000 × $\frac{12}{15}$ = £12,000. Thereafter, the normal rules apply, so tax for 2000–1 is based on profits for the accounting year ending in that tax year – i.e. £16,000.

For the first year of business, 1998–9, Peter's actual profits are taxed. This means his profits for the period from 1 October 1998 to 5 April 1999 – a period of roughly six months. Therefore, he takes £15,000 × $\frac{6}{15}$ = £6,000. To summarise, the profits to be taxed in the first three years of business are:

1998–9 tax year ($\frac{6}{15}$ × £15,000)	£6,000
1999–2000 tax year ($\frac{12}{15}$ × £15,000)	£12,000
2000–1 tax year	£16,000

Splitting your profits between tax years

Sometimes, you are taxed on your actual profits for the tax year, or your profits for 12 months, rather than profits for an accounting period. This can happen in the opening and closing years of a business. To find the relevant amounts, you may need to take a proportion of the profits for one or more accounting years. Where just one accounting period needs to be apportioned, you can do this as follows:

$$\begin{array}{ccccccc}
\text{profits for} & = & \text{profits for} & \times & \text{number of} & \div & \text{total} \\
\text{tax year} & & \text{accounting} & & \text{months of} & & \text{months in} \\
& & \text{period} & & \text{accounting} & & \text{accounting} \\
& & & & \text{period} & & \text{period} \\
& & & & \text{falling into} & & \\
& & & & \text{the tax year} & &
\end{array}$$

If two periods straddle the tax year, you will need to add to the sum above a proportion of the second accounting period's profits worked out in the same way.

Your tax office will usually accept apportioning done on a monthly basis, but strictly speaking it can insist that you do the sums on a daily basis. You should, in any case, choose the daily basis if it would produce a lower tax bill.

Overlap profit

Part of your profits may be taxed twice under the opening-year rules. For example, Peter (see Example 1) was taxed twice on part of the profits for his first accounting period:

$$(\tfrac{6}{15} \times £15,000) + (\tfrac{12}{15} £15,000) = £18,000.$$

That's £3,000 more than his profits for that period. It is called his *overlap profit*. Businesses already established on 6 April 1994 were subject to 'transitional rules' in 1996–7 in order to shift them on to the new system of self-assessment introduced in that tax year. They are treated as having 'transitional overlap profit' for the period from the accounting date falling within the 1996–7 tax year up to 5 April 1997. For example, a business with a normal year-end of 31 December would have a transitional overlap period of three months from 1 January 1997 to 5 April 1997, giving overlap profit of $\tfrac{3}{12}$ of the profit for the accounting year to 31 December 1997. Transitional overlap profit is treated like ordinary overlap profit. It compensates you for the abolition of 'closing year' rules under the old system.

You eventually get tax relief on your overlap profit, but usually not until your business ceases, by which time inflation may have seriously eroded the value of the relief. You may get the relief earlier if you change your accounting date.

EXAMPLE 2

Beth runs a design consultancy as a sole trader. She has been in business since 1992 and makes up her accounts each year to 30 September. In 1995–6 and earlier years, she was taxed on the old 'preceding year basis' which meant that tax for one year was based on profits for the accounting period which ended in the previous year. Since 1997–8, she has been taxed under the new system brought about as a result of the intro-duction of 'self-assessment'. To make the switch from one system to another, transitional rules applied in 1996–7. They meant that Beth was taxed on half the profits for the two-year period ending 30 September 1996. Her tax position for the relevant years can be summarised as follows:

Tax year	Accounting period on which tax is based	Basis of assessment	Taxable profits
1995–6	1.10.1993 – 30.9.1994	Preceding year	£18,300
1996–7	1.10.1994 – 30.9.1996	Transitional year	$\frac{1}{2} \times$ (£19,100 + £19,800) = £19,450
1997–8	1.10.1996 – 30.9.1997	Current year	£20,000

Beth has transitional overlap profit for the part of her accounting period taxed in 1997–8 which falls before 6 April 1997 – i.e. the period 1 October 1996 to 5 April 1997. This is six months, so her transitional overlap profit is $\frac{6}{12} \times$ £20,000 = £10,000.

Choosing your accounting year-end
The date you choose for drawing up your accounts is an important decision for tax planning.

- If you expect your profits to rise steadily, consider a year-end early in the tax year. This will maximise the delay between earning your profits and paying tax on them, which is good for your cash-flow.
- A year-end early in the tax year also gives you plenty of time to sort out your tax accounts before sending them to your tax office.
- But a year-end early in the tax year means carrying forward higher overlap profits.
- If you want your income tax affairs to be as simple as possible, opt for fiscal accounting (see p. 106).

- If you are registered for VAT (see p. 126) it keeps matters simple if your accounting date coincides with the end of a VAT quarter.

Closing a business

For the year in which your business closes down you are taxed on profits for the period running from the end of the last accounting year to the date of closure. From these profits, you deduct any overlap profit (see p. 108) due to you, before tax is worked out. This is called 'overlap relief'.

Income and expenses after you close down

If you get any income from your business after you have closed, it will be taxed under Schedule D Case VI as earned income in the tax year in which you get it. However, if you receive it within six years of closing down, you can choose within two years to have it treated as income you got on the last day of your business.

Usually, if bills come in after you have closed down, you can claim tax relief on them only if you also have some late income from the business against which you can set the expenses. But since 29 November 1994 you have been able to set certain expenses against any other income or gains which you have in the year the bill turns up. The expenses which qualify are:

- the costs of putting right a defective product or service which you supplied, the cost of insuring for such claims against you and legal costs connected with such claims
- debts which you had taken into account in drawing up the profits of your business but which now turn out to be bad debts; and the costs of collecting debts that had been included in your profits.

Paying the tax

Tax is paid in two equal instalments. The first is due on 31 January within the tax year to which the payment relates, the second on 31 July after the end of the tax year to which the payment relates. These are 'payments on account', based on the previous tax year's tax bill. If the tax you owe turns out to be more, you'll have to make a balancing payment the following January. If it's less, you'll be able to set the over-payment against the instalment due the following January. For the payment timetable for 2000–1, see p. 27.

Filling in your tax return

When you submit your tax return, you don't always need to send a balance sheet and you don't need to have your accounts audited. If your total turnover is less than £15,000 a year, you can submit only *three-line accounts* giving your total turnover, total business purchases and expenses, and your net profit. If your turnover is £15,000 or more, you'll have to give full details of your accounts on the tax return. Make sure the records you have provide you with all the information you will need to fill in your tax return, which is sent out in April. The accompanying help-sheets guide you through the questions you will need to answer. You can also get a copy of the Inland Revenue's booklet *A guide to keeping records for the self-employed* (SA BK3). Alternatively, check with your accountant if you use one. Basically, make sure you keep records of:

- all receipts and expenses
- all goods purchased and sold
- all supporting documents relating to the transactions of the businesses such as accounts, books, deeds, contracts, vouchers, receipts and computer records.

You will need to keep these records for five years and ten months following the tax year to which they relate. There are stiff penalties for failure to keep records.

Avoiding problems
There are some simple rules to cut down the chances of a tax inspector's enquiry into your affairs.

- Find out the profit margin for people in similar businesses and, if yours is lower, send a note saying why.
- If the income you take out of the business is very low, e.g. because you are living on savings, tell your tax inspector why this is so.
- Try to send your accounts in on time.
- Don't miss out simple things, such as National Savings Investment account interest, from your tax return.
- Do not leave boxes blank. If you do not have the data asked for, put an estimate. In the space provided for comments, explain why you have estimated the figure and when the actual data will be available.
- If you've made a loss, explain it.

Working out taxable profits

You pay tax on the taxable profits of your business. If you were working out your taxable profits from scratch, it would be your takings during your accounting year – i.e. cash received during the year for the sales you make, plus:

- money owed *to you* at the end of the accounting year
- money owed *by you* at the beginning of the year
- the increase in value of your stocks during the year (see p. 116)

less the following deductions:

- allowable business expenses – see below
- money owed *to you* at the beginning of the year
- money owed *by you* at the end of the year
- capital allowances – see p. 117
- losses – see p. 122.

In practice, you may start off by working out your profit under normal accounting rules. You then turn this into your taxable profits by adding back things which aren't allowable business expenses (for example depreciation and your wages) and deducting things on which you can get tax relief (capital allowances).

In a very few cases (for example a barrister) in the past, your sales figure might have been taken as the cash you received during your accounting year for work done – regardless of when you actually did the work. So you could ignore money owed at the start or end of the accounting year.

However, from 1999–2000 onwards, the option to draw up your accounts on this cash basis has been withdrawn for most people. You must switch to the normal rules. If this results in an extra tax bill, special rules apply so that the bill can be paid over a period of ten years up to 2010. Barristers and legal advocates are still able to use the cash basis during the first seven years that they practice.

If you take items out of stock for your own use you normally have to include these in sales at the normal selling price.

Other income

If you have any other income which is not part of your trading income, it is not part of the taxable profits of your business. How any non-trading income is taxed depends on where it comes from. For example, bank interest is taxed as investment income.

Allowable business expenses

An expense is allowable only if incurred *wholly and exclusively* for the business. The list overleaf gives expenses you will probably be allowed and those you will not. But business needs vary widely, and an expense allowable for one business may not be for another. If in doubt, claim.

Note that the *wholly and exclusively* rule does not mean that you can't claim anything if, for example, you sometimes use your car for business, sometimes for private purposes. If the car is used wholly for business purposes on some occasions, then you can normally claim the proportion of car expenses which is attributable to business use; you'll have to agree the proportion with your tax inspector. You can usually claim the same proportion of your car expenses as your business mileage bears to your total mileage.

However, if you use the car for a trip which is part pleasure, part business, you may not be able to claim any of the costs of the trip as an allowable expense. This is known as the *dual-purpose rule*. For example, you can't normally claim the expenses of a business trip which is combined with a holiday. However, if you attend a conference during the trip, the conference fee will be allowable.

You can normally claim part of your home expenses, such as heating, lighting and insurance, if you use part of your home for business. Home expenses are usually shared out on the basis of the number and size of rooms. If you claim costs of using part of your home exclusively for business, beware of a possible capital gains tax bill if you sell your home.

Capital expenditure, such as what you spend on buying cars and machinery and improving property, is not an allowable expense, nor is depreciation, such as that on cars. But you may get capital allowances – see p. 117.

Pre-trading expenses
If you spend money, e.g. rent and rates on your business premises, expenses incurred up to seven years before your business actually starts will probably count as pre-trading expenditure. It will be treated as a loss in your first year of trading, and you can get loss relief – see p. 122.

Business expenses

Basic costs and general running expenses
• **normally allowed** cost of goods bought for resale and raw materials used in business (see p. 116 for how much to claim); discounts allowed on sales; advertising; delivery charges; initial cost of computer software with a limited useful lifetime (see p. 118); heating; lighting; cleaning; business rates; proportion of the council tax on a second home if let out or used for business; telephone; rent of business premises; replacement of small tools and special clothing; postage; stationery; relevant books and magazines; accountants' fees

(mostly) including fees for assisting with self-assessment; bank charges on business accounts; VAT if you're not registered (see p. 128)

• **not allowed** initial cost of buildings, machinery, vehicles, equipment, permanent advertising signs – but see *Capital allowances*, on p. 117; any money paid as a result of extortion (on or after 30 November 1993); accountants' fees for dealing with an Inland Revenue enquiry which reveals negligence or fraud

Use of home for work

• **normally allowed** proportion of telephone, lighting, heating, cleaning, insurance; proportion of your mortgage interest or rent (and domestic rates in Northern Ireland) if you use part of home *exclusively* for business; proportion of your council tax – though the rules are not clear on whether you can simply work from home or must use part of the home *exclusively* for business for this to be allowable: if you do use part of your home exclusively for business, watch out for capital gains tax and be aware that you could be charged the uniform business rate which is collected by your local authority

• **not allowed** council tax relating to non-business use of your main home

Wages and salaries

• **normally allowed** wages, salaries, redundancy and some leaving payments paid to employees; payments on counselling for employees made redundant; pensions for ex-employees and dependants; cost of alternative transport for employees whose car-sharing arrangements temporarily break down

• **not allowed** your own wages or salary, or that of any business partner

Workplace nurseries

• **normally allowed** cost of childcare provision for employees' children

• **not allowed** cost of premises and equipment – but see *Capital allowances,* on p. 117

Tax and National Insurance

• **normally allowed** employer's National Insurance contributions for employees; VAT on allowable expenses if you're not a registered trader for VAT (and, sometimes, even if you are – see p. 128)

• **not allowed** income tax; capital gains tax; inheritance tax; your own National Insurance

Entertaining

• **normally allowed** entertainment of own staff, e.g. Christmas party

• **not allowed** any business entertainment

Gifts
• **normally allowed** gifts costing up to £15 a year to any single person so long as the gift advertises your business and is not food, drink, tobacco or vouchers for goods
• **not allowed** most other goods

Travelling
• **normally allowed** cost of travel and accommodation on business trips; travel between different places of work; *running costs of own car*: whole of cost, excluding depreciation, if used wholly for business, proportion if used privately too; provided trips are exclusively for business purposes, the cost of travel to and from the UK to carry on business performed wholly outside the UK
• **not allowed** travel between home and business; parking costs; motoring fines; meals, except the reasonable cost of evening meals and breakfast on overnight trips; cost of buying a car or van – but see *Capital allowances*, on p. 117

Interest payments
• **normally allowed** interest on, and costs of arranging, overdrafts and loans for business purposes – see p. 117
• **not allowed** interest on capital paid or credited to partners; interest on overdue tax

Hire purchase and leasing
• **normally allowed** hire charge part of payments (i.e. the amount you pay *less* the cash price); rent paid for leasing car or machinery, for example, though it may be restricted for expensive cars
• **not allowed** cash price of what you're buying on hire purchase (you may get *capital allowances* on cash price – but see p. 117)

Hiring
• **normally allowed** reasonable charge for hire of capital goods, including cars

Insurance
• **normally allowed** business insurance, e.g. employer's liability, fire and theft, motor; life insurance, personal accident insurance, permanent health insurance and private medical insurance for employees
• **not allowed** your own life, accident, permanent health and private medical insurance

Trade marks, designs and patents
• **normally allowed** fees paid to register trade mark or design or to obtain a patent
• **not allowed** cost of buying a patent from someone else – you may get *capital allowances*, see p. 122

Legal costs
• **normally allowed** costs of recovering debts, defending business rights, preparing service agreements, appealing against rates on business premises, renewing a lease with the landlord's consent for a period of under 50 years (but not if a premium is paid)
• **not allowed** expenses (including stamp duty) for acquiring land, buildings or leases; fines and other penalties for breaking the law; costs of fighting a tax case

Repairs
• **normally allowed** normal repairs and maintenance to premises or equipment
• **not allowed** cost of additions, alterations, improvements

Debts
• **normally allowed** specific bad debts and, in part, doubtful debts
• **not allowed** general reserve for bad or doubtful debts

Subscriptions and contributions
• **normally allowed** payments which secure benefits for your business or staff; genuine contributions to approved local enterprise agency; payments to professional bodies which have arrangements with the Revenue (in some cases only a proportion); contributions to Training and Enterprise Councils, Business Links, etc. made before 1 April 2000
• **not allowed** payments to political parties, churches, charities (but small gifts to *local* churches and charities may be allowable)

Training
• **normally allowed** subject to certain conditions, cost of training employees to acquire and improve skills needed for their current jobs; cost of training employees who are leaving or who have left in new work skills

Secondments and donations
• **normally allowed** cost of seconding employees on a temporary basis to certain educational bodies, including local education authorities and institutions maintained by them, and to charitable institutions; value of goods donated to the world's poorest countries for projects undertaken for educational or medical purposes

Stock

You can claim as an allowable expense the cost of raw materials you use in your business, and the cost of things you buy for resale. But you can claim only the cost of business materials which you actually sell during your accounting year – i.e. the value of your stocks of these things at the start of the year *plus* anything you spend on buying more during the year, *minus* the value of your stocks at the end of the year.

If you have stocks which can be sold only for less than you paid for them, you will normally be allowed to value them at what they would fetch if sold now. This means that for tax purposes you can value stock *at the lower of cost or market value*. No other method of valuing stock is allowed by your tax inspector, regardless of what is allowed under accounting rules.

When you value your stocks at the start and end of the accounting year, you need to add in the value of *work-in-progress*. This is the value of work which has begun, but which isn't completed, for example products half-way through the manufacturing process, or part-completed work if you're a builder, solicitor, engineer, etc. Work-in-progress can be valued in one of the following ways:

• cost of raw materials used
• cost plus overheads
• cost plus overheads plus profit contribution.

Once you've chosen a way of valuing work-in-progress, this is how it must be valued each accounting year.

If you are closing a business, your stock will be valued either at the price it's sold at, if sold to someone else in business, or at the price it would fetch if sold in the open market.

Capital allowances

When you work out your taxable profits, you can't deduct anything you spend on capital assets or equipment, for example machinery or cars. Money spent in this way is not an allowable business expense. But you can still get tax relief on these sorts of things by claiming *capital allowances* on:

• plant and machinery (e.g. vans, machines, computers)
• motor cars
• buildings (e.g. industrial, agricultural, hotels, in enterprise zones)
• patents, know-how and scientific research.

Expenditure must be *wholly and exclusively* for the business. But on anything used partly for business, partly privately, you will get a proportion of the capital allowance, depending on the proportion of business use. If you buy equipment for private use and then use it in your business, you can claim a capital allowance on its market value at the time you start using it for business.

How you pay for the equipment doesn't make any difference to the capital allowance. If you pay by a loan or by bank overdraft, the interest is an allowable business expense, not part of the cost of the asset. In the same way, hire-purchase charges are a business expense.

If, instead of buying an asset, you choose to lease it, you can claim the lease rental as an allowable expense, as long as you are using the asset in your own business. The person or company from whom you lease can normally claim the capital allowances. The first-year allowances for items bought to lease out is 25 per cent.

VAT

For how to deal with VAT on items on which you claim a capital allowance, see p. 126.

Computers and other plant and machinery

For expenditure made between 2 July 1997 and 1 July 1998, you could generally claim a capital allowance of 50 per cent of the cost of the plant or machinery for the accounting year in which the purchase falls. For expenditure from 2 July 1998 onwards, this first-year allowance reduces to 40 per cent. Originally, the 40 per cent first-year allowance was to last only a couple of years, but it has now been made permanent.

To encourage e-commerce, the government also announced an even higher first-year allowance when you buy information and communications technology equipment. This includes computers, software (whether or not it is bought at the same time as hardware) and Internet-enabled mobile phones. For spending on these items from 1 April 2000 to 31 March 2003, you can claim 100 per cent first-year allowance – in other words, you can deduct the full cost of the item from your profits for the year in which you make the purchase.

In addition to this temporary change, software with a useful life of less than two years can be claimed as an allowable expense, which has the same effect as a 100 per cent capital allowance. Anything you spent modifying your computer or software to cope with the year 2000 date change (the 'millennium bug') will almost always be accepted as an allowable business expense.

To qualify for the higher rates of first-year allowance, your business (whether you are self-employed, in partnership or operating as a company) must count as small or medium-sized – otherwise, the first-year allowances is 25 per cent. Your business must meet at least two out of the following three criteria:

- turnover is no more than £11.2 million a year
- the assets of the business come to no more than £5.6 million
- you employ no more than 250 people.

The rest of the cost of the plant and machinery is written off over the following years at up to 25 per cent of the remaining value each year. This is how it works. The cost of plant or machinery you buy goes into a *pool of expenditure*. At the end of the year of purchase, you can claim up to 100, 40 or 25 per cent (as appropriate) of the value of the pool as a *writing-down allowance* – this can be deducted from your profits for that year.

In the next and following years, you can claim up to 25 per cent of the value of the pool as a capital allowance, which you deduct from your profits for the year.

The pool is reduced by what you claim: what's left is known as the *written-down value*, and becomes your pool for the start of the next accounting year. At the end of the year you can claim the appropriate percentage of purchases you make during the year plus 25 per cent of whatever the pool is now worth. Note that you can claim less than the full capital allowances you're entitled to claim – see Example 5.

If you sell something on which you have claimed capital allowances, the proceeds (up to the original cost of the item or sometimes the market value) must be deducted from your pool of expenditure before working out your writing-down allowance for the year in which you sell. If the proceeds come to more than the value of your pool, the excess (the *balancing charge*) is added to your profit.

You can claim capital allowances in full only on expenditure which is *wholly and exclusively* for the business. Things bought partly for business, partly for private use, should be kept separate from other business assets in their own pools. You can claim a proportion of the maximum capital allowances, in line with business use.

EXAMPLE 3

Herbert works out what he can claim in capital allowances for his accounting year ending on 30 April 2000. His pool of expenditure at the start of the year was £6,782. In August 1999 Herbert had bought a new van, costing £8,880, trading in his old van for £2,650. He also bought some shelving for his stock room for £960.

Herbert's pool of expenditure on 30 April 2000 is £4,132, i.e. £6,782 *less* the £2,650 he received for the van. He claims a writing-down allowance of £1,033, i.e. 25 per cent of £4,132. He also claims first-year capital allowances of £3,936. This is made up of £3,552 (40 per cent of the £8,880 he paid for the van) and £384 (40 per cent of the £960 he paid for the shelving). The total capital allowances he claims are £4,969.

Herbert's pool of expenditure at the start of the next accounting year is £9,003, i.e. £4,132 (his pool of expenditure on 30 April 2000) *plus* the £8,880 he paid for the van and the £960 he paid for the shelving, *less* the £4,969 he has claimed in capital allowances.

EXAMPLE 4

Bill's accounting year runs from 1 August 1999 to 31 July 2000. On 14 April 2000, he bought a new Internet-ready computer for use in his business at a cost of £950. In the past when he bought a computer, he elected to put it in its own separate pool as an asset with a life of less than five years – see p. 120. This time, he can claim 100 per cent first-year allowance of £950, leaving nothing to carry forward in an expenditure pool.

EXAMPLE 5

Mary bought some machinery costing £10,000 in her accounting year to 30 June 2000. She could claim first-year allowance of £4,000 – 40 per cent of £10,000. However, her taxable profit for the year is just £2,000. (She has other income which uses up her personal allowance.) Claiming the full capital allowance against her profit would create a loss. Tax relief for the loss would be available in the normal way but, instead, Mary can simply claim a smaller capital allowance this year. She claims £2,000.

She then carries forward a higher value pool of expenditure of £8,000 (£10,000 *less* £2,000) as a basis for next year's capital allowance claim.

Cars

Higher first-year allowances are not available on cars, lorries and vans. The maximum you can claim in the year of purchase is a 25 per cent writing-down allowance, followed by 25 per cent for each year you own the vehicle for business purposes.

In the past, cars had to go into a separate pool of expenditure. However, the separate pool is abolished for cars costing up to £12,000 from 6 April 2000 (or from 6 April 2001 if you choose to delay the change – for example because you want extra time to alter your accounting procedures). Any balance brought forward in the separate car pool is added to your main pool of expenditure from the date of the change.

A car (but not a lorry or van) costing more than £12,000 has its own pool of expenditure. In this case, the maximum writing-down allowance can be up to 25 per cent, subject to a limit of £3,000.

Assets with a life of less than five years

Computer equipment is commonly treated as a short-life asset because the pace of change is so great that it tends to become obsolete within just a couple of years. However, for purchases from 1 April 2000 to 31 March 2003, there is no need to elect for computers and similar equipment to be treated as short-life assets if they qualify for the 100 per cent first-year allowance (see p. 118). However, for other items that last only a few years, for example video equipment, you could find yourself still claiming capital allowances for the cost after you have got rid of them. Suppose, for example, you bought a CCTV system for £5,000 in August 2000 and claimed the full capital allowance on it each year. The following table shows what the written-down value would be year by year:

Year	Capital allowance	Written-down value at end of year
1	£2,000 (40%)	£3,000
2	£750 (25%)	£2,250
3	£563 (25%)	£1,687
4	£422 (25%)	£1,265
5	£317 (25%)	£948

If you scrapped the system after four years, there would still be a written-down value of £1,265 in your pool of expenditure and, in the normal way, you'd write this off only over several more years.

With equipment which you expect to scrap or sell within five years, you can opt to write off the value of the equipment when you get rid of it. You must keep each such *short-life asset* in its own pool of expenditure.

- If you sell it for less than its written-down value, the difference can be subtracted from your profits for the year, as a *balancing allowance* (if you scrap it, you can claim the whole written-down value as a balancing allowance).
- If you sell it for more than its written-down value, the difference is added to your profits as a balancing charge (see p. 119).
- If you still have the equipment after five years, its written-down value is added to your main pool of expenditure as if it had never been treated separately.

Buildings

You can claim writing-down allowances on some buildings at 4 per cent of their original cost excluding land:

- industrial buildings, e.g. factories, warehouses
- homes built for letting on assured tenancies, provided certain conditions are met
- agricultural buildings, including farmhouses, farm buildings, cottages, fences, roads
- hotels or hotel extensions of ten bedrooms or more which meet certain conditions.

With industrial buildings and hotels in enterprise zones, you can claim 100 per cent of the cost in the first year, including the cost of fixed plant or machinery in the buildings. If you claim less than 100 per cent, you can claim a writing-down allowance of up to 25 per cent of the original cost, starting the following year.

Patents, know-how and scientific research

You can claim a first-year capital allowance of 40 per cent, and subsequently a 25 per cent writing-down allowance, on the cost of buying a patent to use in your business. Note that you cannot claim an allowance for the cost of creating and registering your own patent (though you may be able to claim expenses for these).

You can claim the same capital allowances for the cost of know-how – any industrial information or techniques likely to assist in manufacturing, mining, agriculture, forestry or fishing. And you can claim 100 per cent of the cost of capital expenditure for the purposes of scientific research (though not on land or houses), in the year of expenditure only.

Combining capital and other allowances

Claiming your full capital allowances each year could cause other allowances and reliefs to be wasted. When deciding how much to claim, first work out by how much personal and any other allowances and any loss relief (see below) will reduce your profits. Capital allowances are not wasted if you claim less than the full amount. What you do not claim will remain in your capital pool, making larger allowances possible in future years.

Since 1997–8 (and for all businesses starting on or after 6 April 1994), capital allowances have been given as a straightforward trading expense deducted along the way to calculating your taxable profit (or your loss) for the year.

Losses

If you make a loss in your business, there are several things you can do with it. The options open to you depend on whether your business is new, ongoing or closing down. You must choose one option to apply to your losses for any one year, but if, after applying that option, some losses remain, you can choose a further option to deal with the remainder.

Since 1997–8, a single system of loss relief has applied to all businesses. Losses are calculated in the same way as profits – i.e. a loss for a given tax year will be the loss for the accounting period ending within that tax year.

New businesses

As well as the reliefs available to an ongoing business (see below), there is a special option if you make a loss during the first four tax years of your business. You can set it against other income (including earnings from a job) in the three tax years before the year in which the loss was made, and so get a tax rebate. You start by setting the loss against the earliest year first.

To get this relief, you must be able to show that you have been trading on a commercial basis and can be expected to make profits within a reasonable period.

Claim this relief within one year and ten months of the end of the tax year to which the loss relates.

Ongoing businesses: relief against other income and gains for the previous year

You can ask for a loss made in one tax year to be set against income for the previous tax year. Once again, this could mean that you are unable to use other deductions and allowances. If, having reduced your income to zero, some loss still remains, it can be set against any capital gains for the previous tax year.

If you have asked for losses made in 1999–2000 and in 2000–1 to be set against your 1999–2000 income, the 1999–2000 loss will be set off first.

The time limit for claiming this relief is one year and ten months from the end of the tax year to which the loss relates – i.e. 31 January 2003 for the 2000–1 tax year.

Ongoing businesses: relief against other income and gains for the same year

You can ask for a loss made in your accounting year ending in the tax year to be set off against any other income you have for the year. If you choose this option, the whole of the loss or as much of the loss as is required to reduce your total income to zero must be used in this way. This means that other deductions and allowances which you qualify for could be wasted – see Example 6. If, having set the loss against income, part still remains, you can set it against any taxable capital gains you have in the same tax year.

The time limit for claiming this relief is one year and ten months from the end of the tax year to which the loss relates – i.e. 31 January 2003 for the 2000–1 tax year.

Ongoing businesses: relief against future profits

You can set the loss against the income of the business in future years. The losses can be carried forward indefinitely until used up. The advantage of doing this is that it is relatively straightforward, but there are disadvantages too:

- the loss can be set off only against income from the same business
- there may be a long delay before the loss can be translated into cash savings – see Example 7
- the whole loss has to be set off against the available profits before any deductions or allowances which may, therefore, be wasted.

Claim within five years and ten months of the end of the tax year you made the loss – i.e. by 31 January 2007 for a loss in 2000–1.

EXAMPLE 6

Suppose you have other income of £13,000, and deductions and allowances of £5,000. In this case your taxable income will be £8,000. If you have losses of £10,000, and ask for them to be set against other income in the same tax year, the whole loss will first be set against your other income, reducing your taxable income to £3,000. This means that £2,000 (£5,000 *less* £3,000) of your deductions and allowances for the year will be wasted. It may be better to ask to carry forward the loss to set against future profits, so that you get the full benefit of your deductions and allowances for this year.

EXAMPLE 7

In June 1997, Jessica set up a new business on which she made a loss of £8,500 in 1998–9. In December 2000 she decides what to do with the loss. Three of her options must be claimed by 5 January 2001, i.e. one year and ten months from the end of the tax year in which she made the loss. Below we show all her income and capital gains for six tax years.

Jessica could get a tax refund of £995 by setting the loss against income and gains in the previous three tax years (1995–6, 1996–7 and 1997–8). But she saves £1,892 by setting the loss against future business profits – £2,200 in 1999–2000 and her estimated profit of at least £6,300 in 2000–1.

	1995–6	1996–7	1997–8	1998–9	1999–2000	2000–1
Income and capital gains before any loss relief						
Capital gain	£0	£0	£9,500	£8,800	£0	£0
Job	£6,500	£6,500	£6,500	£6,500	£6,500	£6,500
Business	n/a	n/a	£400	–£8,500	£2,200	£6,300
Tax	£595	£547	£1,261	£921	£808.95	£1,668.90
Against income for three previous tax years – £995 saved						
Capital gain	£0	£0	£9,500			
Job	£0	£4,500	£6,500			
Business	n/a	n/a	£400			
Tax	£0	£147	£1,261			
Against income and gains for previous year – £939 saved						
Capital gain			£7,900			
Job			£0			
Business			£0			
Tax			£322			
Against income and gains for same year – £921 saved						
Capital gain				£6,800		
Job				£0		
Business				loss		
Tax				£0		
Against future profits – £1,892 saved						
Capital gain					£0	£0
Job					£6,500	£6,500
Business					£0	£0
Tax					£302.95	£282.90

You as employer

When you employ staff on a permanent basis you have several duties as an employer. You must act as a collector of taxes and deduct income tax and Class 1 National Insurance (see p. 142) from your employee's pay. From 6 April 2000, if these taxes you must hand over average no more than £1,500 a month, you are allowed to pay them quarterly instead of at the more usual monthly intervals.

In 2000–1, if you pay someone less than £76 a week you do not need to worry about their tax and National Insurance. For more information on being an employer, get Inland Revenue leaflet CWL3 – *Thinking of taking someone on*. Complete form P223 at the end of the leaflet in order to receive the *New Employer's Starter Pack*. For more complex cases, you may need booklet CWG2 – *Employer's further guide to Pay As You Earn and National Insurance*.

During the 2001–2 tax year only, small businesses that file their end-of-year PAYE return (form P35 and any P14) electronically and pay any tax due electronically (for example by debit card or direct transfer from their bank), or use an Internet payroll service, can qualify for a one-off £50 tax discount. An extra £50 discount will be available if you are paying tax credits to your employees (under the working families' tax credit or disabled person's tax credit schemes).

Employing a nanny

If you pay people to work in your home – such as a nanny, nurse or housekeeper – you may count as an employer and may have to deduct tax and National Insurance. Get the *New Employers' Starter Pack* (see above). But there is no tax to pay on living accommodation if it's the sort of job where accommodation is normally provided. And there's no tax to pay on free or cheap meals if they are provided to all employees, which would be the case if, say, you employed just one live-in nanny.

Your spouse

You may be able to save tax by employing your spouse. If he or she has no other income, you can pay your spouse up to £4,385 in the 2000–1 tax year before any tax is due on it and before you must pay National Insurance. But if earnings exceed £76 a week – equivalent to £3,952 a year – in the 2000–1 tax year, your spouse will have to pay National Insurance.

In stages, the limit at which employees start to pay National Insurance is being raised. By 2001–2 it will be the same as the threshold at which employers start to pay National Insurance and the same as the threshold at which income tax starts to be paid. The government predicts that this limit will be £87 a week by 2001. This means that by 2001–2 you will be able to pay your wife or husband an estimated £87 a week (£4,524 a year) completely free of tax and National Insurance.

Value added tax (VAT)

The current rate of VAT is 17.5 per cent (5 per cent on domestic fuel). There are some goods on which the rate is zero, for example most food, books, newspapers, children's clothing and transport. And some goods and services are *exempt*, for example land, insurance, postage, education, and so on.

If you are registered for VAT, you will be able to claim back VAT where it is levied on your business expenditure. By doing this, you are lowering your costs. But, you must add VAT on to all the bills you send out or sales you make if, of course, they are items on which VAT is payable at 17.5 per cent. By doing this you are increasing your selling prices, but not your income, because you have to hand over the VAT to Customs and Excise. However, you need not worry about the effect of increased prices on your customers if they are businesses and registered for VAT. VAT-registered customers can simply claim back any VAT you add to the bill.

Handing over VAT on income you haven't yet received can cause cash-flow problems. But businesses with a yearly turnover below £350,000 have the option of handing over VAT only on income actually received. (This is known as *cash accounting* by Customs and Excise.)

During 2001–2, small businesses which file their VAT returns electronically and pay any tax due electronically (for example, by debit card or direct transfer from their banks) can qualify for a one-off £50 tax discount.

Registering for VAT

From 1 April 2000 you have to register for VAT if, at the end of any month, the value of your taxable supplies in the last year exceeds £52,000. You must also register if at any time you think it likely that the value of your taxable supplies over the next 30 days will exceed £52,000. Taxable supplies in this case means any supplies which are not exempt – so it includes zero-rated goods and services.

Below these levels, you can choose whether or not to register. Your choice depends upon:

- how much you can cut your costs by claiming VAT back on goods and services you buy for use in your business (which you can do if you register)

- whether your customers will be able to claim back VAT which you must add to your selling prices, and
- how tedious you find the record-keeping necessary to be registered for VAT.

For more information about VAT, contact your local VAT office (under *Customs and Excise* in the phone book).

Keeping records

If you are registered, you have to keep careful records.

- You must give your customer a bill (and keep a copy yourself) which shows, among other things, your VAT registration number, your name and address, the amount payable before VAT and the amount of VAT due. (If you're a shopkeeper and the bill, including VAT, is £100 or less, you needn't show all these).
- You must keep a VAT account in your books which shows the amount of VAT you are reclaiming and the amount of VAT you are handing over.
- You must fill in a form (VAT return) every three months (normally) and send it to Customs and Excise, showing what you are claiming and what you are handing over. Businesses which have been registered for VAT for at least a year, pay VAT regularly and have a yearly turnover of below £350,000 can opt for a yearly return (but you have to pay an estimated amount of VAT monthly by direct debit).

If you have charged more VAT on your sales than you can claim on your purchases, then you have to send the difference to the VAT Collector. If you can claim more on what you've bought than you can charge on what you have sold, the VAT Collector will pay you the difference.

Business expenses and capital allowances

If you *are not* a registered trader for VAT, include any VAT when claiming the cost of allowable business expenses. Also include VAT in the cost of things on which you can claim a capital allowance.

If you *are* a registered trader for VAT, *don't* include VAT when claiming business expenses or capital allowances. However, you should include in your claim for expenses or capital allowances any VAT which you can't claim back through the normal VAT system, for example because it relates to part of your sales exempt from VAT.

But with cars (unless you're a car trader), include VAT in the cost you base your claim on for business expenses and capital allowances. The reason is that VAT on cars you buy can't be reclaimed, even if the expense is related to part of your business liable to VAT. Since 1 August 1992, however, private taxi and self-drive hire firms and driving schools have been permitted to recover the VAT they pay on cars purchased for their businesses.

Partnerships

If you are a business in a partnership with others, much of what has gone before about expenses and capital allowances is relevant.

The partnership itself has no identity for tax purposes. Instead, each partner is treated as if running his or her own individual business. Their profits from the business are their share of the partnership profits as set out in the partnership agreement. The partners are responsible for completing a tax return for the partnership as a whole – though for practical purposes usually one partner will be nominated to take on this task – and the profits are worked out in the same way as those for a sole trader's business. Part of the return, called the *partnership statement*, is issued to each partner so that they can work out their individual tax bills.

When a new partner joins a partnership, the normal opening year rules apply to that partner as if he or she had started a new business (see p. 106). Similarly, when a partner leaves, the normal closing year rules apply to that partner (p. 109). This means that, although all the partners have the same accounting year-end (i.e. that for the partnership as a whole), they might be taxed on a different basis – for example actual basis or profits for the accounting year ending in the tax year – according to the particular rules applying to each partner. It also means that different partners will normally have different levels of overlap profit (see p. 107) which they carry forward until they cease to be partners (or, possibly, until the partnership accounting date is altered).

If the partnership makes a loss, the partners share the loss in accordance with the partnership agreement. Each partner decides individually how he or she wishes the loss to be treated – for example, one partner could decide to carry his or her loss forward to set against future profits from the partnership and another partner could decide to set it off against other income and capital gains for the tax year in which the loss was made.

In contrast to the old pre-1997 system, each partner is now responsible only for his or her own tax on his or her share of the partnership profits and cannot be asked to pay the tax bill of any other partner.

Pensions for partners

Special rules apply where a pension is paid to a partner, or to a widow(er) or dependant of a partner.

- Take the partner's *actual profits* – i.e. what he or she actually declared in the tax return – for the last seven years in which he or she spent substantially the whole time in acting as a partner.
- Separately for each year, multiply the profits by the retail prices index (RPI) for December in the final tax year and divide them by the RPI for December in the year in which the profits were charged to tax.
- Take the average of the three highest figures and divide by two.

The result is the maximum pension which counts as earned income (though it can be increased by the RPI every December). Payments above that limit are investment income. The payments reduce the partnership's income for tax purposes, but payments *within* the limit can't reduce the partnership's (or anyone else's) investment income.

Limited partners
The losses a limited partner can set against other income are limited broadly to the amount of capital he or she has contributed.

Useful Inland Revenue reading

You can ring the Inland Revenue Orderline* for helpsheets, leaflets and notes.

Leaflets and notes

IR56	Employed or self-employed? A guide for tax and National Insurance
CWL1	Starting your own business?
CWL2	National Insurance contributions for self-employed people
SA/BK3	Self assessment – a guide to keeping records for the self-employed
CIS FACT 5	The new construction industry scheme – a handy guide
IR40	Construction industry scheme – conditions for getting a subcontractor's tax certificate
IR116(CIS)	A guide for subcontractors with tax certificates
IR117(CIS)	A guide for subcontractors with registration cards
SA103	Notes on self-employment
SA103L	Notes on Lloyds Underwriters
SA104	Notes on partnership

SA801   Notes on partnership land
SA802   Notes on partnership foreign
SA803   Notes on chargeable partnership assets
SA804   Notes on partnership savings and investments

Helpsheets

When you receive a helpsheet, make sure it relates to the tax year for which you want information.

IR220   More than one business
IR222   How to calculate your taxable profits
IR223   Rent a room for traders
IR224   Farmers and market gardeners
IR227   Losses
IR229   Information from your accounts
IR231   Doctor's expenses
IR232   Farm stock valuation
IR288   Partnerships and capital gains tax
IR380   Partnership – foreign aspect

Concessions

Extra-statutory concessions let you off paying tax that is technically due. Booklet IR1 gives details of each concession.

A29   Farming and market gardening – relief for fluctuating profits
A37   Tax treatment of directors' fees received by partnerships and other companies
B1   Machinery or plant – changes from renewals to capital allowances basis

Your UK tax status when you go abroad

For tax purposes, the UK is made up of England, Scotland, Wales and Northern Ireland but not the Channel Islands or the Isle of Man. You can live abroad and still be liable to pay UK tax on all your income because you may still count as resident in the UK. The UK tax system aims to:

- tax income originating from anywhere in the world if it's paid to people who are resident in the UK – but see p. 135
- tax income originating from within the UK even if it's paid to non-residents, but income originating from outside the UK is free of UK tax if you count as non-resident (see below)
- tax capital gains originating from anywhere in the world if they are made by people who are resident in the UK *and* by those who are ordinarily resident in the UK. But you don't have to pay tax on capital gains originating from outside the UK if the money is not sent to the UK *and* you are not domiciled in the UK, even if you are resident and/or ordinarily resident.

Do you count as non-resident in the UK?

Interpretation of the terms *resident* and *ordinarily resident* is ultimately up to the courts. Your residence status is decided separately for each tax year. You can be resident or ordinarily resident in two or more countries, or none at all. Your status depends on your circumstances and need not be the same as that of your married partner.

- **One-tax-year rule** You will be non-resident if you are abroad for a complete tax year. But if you count as ordinarily resident and are away for, say, 18 months, you will be non-resident only for the period covering a complete tax year – not the other six months – unless one of the following rules applies. (If you do not count as ordinarily resident, you may also count as non-resident for the whole 18 months.)

- **Working-abroad rule** If you left the UK to work abroad full-time under a contract of employment or to work full-time in a trade, profession or vocation, or possibly if you have several part-time jobs abroad, you count as non-resident and not ordinarily resident for the whole of your period away if the period spent abroad includes a complete tax year. Your absence from the UK starts from the day after you leave to the day before you come back. You can keep a UK home without affecting your non-resident status. An accompanying spouse may also count as non-resident even if he or she is not in full-time employment – subject to the same rules on visits back to the UK (see below).
- **Three-year rule** If you don't work abroad, you will be non-resident and not ordinarily resident if you can show that you have left the UK for three years. You can have your UK tax liability reviewed from the date you originally left the UK and claim overpaid tax if it is confirmed that you are non-resident.
- **Evidence that you have left the UK permanently** You can claim to be non-resident before three years are up if you are away for at least one complete tax year and can provide evidence that you have left the UK permanently – for example, that you have taken steps to acquire accommodation abroad to live in as a permanent home. If you keep your UK home you will have to show that this is consistent with your aim in moving abroad.
- **Settled-purpose rule** You can claim to be non-resident before three years are up if you are away for at least one complete tax year and have gone abroad with a *settled purpose*. Discuss this with your tax inspector if you think this applies to you.

Visits back to the UK

You can be non-resident and not ordinarily resident and still visit the UK. But visits are limited to 182 days in any one tax year made up as one visit or a succession of visits and only 90 days a year on average over a four-year period (or the period you are away if this is less than four years). If you exceed these limits you will be treated as resident. The days of your arrival and departure do not normally count as days spent in the UK, nor do days spent in the UK because of exceptional circumstances, such as the illness of a close family member.

UK tax if you're non-resident

Even if you are non-resident for tax purposes, you still have to pay UK tax at the normal rate on:

- UK earnings
- the profits of a trade or profession which is not carried on wholly outside the UK
- UK pensions – but see p. 137
- UK investment income – but see below
- UK rental income – but see below
- UK and foreign capital gains, in certain circumstances – see below.

You may be able to reduce the UK tax bill if you have to pay tax on the same money in another country – see p. 138.

UK investment income if you're non-resident

The UK tax charge on UK investment income is limited to the tax (if any) which is deducted at source (but only for complete tax years in which you are non-resident). However, the rules are different if you are non-resident but receive investment income through your business in the UK. Consult your tax office.

If you are not ordinarily resident, you can have interest paid without tax deducted – ask a bank or building society for form R105. The interest is still liable for UK tax, but if you are non-resident for a complete tax year you will not have to pay UK tax on interest paid without deduction of UK tax at source. Non-residents do not have to pay UK tax on income or gains from gilts (British Government stocks).

UK rental income if you're resident or non-resident

If you are renting out a UK property while you are abroad, your tenant or the letting agent may be required to deduct basic-rate tax from the rental income before paying it to you – even if you are resident in the UK for tax purposes.

However, whether you are resident or non-resident, this will not usually apply if:

- you are abroad for less than six months, or
- your tenant pays less than £100 a week in rent, or
- you have applied to the Revenue's Financial Intermediaries and Claims Office (FICO)* to have the rental paid with no tax deducted – you can apply if you have never had to pay UK tax or do not expect to have to pay it, or if your UK tax is up to date.

Whatever your position, you are likely to have to complete a UK tax return and may have to make payments on account against your tax bill.

UK capital gains tax if you're non-resident

You may have to pay capital gains tax on assets disposed of during absences of less than five complete tax years, if you dispose of assets you owned before leaving the UK. The disposal will be assessed for tax in the tax year of your departure for gains made in that year and in the tax year of your return for other gains.

The five-year rule applies only to those who left the UK after 16 March 1998. Those who left the UK by that date can avoid UK capital gains tax from the date they became non-resident for tax purposes.

UK tax allowances if you're non-resident

Many people who are non-resident can claim UK tax allowances to set against their UK income, including:

* citizens of Britain, Commonwealth and European Union (EU) countries, Iceland, Liechtenstein and Norway
* residents of the Channel Islands and the Isle of Man
* citizens and residents of countries with which the UK has a double taxation agreement (see p. 138)
* employees and ex-employees of the British Crown (e.g. civil servants and members of the armed forces) along with their widows and widowers, civil servants in territories under the protection of the British Crown, employees of UK missionary societies
* former UK residents who have moved abroad for their health or the health of a member of their family who lives with them.

A non-resident husband who qualifies for the married couple's allowance can give the unused part of the allowance to his wife if he does not use all of the allowance against his own UK income.

UK tax on foreign income if you are a UK resident

Broadly speaking, income from another country is taxable in the UK if you are resident in the UK. If you cannot take income out of the other country – for example because of a ban or a war – you can ask the Revenue to let you off paying tax on it until the money can be sent to the UK. Once you can get the money out of the other country you will have to pay tax on it, even if you choose not to send the money to the UK.

Some people who are *resident* in the UK may not be *ordinarily resident* or *domiciled* (see p. 138) in the UK. They may not have to pay tax on income originating from outside the UK if it is not sent (*remitted*) to the UK. The rules are complicated. Contact your tax inspector if you believe this may apply to you.

Below we give details of when UK residents working abroad may not have to pay tax on their earnings. For details of how investment income from outside the UK is taxed, see p. 216.

Seafarers

You can have your non-UK earnings tax-free under the *foreign earnings deduction* if you are a seafarer – i.e. someone who performs their employment duties on a ship. A gas or oil rig, however mobile, does not count as a ship. Whether you qualify for the deduction depends broadly on how long you spend outside the UK (which means working on a vessel on a voyage, or part voyage, which begins or ends outside the UK). You must be away for a qualifying period of 365 days or more (not necessarily coinciding with the tax year). This period can include visits back to the UK, providing they are for no more than 183 days or one-half of the days in the qualifying period.

Crown employees

Crown employees (for example UK diplomats and members of the armed forces) working abroad are, for most income tax purposes, taxed as if they worked in the UK. But any extra allowance paid for additional living costs when working abroad isn't taxable.

Travelling expenses

You don't have to pay tax on what your employer pays towards the cost of travel to a job abroad (and back again when you've finished), or between countries where you're working. If your employer doesn't pay and the duties of the employment are carried out wholly abroad, you can get tax relief against your taxable earnings from your job abroad for the costs you incur.

You can make any number of visits to the UK, paid for or reimbursed by your employer, without being taxed on the travel expenses, providing your job can be performed *only* outside the UK and you go abroad purely for work purposes. And, providing you're working abroad continuously for at least 60 days' you will not be taxed on the cost of up to two return trips each tax year made by your wife or husband and children under 18, if paid for or reimbursed by your employer.

If *you* pay for these visits to the UK, the cost of your own travel will normally count as an allowable expense only if your workplace abroad falls within the legal definition of a 'temporary workplace' (see p. 69). Family visits which you pay for will not be an allowable expense.

You won't be taxed on costs your employer meets for travel at the beginning or end of your journey in the UK (for example to and from the airport).

Board and lodging abroad

If your job is done wholly abroad, and your workplace abroad falls within the legal definition of a temporary workplace, then if your employer pays (or reimburses) the cost of board and lodging which enables you to carry out your duties, there'll be no tax to pay on this fringe benefit. But you *will* be taxed on the cost to your employer of board and lodging for your husband or wife and children, and of any board and lodging for a holiday abroad. If your employer doesn't pay, you can't claim any board and lodging as an *allowable expense*.

If your job is done partly in the UK and partly abroad, there'll normally be no tax to pay on what your employer pays towards *your* board and lodging, and if your employer doesn't pay, you may be able to claim the cost as an allowable expense.

Golden handshakes and pension lump sums

Redundancy payments made to UK residents after working abroad and lump sums from foreign pension schemes may be wholly tax-free, however large, if any of the following apply:

- you worked abroad for at least three-quarters of the time you did the job
- you worked abroad for all of the last 10 years (if you were in the job for under 20 years)
- you did the job for over 20 years, and at least 10 of the last 20 years *and* at least half the total time was spent working abroad.

Where the payment isn't wholly tax-free, part may be. An amount will be deducted from the payment equal to:

$$\frac{\text{number of months you worked abroad} \times \text{the amount which would otherwise have been taxable}}{\text{total number of months' service}}$$

You count as working abroad if you were non-resident and not ordinarily resident, if you got the foreign earnings deduction or if your earnings were 'foreign emoluments' (earnings of non-UK residents from employers who are not resident in the UK).

Paying tax twice – in the UK and abroad?

You can claim *tax credit relief* if you are liable to tax in the UK and abroad on the same income. Roughly speaking, you work out the UK tax on your income, including foreign income on which tax has been paid. Then you work out the UK tax on your income excluding the foreign income. Deduct the one from the other and this difference between the two amounts of tax is the amount of relief you can claim, i.e. you don't have to pay the extra tax on the higher bill.

However, the difference could be greater than the actual amount of foreign tax paid, for example because foreign tax paid is 15 per cent while UK tax due is 40 per cent. In this case you can claim relief only for the actual amount of foreign tax deducted and not the whole difference between the two tax bills, so in the 15 per cent/40 per cent example you would end up paying 25 per cent tax in the UK.

However, the *double taxation agreements* with some countries put a limit on the tax credit relief you can claim on particular types of income. You may be able to apply to the tax authorities of the other country for a refund if there's a limit on what you can claim in the UK. In some agreements, tax credit relief is prohibited. Contact your tax office for details of specific double taxation agreements.

UK residents can claim relief in the absence of a double taxation agreement, provided the foreign tax corresponds to UK income or capital gains tax. Special rules apply in some cases for residents of the Channel Islands or the Isle of Man.

You may be able to claim relief on income and on capital gains. But if you claim relief and the tax payable in the other country is then reduced, you must notify your tax office who may claw back some of the relief.

Where you are domiciled

You start off life with a domicile of origin inherited from your father (or, in some cases, your mother), and you have a domicile of dependence. You can then change your domicile to a new domicile of choice, but only by living in a new country with the intention of remaining there permanently or indefinitely.

You'll generally be considered to be *domiciled* in the UK if this is where you have your permanent home and where you're likely to end your days. Registering and voting as an overseas elector is not normally taken into account in determining whether you are domiciled in the UK.

If you're considered to be domiciled in the UK, it will largely affect your liability to capital gains tax and inheritance tax as well as having implications for income tax, even if you're currently living abroad. See booklet IHT 18 – *Inheritance tax: Foreign aspects*.

Useful Inland Revenue reading

You can ring the Inland Revenue Orderline* for helpsheets, leaflets and notes.

Leaflets and notes
IR20   Residents and non-residents – liability to tax in the UK
IR138   Living or retiring abroad? A guide to UK tax on your UK
            income and pension
IR139   Income from abroad? A guide to UK tax on overseas income
IR140   Non-resident landlords, their agents and tenants
SA109   Notes on non-residence
IHT18   Inheritance tax – foreign aspects

Helpsheets
When you receive a helpsheet, make sure it relates to the tax year for which you want information.

IR205   Foreign earnings deduction
IR205(s) Foreign earnings deduction for seafarers
IR211   Employment – residence and domicile issues
IR278   Temporary non-residents and capital gains tax
IR300   Non-residents and investment income
IR302   Dual resident
IR303   Non-resident entertainers and sports persons
IR304   Non-residents – relief under double taxation agreements

Concessions
Extra-statutory concessions let you off paying tax that is technically due. Booklet IR1 gives details of each concession.

A10   Lump sums paid under overseas pension schemes
A11   Residence in the UK – year of commencement or cessation
           of residence

A12 Double taxation relief – alimony etc. under UK court order or agreement, payer resident abroad

A14 Deceased person's estate – residuary income received during administration period by non-resident

A25 Crown servants engaged overseas

A78 Residence in UK – accompanying spouse

National Insurance

If you work, you will usually have to pay National Insurance on your earnings in addition to any income tax. The main exceptions are:

- where you are under the age of 16
- where your earnings are very low
- where you are over state pension age (currently 65 for men and 60 for women).

Insurance or tax?

National Insurance was first levied as a way of paying for the welfare state. Contributions formed a fund to provide income for people in their old age, when they were too sick to work, when unemployed and so on.

Today, the link to the welfare state still exists. The National Insurance Fund is used to pay the following state benefits: state retirement pensions, widows' benefits (and bereavement benefits due to be introduced from April 2001), incapacity benefit, maternity allowance and contributory jobseeker's allowance. Your entitlement to these depends on whether you have paid enough Class 1, Class 2 or Class 3 National Insurance. Class 4 National Insurance gives you no rights to benefits. It is a straightforward tax.

If you are an employee

Employees, including company directors, pay Class 1 National Insurance. It is levied only on earnings, not on unearned income. If you are a director of your own company, you may be able to save tax by paying yourself share dividends (which count as unearned income) rather than earnings.

Benefits

Class 1 entitles you to contributory jobseeker's allowance, incapacity benefit, maternity allowance, widows' benefits, state basic pension and state-earnings related pension. You will have to pass contributions tests which differ for each benefit.

Which earnings are taxed?

Class 1 is due on all wages, salaries, commission, profit-related pay and overtime payments and on sick pay and maternity pay from your employer. It is based on your gross earnings – in other words before deducting tax, payments to pension schemes, donations to charity under payroll giving, expenses incurred in doing your job and so on.

Employees do not usually pay Class 1 on *benefits in kind* (i.e. perks such as a company car) or expense payments they receive. But they do pay Class 1 on benefits in kind that can be easily converted to cash – for example, commodities, gold bullion and gemstones. Employers pay National Insurance on most benefits in kind, whether or not they can be converted to cash.

What you pay in 2000–1

You pay Class 1 at a rate of either 10 per cent or 8.4 per cent but only on earnings between:

- **the employees' earnings threshold** – £76 a week, £329 a month, £3,952 a year, *and*
- **the upper earnings limit** – £535 a week, £2,319 a month, £27,820 a year, *so*
- **the maximum on which Class 1 would be deducted** if you have only one job is £24,327: £535 – £76 = £459, multiplied by 53 (the number of weeks in the year plus the remaining part of a week); 10 per cent of £24,327 is £2,432.70, 8.4 per cent is £2,043.47.

The 10 per cent rate builds up entitlement to both a state basic pension and a state earnings-related pension. The 8.4 per cent rate builds up entitlement to a state basic pension but not a state earnings-related pension. You pay 8.4 per cent only if you belong to an employer's pension scheme which is *contracted out*. Not all employers' pensions are contracted out. Because the state will pay you less pension when you retire, you (and your employer) pay Class 1 National Insurance at a lower rate.

Employees can also be contracted out of the state earnings-related pension scheme (SERPS) through other types of pension arrangements – a personal pension, an FSAVC plan and a stakeholder pension (available from April 2001). But with these, you pay Class 1 at the 10 per cent rate. Part of what you pay is returned as a rebate paid direct to the pension scheme or plan.

If your earnings are less than the employees' earnings threshold, you do not pay National Insurance. But you will still be building up rights to benefits provided your earnings are not less than a *lower earnings limit* – £67 a week, £291 a month, £3,484 a year in 2000–1.

EXAMPLE 1

Phil earns £1,700 a month as a supermarket manager. He pays Class 1 National Insurance on the amount of these earnings above the employees' earnings threshold (£329 a month in 2000–1). As the pension scheme at work is not contracted out (see above), he pays at the full rate of 10 per cent. Here's how Phil's monthly National Insurance deduction is worked out: £1,700 – £329 = £1,371, and 10 per cent of £1,371 is £137.10.

How you pay
Class 1 is automatically deducted from your pay by your employer through the Pay-As-You-Earn (PAYE) system. Your payslips and P60 show how much National Insurance you have paid.

Married womens' and widows' reduced rate
In 2000–1, some women employees pay National Insurance at a reduced rate of 3.85 per cent on earnings between the employees' earnings threshold and the upper earnings limit. Married women used to be able to elect to pay Class 1 National Insurance at a reduced rate. The reduced rate gives no entitlement to benefits. It was assumed that married women could rely on their husband's (or late-husband's) payments for a state pension.

The option ceased to be available after 11 May 1977, but if you elected to pay a reduced rate by that date you can continue to pay it. However, you can voluntarily switch to paying normal Class 1 National Insurance and so build up your own rights to benefits – use the form in leaflet CA13 – *NIC for married women*. You automatically lose the right to pay reduced rate if:

- you divorce
- you are a widow and you remarry

- you have no earnings for two years running
- you have very low earnings for two years running.

If this applies to you, tell the Inland Revenue as soon as you can. If you delay, you will have to make up any National Insurance underpaid since the date your circumstances changed.

If you are self-employed

Self-employed people pay Class 2 and Class 4 National Insurance.

Benefits
Class 2 entitles you to incapacity benefit, maternity allowance, widows' benefits, state basic pension but not the state earnings-related pension. You will have to pass contributions tests which differ for each benefit. Class 4 does not entitle you to any benefits.

Which earnings are taxed?
Whether or not you need to pay Class 2 depends on the profits from your business during the tax year. If the tax year does not coincide with your accounting year, you must apportion the profits for each accounting year – see Example 2.

But Class 4 National Insurance is due on the same basis as income tax – i.e. it is paid on your profits for the accounting year ending within the tax year. See Chapter 6 for special rules applying to the opening and closing years of a business.

What you pay in 2000–1
- Class 2 National Insurance is paid at a flat rate of £2 a week. But if your profits are less than £3,825 (the small earnings exception) you can opt not to pay Class 2 National Insurance. If you do this, you will not be building up any rights to benefits.
- Maximum Class 2 is £106 (52 weeks plus the remaining part of a week in 365 days).
- Class 4 National Insurance is payable on profits for the year that fall between the lower profits limit of £4,385 and the upper profits limit of £27,820. The rate is 7 per cent. The maximum Class 4 you would pay is £27,820 – £4,385 = £23,435. 7 per cent of £23,435 is £1,640.45.
- You pay no Class 4 National Insurance if your profits for the year are less than the lower limit.

EXAMPLE 2

Justin runs his own carpentry business. The business has been through a bad patch. In the two most recent accounting years, his profits are:

- 1 August 1999 to 31 July 2000 – £2,800
- 1 August 2000 to 31 July 2001 – £4,100

Justin must work out the portion of each accounting year's profits which falls within the 2000–1 tax year to work out whether he must pay Class 2 National Insurance. The 2000–1 tax year runs from 6 April 2000 to 5 April 2001. It covers 117 of the 365 days in his 1999–2000 accounting year and 248 of the 365 days in his 2000–1 accounting year.

- He divides £2,800 by 365 and multiplies the answer by 117 to get £897.53.
- He divides £4,100 by 365 and multiplies the answer by 248 to get £2,785.75.
- £897.53 plus £2,785.75 comes to £3,683.28 – the profits on which to base Class 2 National Insurance in 2000–1.

Justin's profits are less than the £3,825 threshold for claiming the small earnings exception. He applies not to pay Class 2 National Insurance in 2000–1.

EXAMPLE 3

Chris runs her own book-keeping business. Her profits are above the small earnings exception, so she pays £2 a week Class 2 contributions (£104 over the whole year).

Profits for her accounting year ending in 2000–1 were £22,585, a figure below the upper profits limit of £27,820 at which Class 4 National Insurance ceases to bite. But Chris can deduct the lower profits limit of £4,385 from £22,585 to get £18,200; 7 per cent of £18,2000 is £1,274, so £1,724 is the Class 4 National Insurance she must pay for the year.

How you pay

Let the Inland Revenue know you have earnings from self-employment by completing the form in leaflet CWL1 – *Starting your own business*. The form asks how you want to pay Class 2 National Insurance. You can pay either by quarterly bill or monthly by direct debit. Class 4 National Insurance is paid along with your income tax through the self-assessment system – see p. 27.

Married women, widows and class 2

Certain self-employed women pay no Class 2, regardless of the level of profit they make. Married women were previously able to opt not to pay Class 2 (though they have always had to pay Class 4). By not paying Class 2, they are not building up any rights to benefits. It was assumed that married women could rely on their husband's (or late-husband's) payments for a state pension.

The option ceased to be available after 11 May 1977. If you opted not to pay Class 2 by that date, you can continue not to pay. Alternatively, you can start paying Class 2 and build up entitlement to benefits – use the form in leaflet CA13 – *NIC for married women*. With contributions down to £2 a week in 2000–1, you should consider whether it's worth paying to gain access to benefits. You lose the right not to pay Class 2 if:

- you divorce
- you are a widow and you remarry
- you have no earnings for two years running
- you have very low earnings for two years running.

If this applies to you, tell the Inland Revenue as soon as you can. If you delay, you will have to make up any National Insurance underpaid since the date your circumstances changed.

You as employer in 2000–1

As well as deducting National Insurance from your employees' pay, you may have to pay employers' National Insurance.

- You pay nothing on earnings up to £84 a week.
- You pay 12.2 per cent on earnings above £84 unless you run a contracted-out employer's pension.
- If you run a contracted-out employer's pension, you pay a variety of lower rates depending on the type of pension scheme

and the level of the employee's earnings. You pay the lower rates on earnings between £84 a week and £535 a week in respect of employees who belong to the contracted-out pension scheme and 12.2 per cent on earnings above £535.
- From 6 April 2000, employers (but not employees) pay National Insurance on the taxable value of most benefits in kind they provide. This already applied to the provision of a company car and/or fuel for private use before that date.

Periods with no earnings

You may be credited with National Insurance which can help you qualify for contributory state benefits if you are not working. Credits are usually given automatically. You may get credits towards:

- state basic pension and widows benefits for the years in which you reached ages 16, 17 and 18
- jobseeker's allowance and incapacity benefits, when an approved training course comes to an end
- all the contributory benefits, if you are unemployed or unable to work because of illness or disability, provided you 'sign on' or are claiming benefit
- all the contributory benefits, if you are a man aged 60 to 64 and not working – you do not have to 'sign on' or claim benefits to get these credits
- state basic pension if, for example, you are caring for children or an elderly relative – you get this *home responsibilities protection* automatically if you are getting child benefit. In other circumstances you may need to make a claim (contact your local Benefits Agency).

Should you pay voluntary Class 3 National Insurance?

If you do not qualify for National Insurance credits, a period without work usually appears as a gap in your National Insurance record. As a result, you might fail to qualify for a state benefit you need or may get only a reduced amount of benefit. Gaps in your record can occur, for example, for years spent studying at university, breaks taken to travel, and time spent working overseas unless the UK has a recip-rocal agreement with the country where you are working – as it does with other EU countries, for example.

You can fill gaps by voluntarily paying Class 3 National Insurance. You can pay at the time the gap is created, and you can also go back up to six years to fill earlier gaps in your record.

Married women and widows cannot pay Class 3 for periods when they had opted to pay the married women's reduced rate National Insurance (see p. 143) or opted out of paying Class 2 National Insurance (see p. 145).

Your local Benefits Agency can help you check your current benefit entitlement and whether it is worth you paying voluntary National Insurance.

Benefits
Class 3 counts towards state basic pension and widows' benefits.

What you pay in 2000–1
Class 3 is paid at a flat rate of £6.55 a week. If you are filling earlier gaps in your record, the rate you pay depends on when the gap arose.

- For gaps within the last two years you normally pay at the Class 3 rate for the earlier year.
- For gaps within the last three to six years you normally pay either the rate for the earlier year or the rate for the year you make the payment – whichever is the higher rate.

EXAMPLE 4

Max took a year off work in order to travel and visit family overseas. His travels covered two different tax years to create a 13-week National Insurance gap in 1994–5 and a 39-week gap in 1995–6. Neither year will count towards his state basic pension and widows' benefits unless he makes up the gap by paying Class 3 National Insurance.

There is a six-year time limit. Max has until 5 April 2001 to fill the 1994–95 gap and until 5 April 2002 to fill the 1995–6 gap.

The Class 3 contribution rate is £6.55 a week in 2000–1. It was lower in 1994–5 at £5.55 and lower in 1995–6 at £5.65. Max decides to pay for the whole 52-week gap, so must pay at the higher 2000–1 rate. He must pay £6.55 x 52 = £340.60.

How you pay
You can pay by quarterly bill or monthly by direct debit if you are paying Class 3 on a regular basis. You can also pay lump sums by cheque if you are making good gaps in your past record.

Earnings from more than source

More than one business

If you run more than one business as a self-employed person, all your businesses are treated as a single business for National Insurance purposes.

Working for more than one employer

Each job is treated separately for National Insurance purposes, so each employer deducts National Insurance as if you worked only for that employer. But the maximum you have to pay in National Insurance on your earnings from all the jobs is 53 times the full Class 1 rate that would be payable if your earnings equalled the weekly upper earnings limit – £535 a week in 2000–1. The total National Insurance bill for the year on all your jobs is limited in 2000–1 to:

- £535 – the weekly upper earnings limit, *minus* £76 – the weekly employees' earnings threshold: £535 – £76 = £459
- multiplied by 53: £459 x 53 = £24,327
- multiplied by 10 per cent, the full Class 1 rate: £24,327 x 10 per cent = £2,432.70, so
- the maximum Class 1 if you have more than one job is £2,432.70.

You can apply for a refund (see below) if you pay more than £2,432.70 in 2000–1. And you can apply for a deferment in advance if you expect that you will end up paying too much National Insurance. Earnings from some of your jobs will be paid with less National Insurance deducted or none at all if the Inland Revenue agrees to a deferment. The Revenue – not you – decides which of your jobs will be treated in this way. To apply for a deferment, complete the form in leaflet CA72 – *National Insurance Contributions – deferring payment*.

Are you self-employed *and* employed in 2000–1?

Your self-employment and the job or jobs you do for employers are each treated separately for National Insurance. Your employer(s) deduct Class 1 National Insurance in the usual way and you are responsible for Class 2 and possibly Class 4 National Insurance in respect of your self-employment. But special rules put a maximum on the total National Insurance on your earnings from all sources.

- **Rule 1** £2,432.70 is the maximum anyone has to pay in Class 1 and Class 2 contributions. The £2,432.70 figure is based on 53 times Class 1 at the 10 per cent rate you'd pay if your earnings equalled the weekly upper earnings limit – see p. 149.
- **Rule 2** £1,746.45 minus what you must pay in Class 1 and Class 2 is the maximum you have to pay in Class 4. The £1,746.45 figure is based on the maximum Class 4 (£1,640.45) if your earnings are at or above the upper profits limit, plus £106 (53 multiplied by £2, the Class 2 rate).

To work out whether your National Insurance bill is (or is likely to be) more than the maximum, treat all Class 1 National Insurance as if you had paid at the 10 per cent rate. If you paid at the 8.4 per cent contracted-out rate or the 3.85 per cent married women's reduced rate, you need to scale-up the amount you paid before checking the total against the maximum for the year. For how the rules work in practice, see Example 5 and Example 6.

You can apply for a deferment if you expect that you will end up paying too much National Insurance. The Inland Revenue can make special arrangements for you to pay less Class 2 National Insurance or none at all. Class 4 National Insurance can also be deferred until it is clear what amount, if any, is due. To defer Class 2 and Class 4 National Insurance, use the form in leaflet CA72 – *National Insurance contributions – deferring payment*. And if you have overpaid you can claim a refund.

EXAMPLE 5

Jack was mainly self-employed in 2000–1. He was also employed in a bar where he worked for 21 weeks and earned £200 a week. But the bulk of his earnings came from his work as a self-employed garden contractor. His profits were £25,500. His National Insurance position is as follows.

- Class 1 on his bar earnings is 10 per cent of £2,604 (£200 minus the weekly employees' earnings threshold of £76 = £124: £124 x 21 = £2,604). 10 per cent of £2,604 is £260.40.
- Class 2 on his self-employed earnings is 52 x £2 = £104.
- His total Class 1 and Class 2 comes to £260.40 + £104 = £364.40.
- Based on his self-employment profits, he would pay Class 4 of £1,478.05. That's 7 per cent of £21,115 (his profits of

---

£25,500 minus the £4,385 lower profits limit). But under Rule 2, the maximum Class 4 is restricted to £1,746.45 minus the amount he must pay in Class 1 and Class 2. £1,746.45 − £364.40 = £1,382.05. So Jack pays £1,382.05 in Class 4, £96 less than he would otherwise have paid.

Jack pays £1,746.45 in total – £260.40 in Class 1 plus £104 in Class 2 plus £1,382.05 in Class 4.

EXAMPLE 6

Elspeth was mainly an employee in 2000–1. She was deputy head at a private school. Her salary was £29,000. But she also writes maths textbooks on a self-employed basis. Her profits were £12,000. Her National Insurance position is as follows.

- Class 1 on her school salary is 8.4 per cent of £23,868 (the upper earnings limit of £27,820 minus the employees' earnings threshold of £3,952). 8.4 per cent of £23,868 is £2,004.91. Elspeth pays at the 8.4 per cent rate because she belongs to a contracted-out pension at work. But for working out how much National Insurance she must pay in total, she can use the 10 per cent rate. 10 per cent of £23,868 is £2,386.80.
- Class 2 on her self-employed earnings is 52 x £2 = £104.
- Her total Class 1 and Class 2 comes to £2,386.80 + £104 =£2,490.80. But the maximum she must pay under Rule 1 is £2,432.70. Elspeth has paid £58.10 too much in Class 1 and Class 2.
- Based on her self-employment profits, she would pay Class 4 of £533.05. That's 7 per cent of £7,615 (her profits of £12,000 minus the £4,385 lower profits limit). But under Rule 2, the maximum Class 4 is restricted to £1,746.45 minus the amount she must pay in Class 1 and Class 2. This comes to less than zero. So Elspeth pays no Class 4.

Elspeth pays £2,050.81 in total – £2,004.91 in Class 1 deducted at the contracted-out rate of 8.4 per cent plus £104 in Class 2, minus £58.10 that is over the maximum for Class 1 and Class 2.

Solving problems

Enquiries and information

Local Inland Revenue offices deal with enquiries and can provide leaflets and forms.

The National Insurance Contributions Office (NICO)* is part of the Inland Revenue. It administers National Insurance and holds your National Insurance records.

If you have enquiries about your rights to benefits as a result of paying National Insurance, contact your local Benefits Agency.

Challenging decisions

If you do not agree with the amount of National Insurance you are being asked to pay, you can appeal – contact your local Inland Revenue office. If the dispute cannot be resolved informally, a formal decision will be made by an officer of the Board of the Inland Revenue.

You will receive a notice of the decision. If you are not happy with it, you can appeal within 30 days to the Inland Revenue Commissioners as described in Chapter 2.

Repayment of overpaid National Insurance

You can apply in writing to the Refunds Group at NICO*. An application for a refund of Class 1 or Class 2 National Insurance contributions must be made within six years of the end of the tax year in which the contributions were made. An application for a refund of Class 4 National Insurance must be made within six years of the end of the tax year to which the contributions apply or within two years of the end of the tax year in which they were made.

Where you apply for a refund and you have paid National Insurance of more than one type, refunds follow a strict order of priority:

- Class 4 National Insurance
- married women's reduced rate Class 1 National Insurance
- Class 2 National Insurance
- 10 per cent Class 1 National Insurance
- 8.4 per cent contracted-out Class 1 National Insurance.

You may be entitled to interest on the National Insurance overpaid.

Useful Inland Revenue reading

You can ring the Inland Revenue Orderline* for leaflets and notes.

Leaflets and notes

CA01   National Insurance for employees

CA02   National Insurance for self-employed people with small earnings

CA04   Class 2 and Class 3 National Insurance contributions. Direct debit the easier way to pay

CA07   NIC unpaid and late paid contributions

CA08   NIC voluntary contributions

CA09   NIC for widows

CA10   NIC for divorced women

CA12   Training for further employment and your National Insurance record

CA13   NIC for married women (includes form CF9 for revoking election to pay reduced rate contributions)

CA53   Information about National Insurance contributions

CA65   NIC for people working for embassies, consulates and overseas employers

CA72   National Insurance contributions. Deferring payment (includes forms CA72A and CA72B for requesting deferral)

CWL1   Starting your own business (includes form CWF1 for notifying Inland Revenue and VAT authorities that you are starting up and for arranging to pay National Insurance contributions)

CWL2   National Insurance contributions for self-employed people. Class 2 and Class 4

IR37   Appeals against tax, National Insurance contributions, Statutory Sick Pay and Statutory Maternity Pay

Social security and means-tested tax credits

If you're getting social security benefits, you may think you don't have to worry about tax at all. For many people this will be true, as the majority of benefits are not taxable. But your benefit may be taxable if you are:

- training
- unemployed
- on strike
- sick or disabled
- having a baby
- a pensioner
- a widow.

Is your benefit tax-free or taxable?

Below we show whether a benefit is tax-free or taxable. The list does not include benefits paid by foreign governments to UK residents. As a general rule, a benefit paid by a foreign government will be tax-free if it is broadly similar to a tax-free benefit paid by the UK government. Likewise, it will be taxable if it is generally similar to a taxable benefit paid by the UK government. If you are not sure about the tax status of any benefit, check with your tax office.

If you are training, unemployed or on strike
- **tax-free** part of jobseeker's allowance and part of income support (see p. 157), back to work bonus, jobfinder's grant, youth training allowance and training for work allowance paid to trainees

- **taxable** part or all of jobseeker's allowance, part or all of income support, youth training allowance paid to employees

If you have children or are pregnant
- **tax-free** maternity allowance, maternity payments from the social fund, child benefit, child's special allowance, guardian's allowance
- **taxable** statutory maternity pay (see p. 159)

If you are older
- **tax-free** income support, £10 Christmas bonus, cold-weather payments, winter fuel payment, special pensions paid by the governments of Germany and Austria to UK victims of Nazi persecution
- **taxable** state retirement pension except additions for children, over-80s pension, invalidity allowance paid with retirement pension

If you are a widow
- **tax-free** widow's payment, additions paid for children, war widow's pension including allowances for children and rent
- **taxable** widowed mother's allowance, widow's pension, industrial death benefit

If you are disabled or sick
- **tax-free** short-term incapacity benefit paid at the lower rate, severe disablement allowance, attendance allowance, disability living allowance, disablement benefits paid because of injury at work or an industrial disease, disablement pensions paid as a result of service in the forces or merchant navy or to civilians for war injuries, extra pension paid to police and fire staff on duty beyond what they would have received if retired through ill-health
- **taxable** statutory sick pay and short-term incapacity benefit paid at the higher rate and long-term incapacity benefit except additions paid for children (see p. 159), invalid care allowance except additions for children, invalidity allowance paid with retirement pension

Miscellaneous benefits
- **tax-free** income support (if not on short-time work or on strike), grants for improving or insulating your home, social fund funeral

payment, social fund community care grant, housing benefit, council tax benefit, earnings top-up (currently on trial in some areas), some annuities and pension additions for gallantry awards such as the George Cross.

How is tax on benefits collected?

Most taxable benefits are paid gross – i.e. before any tax is deducted – and are taxed as the earned income of the person claiming benefit. If you're claiming extra benefit for your spouse (or someone living with you as your spouse), it is taxed as your income. For state retirement pensions, this includes the adult dependency addition paid where, for example, the pensioner's spouse has not reached the state pension age. But a married woman's pension is paid direct to her and is treated as her own for income tax, even if it is paid as a result of her husband's contributions.

Tax-free benefits shouldn't be entered on your tax return, but you do need to include any taxable benefit you've received during the tax year.

You will have to pay income tax if your total taxable income, including taxable state benefits, comes to more than your allowances and deductions. Special rules apply if you're off sick (see p. 155) or claiming jobseeker's allowance because you're unemployed – see below. For other benefits, if you are working or getting an employer's pension, any tax due will be collected through Pay-As-You-Earn (PAYE). It will look as if you are paying much more tax than others earning the same amount. But this is because *all* the tax due on your benefits is being collected at the same time as tax on your pay.

If you are not taxed under PAYE, you will be sent a statement telling you how much taxable benefit you received. If you receive incapacity benefit and are due to pay tax, tax will be collected through PAYE if you are still being paid by your employer or receive an employer's pension; if not, any tax due will be deducted by the benefit office before incapacity benefit is paid.

Special PAYE codes
If your taxable state benefits and other income amount to more than your tax-free allowances and you're taxed under PAYE, your earnings (or employer's pension) will have to be taxed at a higher-than-normal rate, e.g. at 25 per cent rather than 23 per cent, to collect the tax on your state benefits. Your tax code will then include the letter K.

Tax if you're unemployed or on strike

People who are unemployed can claim jobseeker's allowance. There are two types of jobseeker's allowance. One type is 'contribution-based' and depends on your National Insurance contributions; it is paid for a maximum of six months. The other type is 'income-based' and depends on your income.

Jobseeker's allowance is made up of personal allowances and various 'premiums' which depend on your circumstances and income. The personal allowances depend on your age, on whether you are part of a couple (married or not) and whether you have dependent children. The income-based premiums and allowances for dependent children are the same for both jobseeker's allowance and income support.

How much of your benefit is taxable?

If you are claiming as a single person, the taxable part of jobseeker's allowance is anything you receive up to the level of the weekly jobseeker's personal allowance for a single person of your age. For 2000–1, the allowances are:

- aged under 18 (usual rate)   £31.45
- aged 18–24   £41.35
- aged 25 or over   £52.20

If you are claiming income-based jobseeker's allowance as a couple, the taxable amount is that for the oldest partner in the table above, unless one of the following applies. You are:

- both under 18, one is disabled   £41.35
- both under 18, with a child   £62.35
- both 18 or over   £81.95

Above these levels, jobseeker's allowance is tax-free. Any personal allowances you receive for dependent children are not taxable, nor are any premiums you receive in addition to your personal allowances.

The taxable amount of jobseeker's allowance for a couple counts as taxable income for the jobseeker only (not for his or her partner).

If you are involved in a strike you won't get jobseeker's allowance for yourself. But you may be able to claim income support for your partner (whether or not you are married) and for any dependent children. This is taxable, but to find out how much is taxable contact your tax office.

157

Tax rebates

If you are unemployed and living on benefits for a full year with no other taxable income, your total taxable benefit will be below your allowances. So there'll be no tax to pay.

Because of the way the PAYE system works, if you become unemployed at some point in the tax year, you may have paid more tax on your earnings than you need have done. But if you're claiming benefits, you won't get your tax rebate at once. Instead, you'll get it when you start work again or (unless you're involved in a strike) at the end of the tax year, whichever comes first. In most cases, the rebate will be paid to you by your benefit office if you are claiming income support, or by your local Job Centre if you are getting jobseeker's allowance. You'll also get a statement showing how much taxable benefit you have been paid.

If you think the figure is wrong ask the benefit office or Job Centre to explain it. If you're still unhappy, you should write to the benefit office or Job Centre within 60 days of the date on which the statement was issued. If you get no satisfaction, ask to fill out a tax return, which the Revenue will check and amend. You can appeal against the amendment in the normal way.

If you are unemployed and not claiming any taxable benefit, you can claim a tax rebate after being unemployed for four weeks. You'll have to claim on form P50, which you can get from your tax office.

Returning to work

If you start work again before the end of the tax year after you have been unemployed, your benefit office or Job Centre will give you a new form P45 showing how much taxable income you've had and how much tax you've already paid. Your new employer will then deduct the right amount of tax, including that due on your benefit, from your earnings for the rest of that tax year or, normally, from a later tax year. You will also be sent a statement of how much taxable benefit you've had.

When you return to work after a strike or if you are still unemployed at the end of the tax year, your benefit office or Job Centre will send you a form P60U which includes details of how much taxable benefit you've had in that tax year. Once you're working, your PAYE code will be adjusted so that any tax you owe on benefits will be collected from your earnings.

If you find a job and have paid too much tax, you should receive a refund with your final payment of jobseeker's allowance, provided that you complete your booklet ES40 (which gives details about signing on) and return it to the Job Centre.

Tax if you're off sick

Employers usually have to pay their employees statutory sick pay for their first 28 weeks of a spell of illness. Statutory sick pay is treated just like your regular earnings, so tax is deducted from it under PAYE. If the amount of sick pay you get is lower than the amount you can earn each week (or month) before paying tax, your employer will give you a refund of some of the tax you've already paid in each pay packet.

If you cannot get statutory sick pay, you can claim short-term incapacity benefit paid at the lower rate, provided that you have paid enough National Insurance to qualify. This is not taxable.

After you have been sick for 28 weeks and are in receipt of either statutory sick pay or short-term incapacity benefit, you can claim short-term incapacity benefit at the higher rate (again, depending on your National Insurance record). This is taxable.

If you receive both incapacity benefit and a pension from a former employer (or pay from your employer) any tax due will be collected through an adjustment to your PAYE code – i.e. tax will be deducted from your pension or pay. If you are not receiving pay or a pension and your incapacity benefit comes to more than your tax allowances, tax will be deducted from your incapacity benefit at source.

Very occasionally, for example if your employer is insolvent, statutory sick pay is paid to you directly by the Department of Social Security (DSS) without any tax deducted. In this case, you will have to declare the benefit on your tax return.

Tax if you're having a baby

Statutory maternity pay is paid by employers to qualifying employees for up to 18 weeks. Statutory maternity pay is taxed in the same way as regular earnings – so tax is deducted under PAYE. If the amount of maternity pay you get is lower than the amount you can earn each week (or month) before paying tax, in each pay packet you will get a refund of some of the tax you have already paid.

If you don't meet all the statutory maternity pay conditions, you might be able to get maternity allowance for up to 18 weeks. You need to have paid enough in National Insurance to get the allowance, but it's not taxable. You might be able to get incapacity benefit if you can't get either statutory maternity pay or maternity allowance – depending on how much you've paid in National Insurance. Incapacity benefit paid at the long-term rate or the short-term higher rate is taxable; if it is paid at the short-term lower rate, there is no tax to pay.

As with statutory sick pay, if you receive any statutory maternity pay directly from the DSS, you should declare it on your tax return.

Working families' and disabled person's tax credits

You can claim working families' tax credit whether you are single or living with a partner (whether or not you are married) if:

- you or your partner work at least 16 hours on average a week
- you have one or more dependent children under 16, or under 19 if in full-time education up to A-level or equivalent standard, living with you
- you are on a low income
- you have capital of no more than £8,000 (£8,000 per couple if you are a couple) – capital includes savings, investments and property for example, but excludes the home you live in.

You get a maximum weekly tax credit of:

- £52.30 per family plus £11.50 if one earner works at least 30 hours a week
- £19.85 for each child up to the age of 11
- £20.90 for each child who is 11 or over
- £25.95 for each child who is 16 or over and in full-time education (see above)
- 70 per cent of eligible childcare costs of up to £100 a week for one child, 70 per cent of up to £150 a week for two children.

Couples can choose which of them will receive the credit. Employees will receive the credit through the Pay-As-You-Earn (PAYE) system. The self-employed have to claim it through their tax office.

The maximum weekly credit is reduced by 55p for every £1 of net income above £90. The definition of net income is complicated. It includes, for example, income you are assumed to receive if your capital is between £3,000 and £8,000.

Disabled person's tax credit works in a similar way to working families' tax credit, though some of the credit levels, income limits and capital limits are different To qualify, you must receive (or have received in the 182 days prior to applying for the credit) one of a range of incapacity or disability benefits and work for at least 16 hours a week.

The working families' and disabled person's tax credits are essentially means-tested state benefits for which you have to apply every six months. They are paid through the Inland Revenue but have little to do with tax and are outside the scope of this book. If you think you may be eligible, get the appropriate leaflets listed below, which include details of how to apply.

Useful Inland Revenue reading

You can ring the Inland Revenue Orderline* for helpsheets, leaflets and notes.

Leaflets and notes
IR41	Income tax and job seekers
IR144	Income tax and incapacity benefit
IR37	Appeals against tax, National Insurance contributions, statutory sick pay and statutory maternity pay
IR120	You and the Inland Revenue. Tax Credit Office (working families and disabled person's tax credit)
WFTC/BK1	Your guide to working families' tax credit
WFTC/FS1	Working families' tax credit
CTC/BK1	Working families' tax credit and disabled person's tax credit
CTC/FS1	Working families' tax credit, disabled person's tax credit and childcare
DPTC/FS1	Disabled person's tax credit
DPTC/BK1	Your guide to disabled person's tax credit
WFTC/AP	If you think a tax credit decision is wrong
WFTC/APNI	If you think a tax credit decision is wrong (Northern Ireland)

Helpsheets
When you receive a helpsheet, make sure it relates to the tax year for which you want information.

IR310	War widow's and dependants pensions

Concessions
Extra-statutory concessions let you off paying tax that is technically due. Booklet IR1 gives details of each concession.

A24	Foreign social security benefits

10 **Pensions**

- Tax relief on payments towards your pension – p. 163
- Employers' pensions: how and when you can benefit – p. 172
- Personal pensions: how and when you can benefit – p. 177
- How pensions are taxed – p. 179
- Useful Inland Revenue reading – p. 181

Most people who pay National Insurance or who are building up credits are already paying towards a state pension in the form of the basic retirement (or 'old-age') pension and, for certain employees, an earnings-related pension. But until the 2001–2 tax year, the tax rules say that only people who have earned income – such as those who have a salary from a job or profits from working for themselves can pay into a pension scheme which will pay them an income in retirement on top of what they get from the state. From 6 April 2001, anyone – whether earning or not – will be able to contribute up to £3,600 a year into the government's new stakeholder pension.

The advantage of saving now to buy a future income by paying into a private pension, whether an employer's scheme or a personal pension, is tax concessions.

- Your pension fund grows in an environment which is largely free of income tax and wholly free of capital gains tax.
- You get full tax relief on the payments you make up to certain limits (see p. 163).
- Any payments an employer makes to your pension are tax-free (but see p. 166).
- You can normally swap part of your pension for a tax-free lump sum when you retire (see pp. 174 and 177).

However, there are drawbacks to paying into a pension.

- You can't normally get at the money you have paid in until you reach a certain age.
- The tax rules dictate how your retirement income is provided.

162

- You have to hand over the bulk of your savings in exchange for an income and cannot get them back.
- There are limits on the size of pension you can have from an employer's scheme.
- The pension (or annuity) income you get is taxable – unlike, for example, certain types of investment income paid from individual savings accounts (ISAS).

The tax rules described in this chapter relate to statutory pension schemes, such as those for public-sector workers, and those approved by the Inland Revenue – most employers' and personal pensions.

Some employers offer pension schemes which are not approved by the Inland Revenue. These do not qualify for the favourable tax treatment described here. 'Unapproved' schemes are aimed mainly at people earning significantly more than £91,800 and/or people who are likely to fall foul of Inland Revenue limits at the time they take their pension.

Tax relief on payments towards your pension

If you pay into a statutory or approved pension scheme, you get tax relief on your payments at your highest rate of tax. So if you pay tax at the basic rate of 22 per cent, a contribution of £100 costs only £78 after tax relief; for a higher-rate taxpayer the cost falls to £60.

However, the Revenue puts limits on how much you can pay in. These are expressed as a percentage of your earnings if you are an employee or your profits if you work for yourself. How much you can pay in each year also depends on whether you are paying into an employer's or personal pension.

You can't belong to an employer's pension (even if it's a non-contributory one) and have a personal pension at the same time unless:

- the personal pension is used only for contracting out of the state earnings-related pension scheme (SERPS), and you are not already contracted out through your employer's pension
- the personal pension covers earnings which are otherwise non-pensionable earnings, e.g. freelance earnings
- you take out a free-standing additional voluntary contribution (FSAVC) plan (see p. 164); in fact, an FSAVC plan is *not* technically a personal pension, and the rules on contributions and benefits are very different

- you take out a stakeholder pension when they become available in April 2001.

You're not disqualified from taking out a personal pension just because your employer provides you with some life insurance cover which will pay out a lump sum if you die, or provides a pension only for your spouse or dependants. You'll still be entitled to take out a personal pension as well.

How much can you pay into an employer's pension?
There are no set limits on what your employer can pay into your pension on your behalf. What *you* can pay is a maximum of 15 per cent of the Revenue's definition of your pensionable earnings. This may be more generous than the earnings which your employer uses to calculate your pension payments. It includes:

- your wages or salary
- other cash payments such as bonuses and commission, but not allowable expenses
- the cash value of any taxable benefits in kind such as a company car or private medical insurance.

As well as the percentage limit, there may also be a cash limit of £13,770 in the 2000–1 tax year. But this will apply only if you earn more than £91,800 (the *earnings cap*) and you joined your pension scheme after 31 May 1989, or the scheme you are in was set up after 13 March 1989. (£13,770 is 15 per cent of £91,800.)

The regular payments your employer requires you to make are much lower than the 15 per cent limit in most cases. But you can use the unused part of the tax relief available to make additional voluntary contributions (AVCs). These can be paid into an AVC scheme that your employer is obliged to run alongside an employer's pension. Alternatively, you can pay them into a freestanding additional voluntary contribution (FSAVC) plan run by a commercial provider such as an insurance company. Topping up your pension through extra payments is worth considering if your main employer's pension plus any state pension is unlikely to provide you with the level of income you think you will need in retirement.

Getting the tax relief
Your employer subtracts the payments towards your pension – including any AVCs you make to your employer's AVC scheme – from your gross pay. Your employer then uses the PAYE system to work out

the tax that's due on the pay that's left. This way, you automatically get tax relief at your highest rate.

If you make AVCs to a free-standing plan from a commercial provider, you automatically get basic-rate tax relief when you make your payments. But if you are a higher-rate taxpayer, you have to claim the higher-rate relief by giving details on your tax return.

EXAMPLE 1

John is 62 and due to retire when he's 65. Because he has changed jobs several times in his working life, his total pension will be a lot less than the amount he thinks he will need to live on. So he arranges to make extra pension payments of £100 a month into his employer's AVC scheme.

He is a higher-rate taxpayer and gets tax relief of £40 on each £100 deducted from his before-tax salary. So the true cost to him is only £60 a month. The money is paid into a special fund for AVCs that his employer has arranged through an insurance company. Over the last five years, the fund has grown by around 12 per cent a year tax-free.

How much can you pay into a personal pension?

The tax limits which apply to payments to a personal pension vary according to:

- your age at the start of the tax year
- when you first started paying into your personal pension(s)
- what the Revenue calls your *net relevant earnings*.

'Personal pension' is a phrase widely used to refer to any private pension bought from a commercial provider. But as far as tax rules are concerned *personal pension* means a private plan that you started to pay into on or after 1 July 1988. The Inland Revenue refers to a private pension from a commercial provider taken out before that date as a *retirement annuity contract* or a plan under Section 620 or Section 226.

The table on p. 166 gives the percentage limits based on your age at the start of the tax year for both personal pensions and retirement annuity contracts. If you have a mixture of both types, the overall limit is the one given for personal pensions. However, you won't be able to pay more into a retirement annuity contract than the limit given for these old-style plans.

Note that payments to a personal pension made by your employer (which is most likely to happen if the employer has set up a group personal pension) count towards the maximum you can pay. But payments made directly by the government if you use a personal pension to contract out of SERPS (the National Insurance rebate) do not affect the maximum you can pay. Employers can't contribute directly to a retirement annuity contract.

Part of the overall limit – up to 5 per cent of your net relevant earnings – can be used to buy pension-linked life insurance.

Maximum percentage of net relevant earnings

age	retirement annuity contract %	personal pension [1] %
up to 35	17.5	17.5
36 to 45	17.5	20.0
46 to 50	17.5	25.0
51 to 55	20.0	30.0
56 to 60	22.5	35.0
61 to 74	27.5	40.0
75 and over	You cannot make further contributions	

[1] You cannot pay more than the applicable percentage of £91,800 – the earnings cap in 2000–1.

Overpayments to a personal pension must be refunded. If you pay too much into a retirement annuity contract, you can leave the money invested but you won't get tax relief on the excess.

Net relevant earnings

For employees, your net relevant earnings are the same as the earnings that can be taken into account for paying into an employer's scheme (see p. 164). You can also include the value of share option schemes and the taxable part of any redundancy payments if you pay into a retirement annuity contract

For the self-employed, your net relevant earnings are your taxable profits being assessed for the tax year and these will normally relate to a particular accounting year. For how tax years relate to accounting years, see Chapter 6.

Taxable profits normally means your business takings (including money owed to you) for your accounting year less allowable business expenses, capital allowances and any losses from earlier years of the business which haven't been set off against other income. Certain payments from your business, including patent royalties, covenant payments and annuities, must be deducted from your taxable profits when working out your net relevant earnings.

If you work for yourself on a freelance basis, your net relevant earnings are the fees you have received less any allowable expenses.

EXAMPLE 2

Harry has been self-employed for some years and his accounting year ends on 31 December each year. His profits for the accounting year ending on 31 December 2000 are £15,700. His tax bill for the 2000–1 tax year is based on taxable profits of £15,700. Harry also has a part-time lecturing job. There is no pension with that job, and in 2000–1 he earns £3,200. Harry's net relevant earnings are £15,700 + £3,200 = £18,900.

Getting the tax relief

- If you are an employee paying into a personal pension, you automatically get basic-rate tax relief at 22 per cent in the 2000–1 tax year, even if you are a starting-rate taxpayer or a non-taxpayer. You get the tax relief by making payments net of tax relief. So for every £78 you pay in, your pension provider claims back £22 (the basic-rate relief) from the Inland Revenue. A net payment £78 equals a gross payment of £100.
- Higher-rate tax relief for employees paying into a personal pension has to be claimed separately. For every gross payment of £100 you can get back £18, i.e. £40 higher-rate tax relief less the £22 claimed directly by the pension provider (see above). Fill in the relevant boxes on your tax return. You normally get the relief by an adjustment to your PAYE code.
- Whether you are an employee or self-employed, payments to a retirement annuity contract have to be made in full. So if you want £100 to go into the pension, you pay £100. Similarly, if you are self-employed and pay into a personal pension, you hand over £100 for every £100 you want to go into the pension. You

get tax relief by filling in a tax return. Your tax bill will take account of the payments and give you both basic-rate and higher-rate tax relief. For how this works, see Chapter 3.

From 6 April 2001, your employment status will not affect the way in which you make pension payments because all payments will be made after deducting basic-rate tax relief.

EXAMPLE 3

David has two pensions: a retirement annuity contract which he started in 1987 and a personal pension that he took out two years later. In the 2000–1 tax year his net relevant earnings are £32,000. Because he turned 46 just before the start of the tax year he can now contribute up to 25 per cent of his earnings to his pensions – a total of £8,000 (25 per cent of £32,000).

David would like to put the full £8,000 into the pension he took out in 1987, but can't because the most he can pay is 17.5 per cent of £32,000, which is £5,600. He decides to pay the maximum £5,600 into this pension and the remaining £2,400 into his personal pension.

Although he has to make the payment to his retirement annuity contract in full, the contribution to his personal pension costs him only £1,872. His pension provider will claim the tax rebate of £528 and pay it into the pension. Since David does not get a tax return, he makes a note to tell his tax office about the £5,600 he has paid in full so that the tax relief can be accounted for in his PAYE tax code.

Backdating payments

You can ask in any tax year to have all or part of the payments you make in that year treated for tax purposes as though you had paid them in the previous tax year (as long as you have sufficient unused relief for the previous tax year). And if you didn't have any net relevant earnings in the previous tax year, you'll be able to get your payments treated as if you had paid them in the year before that. Backdating – or *carrying back* – payments can be a good idea for several reasons.

- If you couldn't afford to make payments to use up all the relief available to you last year, you may be able to catch up this year.

- You can delay making your pension payments until after the end of the tax year but then backdate them. This is useful if you can't finalise your net relevant earnings until some months after the end of the tax year – for example you run your own business and have yet to draw up your accounts.
- If your tax rate has fallen this year compared with last (because your earnings or profits are lower, for example), you can get more tax relief by carrying back.
- If tax rates generally fall, you can take advantage of the fact that rates were higher in earlier years. For example, if you're a basic-rate taxpayer, in the 2000–1 tax year you'll get relief at 22 per cent on a payment made within this tax year. But if you ask for that payment to be backdated to the 1999–2000 tax year, you'll get relief at 23 per cent.

Backdating payments is very straightforward. If you get a tax return, use the boxes provided to carry back your payments; otherwise, ask your tax office for form PP43. Note that you cannot backdate payments to an employer's pension (or an FSAVC plan) unless it is a group personal pension.

Unused relief from the last six years

As well as backdating payments by one year (possibly two), you can take advantage of unused relief by going back further through *carry forward* relief. However, the 2000–1 tax year is the last in which you can use carry forward, which will be replaced with a simpler system from 6 April 2001.

Carry forward relief lets you use unused relief from up to six tax years before the current tax year, or six years before the previous two tax years if you also backdate a payment to either year. You cannot include years when you were a member of an employer's pension unless:

- you also had earnings on which your membership of an employer's pension was not based – for example from a second part-time job or from freelance earnings
- you were a member of an employer's pension but don't count as having been a member if you have no preserved pension rights for that year – for example because you got a refund of pension payments after fewer than two years' membership.

Any pension payment you make first counts towards your current year's limit (or the year to which you backdate a payment). So, for example, if your net relevant earnings for the 2000–1 tax year are £20,000 and your payment limit is 20 per cent, you can pay £4,000 (£3,120 after basic-rate tax relief) into your pension. But you can claim carry forward relief on anything you pay over £4,000 – assuming you have unused relief from earlier years.

In 2000–1, you can go back six tax years to the 1994–5 tax year. But if you backdate a payment to 1999–2000 you can go back to 1993–4. If you backdate to 1998–9 you can go back to 1992–3.

The unused relief must be calculated using the limits that applied in the relevant tax year. For example, if you earned £15,000 in 1994–5 and could pay 17.5 per cent into your pension – your maximum payment was £2,625. If you paid only £1,000, your unused relief would be £1,625.

Make sure you work out your past payments on a gross (before-tax) basis. Otherwise you might overestimate the amount of unused relief you have. For example, if an employee pays £1,500 into a personal pension net of basic-rate tax relief, he or she will have to add back the tax claimed by the pension provider. If the payment was made in 1995–6 when the basic-rate of tax was 25 per cent, a net payment of £1,500 becomes a gross payment of £2,000. See p. 48 for how to convert from net to gross.

Provided you are eligible for carry forward relief, the payments can be made from any money you have – savings or a lump sum you have inherited, for example, as well as earnings. This makes carry forward relief a useful way of boosting your pension payments if you have a sudden windfall. However there are two points to note.

- The amount of tax relief is based on tax rates in the year you make the payment (or the year to which you backdate it) – not the tax rates of the year or years from which the unused relief is carried forward.
- You cannot pay more than your net relevant earnings for the year you make the payment (or to which you backdate it). So, for example, you might have unused relief of £35,000 – and a windfall of £35,000. But if your net relevant earnings are £30,000, you can pay no more than £30,000 to your pension.

In rare cases, a tax bill (an *assessment*) may become final for a tax year more than six years ago, perhaps for example because you have had a dispute with the Inland Revenue which has taken years to resolve. It could mean you have some unused relief. You can carry this forward provided you make payments to the pension plan within six months of the bill becoming finalised.

For help with the calculations, ask your tax office for helpsheet IR330 – *Pension payments*. To claim the relief, fill in form PP42, also available from your tax office or the Inland Revenue Orderline.*

EXAMPLE 4

Arnold took out a retirement annuity contract in 1980, paying £15 a month (£180 a year). He has never increased his payments but has savings of £30,000. With just over ten years to go before retirement, he wonders if it's worth putting some of his savings into his pension. Arnold will be able to use all his unused tax relief for the last six years, but if he backdates some of his payments to last year he can reclaim relief from seven years ago.

Year	Net relevant earnings £	Maximum contribution £	Payment made £	Unused tax relief £
1993–4	10,000	1,750 (17.5%)	180	1,570
1994–5	11,000	1,925 (17.5%)	180	1,745
1995–6	12,000	2,100 (17.5%)	180	1,920
1996–7	17,000	3,400 (20.0%)	180	3,220
1997–8	18,000	3,600 (20.0%)	180	3,420
1998–9	20,000	4,000 (20.0%)	180	3,820
1999–2000	20,000	4,000 (20.0%)	180	3,820
2000–1	23,000	4,600 (20.0%)	180	4,420
		25,375	1,440	23,935

Arnold decides to put £23,935 into his pension – i.e. the maximum payment of £25,375 less the payments already paid of £1,440. This is the full amount of his available unused tax relief since 1993–4 for a retirement annuity contract. In order to get the unused relief for 1993–4 he asks the Revenue to treat £13,985 of this payment as though it were paid in 1999–2000; £13,985 is the amount of income on which he paid basic-rate tax in 1999–2000. This gives a tax rebate of £3,216.55 at the 23 per cent basic rate of tax in 1999–2000. Tax relief on the remaining £9,950 is at the 2000–1 rate of basic-rate tax, 22 per cent. This comes to £2,189. So the tax rebate is £5,405.55 in total. Arnold decides to put this back into his building society account, which, along with the remaining £6,065 (savings of £30,000 less £23,935), still leaves him £11,470.55.

Employers' pensions: how and when you can benefit

In addition to the amount you can pay into your pension, the tax rules also affect:

- how much pension you can have
- whether you can take part of your pension benefits as a tax-free lump sum
- the level of other benefits such as a widow's or widower's pension and death-in-service benefits
- when you can take your pension.

The benefits you get from an employer's pension depend on the rules of the scheme. Common benefits are:

- a pension payable to you on retirement
- regular increases to your pension once it starts to be paid
- the right to swap some of your pension for a tax-free lump sum at retirement (in some pensions you always get a tax-free lump sum – there is no choice)
- a pension for your widow, widower and dependants
- a pension if you choose to retire early, or have to do so because of ill health
- life insurance if you die before retirement.

The maximum benefits you can get are restricted by the Revenue. In practice, the rules set by the employer are often not as generous as the Revenue allows. With a few exceptions, the Revenue limits apply to all types of employers' pensions – i.e. both the *final pay* and the *money purchase* varieties. A final pay pension is linked to your pay. A money purchase pension depends on how the money invested grows and what pension you can purchase at retirement – which depends on the annuity rates at the time.

The basic Revenue limits allow for a maximum pension of $\frac{1}{60}$ of your final salary for each year you have been in the scheme up to 40 years – i.e. a maximum pension of two-thirds of your final pay. They also allow part of this pension to be swapped for a lump sum building up at a rate of $\frac{3}{80}$ of final pay for each year up to 40 – i.e. a maximum lump sum of $1\frac{1}{2}$ times final pay.

However, the tax rules also let you build up a pension and lump sum at a faster rate towards the maximum. This is useful where you will be a member for less than 40 years and your employer is willing to agree more generous pension terms, or where the pension fund built up is enough to buy more than the basic benefits allowed.

These more generous limits are applied to the benefits from your present pension *plus* benefits that you've built up in other private pensions, where you have *retained benefits*. How the faster build-up rates work depends on when the employer's pension you belong to was set up and when you joined it.

Your pension

If you joined after 17 March 1987 you need at least 20 years' service to qualify for the maximum pension. The quickest rate at which the pension can build up is $\frac{1}{30}$ of final pay for each year of service.

If you joined before 17 March 1987 you can build up the maximum two-thirds pension over just ten years. The fastest rate at which it can build up is as follows:

Years of service before retirement age	Proportion of 'final salary'
1 to 5	$^1/_{60}$ for each year
6	$^8/_{60}$
7	$^{16}/_{60}$
8	$^{24}/_{60}$
9	$^{32}/_{60}$
10 or more	$^{40}/_{60}$

If your employer's pension was set up after 13 March 1989 or, if it was set up before then, but you joined it on or after 1 June 1989, there is also a cash limit on the maximum pension you can get. This is set by putting an *earnings cap* on the final pay which can count for pension purposes (£91,800 in the 2000–1 tax year). The maximum pension you can get after 20 or more years' service is £61,200 ($\frac{2}{3}$ of £91,800).

If you take part of your benefits as a cash lump sum, the maximum pension you can have under the Revenue limits is reduced accordingly.

'Final pay' can be defined in various ways, as long as it's not more favourable than either:

- your pay in any of the five years before normal retirement date, *or*
- your average pay for any three or more consecutive years in the 13 years before normal retirement date.

Note that a controlling director's 'final pay' must not be more than would be allowed by the second definition.

'Pay' can mean your salary plus bonuses, commission, director's fees and the taxable value of any benefits in kind. If the first definition is used, payments apart from salary must be averaged over at least three years. If the pension is based on the amount you earned in years before the final one, the figure for pay can be increased in line with any increase in the cost of living from the end of that earlier year until your retirement (known as *dynamisation*). You may want to check the precise rules of your particular employer's pension to find out what your pension might be; there are many variations within the limits allowed by the Revenue.

These rules apply to your pension in the first year of retirement, but the pension can be increased (within limits) each year to compensate for inflation.

Your tax-free lump sum

Your employer's pension rules may allow or require part of the maximum pension to be exchanged for a tax-free lump sum. The maximum lump sum allowed depends on the number of years you've worked for the employer before normal retirement age, and your 'final pay'.

If you joined your employer's pension before 17 March 1987 the limits in the table on the opposite page apply.

If you joined on or after 17 March 1987 your lump sum can be increased by the same proportion as any increase in your pension. However, if you joined between 17 March 1987 and 13 March 1989 or 31 May 1989 (see below) there is a maximum cash limit on the lump sum of £150,000.

If you joined after 31 May 1989, or your employer's pension was set up after 13 March 1989, your lump sum can't be more than $1\frac{1}{2}$ times your final pay up to the earnings cap – i.e. $1\frac{1}{2} \times £91,800 = £137,700$ in 2000–1 – or $2\frac{1}{4}$ times your initial annual pension, including dependants' benefits and benefits gained by AVCs.

Years of service before retirement age	Proportion of 'final pay'
1 to 8	$3/80$ for each year
9	$30/80$
10	$36/80$
11	$42/80$

12	$^{48}/_{80}$
13	$^{54}/_{80}$
14	$^{63}/_{80}$
15	$^{72}/_{80}$
16	$^{81}/_{80}$
17	$^{90}/_{80}$
18	$^{99}/_{80}$
19	$^{108}/_{80}$
20 or more	$^{120}/_{80}$

Note that you cannot use AVCs to boost the tax-free lump sum unless:

• you started payments before 8 April 1987
• your extra payments bought added years in a final-pay pension – added years increase the number of years on which both the pension income and the tax-free lump sum are based.

Widow's and widower's pension

If you die, your widow's or widower's pension is restricted to two-thirds of your final pension, but most employers' pensions offer less than this. Some employers' pensions enable you to take a lower pension when you retire, and leave a higher pension for your surviving partner, but you won't be allowed to leave a pension greater than the one you took when you retired.

Death in service benefits

Some employers give death in service benefits to all employees, others restrict it to pension members. Your dependants can get a tax-free lump sum of up to four times your final pay (subject to the earnings cap – see p. 174 – if it applies to you) to share and each can get a pension. The total pension payable to any individual cannot be more than two-thirds of the maximum pension you could have got had you continued working until retirement on your present salary. The total of all the pensions paid cannot be greater than the maximum pension. In practice, few employers' pensions are this generous.

When you can retire

Employers' pensions set a normal pension age. Nowadays, most have the same age for men and women and this is often 65. However, it is possible to start your pension at a much lower age. Whether or not early retirement will affect your pension will depend on when you joined. The government is reviewing the ages at which people can take private pensions.

If you joined an employer's pension set up after 13 March 1989, or joined any employers' pension after 31 May 1989, the current *tax* rules allow you to take your pension at 50 and there's no requirement for the pension to be reduced (but your employers' rules may not allow this).

If your present employer's pension was set up before 14 March 1989 you can receive your pension at 50 if you're a man or 45 if you're a woman within ten years of retirement. Unfortunately, your benefits must be reduced if you take early retirement. Your pension will be the greater of:

$\frac{1}{60}$ of your final pay × number of years' service
or

$\dfrac{\text{number of years with employer}}{\text{total possible years with employer}}$ × the maximum pension you could
(up to 40) have got

Your maximum lump sum will be worked out in a similar way, and will be the best of:

$\frac{3}{80}$ of your final pay × number of years' service
or

$\dfrac{\text{number of years with employer}}{\text{total possible years with employer}}$ × the maximum lump sum you
(up to 40) could have got

Many employers' pensions pay less than the maximum and may not allow early retirement. These limits apply to the sum of all the pensions you may be entitled to, not the individual employers' pensions themselves.

You can choose to be bound by the new rules and get a full pension if you want and if your employer's pension allows it, but then the earnings cap of £91,800 in 2000–1 will also apply if you do.

To be eligible for an early retirement pension under current tax rules, you must stop working for the employer who runs the scheme.

Early retirement due to ill health

The definitions of ill health relevant to early retirement vary widely. You won't be allowed to get a pension of more than you would have got if you had retired at the normal time with your present pay, but most employers' pensions will give you less than the maximum.

Leaving an employer's pension

When you leave a job, you can either leave your pension rights behind or transfer them. The tax rules do not allow you to take a refund of payments unless you have been a member of a contributory employer's pension for less than two years. In this case, your employer has the right to give you a refund of your own (but not your employer's) contributions. Equally, your employer has the right to give you a preserved pension and is not obliged to give a refund. It all depends on what's written in the rules. Normally, 20 per cent tax will be deducted from any refund by the trustees from contributions you withdraw, but there's no further tax to pay. If the employer's pension is *contracted out*, there will usually be a deduction from your refund to buy you back into the state scheme for the period of contracting out before 6 April 1997. For periods after that date, you can't be bought back into SERPS.

Personal pensions: how and when you can benefit

Your pension

There are no upper limits on the pension you can get by buying an annuity with the fund you have built up in a personal pension or retirement annuity contract. The tax rules allow you to put off buying an annuity until you are 75. But you can take your tax-free lump sum at an earlier age (see p. 178) and, within limits, draw an income direct from the pension fund. The income you can draw will be reviewed every three years to make sure that your pension fund isn't being run down too far. This option is generally cost-effective only with quite substantial funds.

Your tax-free lump sum

If you took out your pension before 17 March 1987 your lump sum can be up to three times your remaining pension, but subsequent rules have been less generous.

If you started a personal pension betweeen 1 July 1988 and 27 July 1989, you are allowed to take a quarter of your fund after you have provided for dependants' pensions. If you started on or after 27 July 1989, you can take a quarter of the fund remaining after any *protected rights* or *contracted out* pension has been provided, for personal pensions which have been partly used to contract-out of SERPS.

For personal pensions taken out between 17 March 1987 and 26 July 1989, there is also a cash limit on the lump sum of £150,000. But in practice the limit is easily avoided. It applies to each personal pension and retirement annuity contract and so you could have several, each with a £150,000 limit. In any case, you can switch at retirement or earlier to a current personal pension without any cash limit. You'll do this automatically if, at retirement, you exercise an *open market option*, which lets you switch to another company in order to get a higher annuity.

Widow's and widower's pension

A contracted-out personal pension must pay a widow's or widower's pension as part of your protected rights. Apart from this any provision for a spouse or other dependant has to be made at retirement, when you purchase annuities with your accumulated fund.

With a personal pension, there is no upper limit for any widow's, widower's or dependants' pensions, but their sum cannot be greater than your pension before your death. With a retirement annuity contract there is no overall limit on dependants' pensions.

When you can retire

With retirement annuity contracts, the earliest age at which you can withdraw your pension is usually 60; with personal pensions, it is 50. The government is currently reviewing these ages.

Early retirement due to ill health

The tax rules allow you to receive your pension as soon as you are too sick to continue working, regardless of your age, but it could be worth little if you have not paid contributions for very long, or your fund has not had time to accumulate.

Many personal pension providers will let you buy a *waiver of premium* benefit, which allows the fund to accumulate as though you were still paying premiums. They are also allowed to offer *permanent disability insurance*, which guarantees you a minimum income if you become incapable of working for health reasons, but few if any providers offer this benefit. Up to 25 per cent of your contributions can be used to provide these sickness benefits, but these premiums will reduce the amount invested for your main pension benefit.

If you die before you draw the pension

A personal pension used to contract out of the state earnings-related pension scheme (SERPS) must provide for a widow's or widower's pension to be paid if you die before retirement and your spouse is aged 45 or more, or is younger but has dependent children to care for.

If these conditions are not met, and in the case of personal pensions which are not used for contracting out, a lump sum will be paid out. This will usually be the value of your invested fund or may be a return of your contributions with interest or bonuses. There are no restrictions on who can receive the lump sum (or how it is used).

How pensions are taxed

Some pensions are tax-free. However, the following pensions are taxable:

- state retirement pension including any graduated pension and additional pension (SERPS)
- non-contributory retirement pension for people of 80 or over who are getting less than the normal state pension
- pension paid by an employer to a former employee or his or her widow or widower, and/or dependants
- income from a compulsory-purchase annuity bought with the proceeds of an employer's money-purchase pension, personal pension or retirement annuity contract
- pensions from abroad.

Tax on state retirement pensions

The state retirement pension is taxable but it is paid without tax deducted. If the basic state pension is your only income, you won't have to pay any tax because the pension comes to less than your personal allowance. But there may be some tax to pay if your state pension, added to any other taxable income you get (for example a pension from your former employer or investment income), comes to more than your total outgoings and allowances.

The amount of pension which will be included in your income is the total of the weekly amounts due over the tax year. Note that this applies even if your pension is paid monthly or quarterly.

Married woman's state retirement pension

A married woman's state retirement pension, if paid direct to her, counts as her income whether based on her own National Insurance contributions or on her husband's contributions. But any *adult dependency addition* paid to a retired husband whose wife has not yet reached state pension age is counted for income tax purposes as his income.

Pensions from former employers

Tax on a pension you get from a former employer is collected under the PAYE system – see Chapter 4.

Annuities from pensions

If an annuity has been provided by an employer's pension scheme you've belonged to, or was bought with the proceeds of a personal pension, the full amount of what you get is taxable. Annuities bought with personal pensions, as well as pensions or annuities paid by employers' pension schemes, are paid under PAYE so the correct amount of tax, if any, should be deducted. By contrast, annuities from older-style plans (retirement annuity contracts) are often paid with tax deducted at 20 per cent. Check whether you can claim a rebate or have extra tax to pay.

An annuity you've bought voluntarily is taxed differently from an annuity which comes from an employer's or a personal pension scheme – see p. 204.

Pensions from abroad

You are normally liable for tax on nine-tenths of any pension from abroad, whether or not it is brought into the UK. With certain pensions, only half the amount is taxable, and certain war widows' pensions are tax-free.

Pensions paid to the victims of Nazi persecution by the governments of Germany and Austria are tax-free.

How tax is collected on pensions

If you get a pension from your former employer, the tax due on all your income will, as far as possible, be collected under PAYE from your employer's pension. The state pension and any untaxed investment income the Inland Revenue expects you to receive over the tax year will be subtracted from you allowances on the PAYE Coding Notice.

You may get a lower PAYE code and appear to pay tax at a higher rate than before you retired. If the amount to be subtracted from your allowances is greater than your total allowances, your PAYE code will contain a 'K' which will instruct your employer to add an amount to your earnings for pension on which tax is to be paid. At the end of the year you should have paid the correct amount of tax. See Chapter 4 for more information about PAYE.

If you don't get a pension paid under PAYE and your state pension plus any other income comes to more than your total outgoings and allowances, you will be sent a statement of the tax you owe to be collected in two interim instalments and a final instalment. If the tax on the excess comes to less than a specified amount (which is announced just before tax returns are issued), the tax is not normally collected.

Useful Inland Revenue reading

You can ring the Inland Revenue Orderline* for helpsheets, leaflets and notes.

Leaflets and notes

IR78   Personal pensions – a guide for tax
IR120   You and the Pensions Schemes Office
IR121   Income tax and pensioners
IR129   Occupational pension schemes – an introduction
PS01   Occupational pensions schemes – a guide for members of tax-approved schemes

Helpsheets

When you receive a helpsheet, make sure it relates to the tax year for which you want information.

IR330   Pension payments

Concessions

Extra-statutory concessions let you off paying tax that is technically due. Booklet IR1 gives details of each concession.

A9   Doctors and dentists superannuation contributions
A49   Widow's pension paid to widows of Singapore nationality
A55   Arrears of foreign pensions
A62   Pensions to employees disabled at work

11 Homes and land

Buying your main home no longer has the advantage of tax relief on mortgage interest. However, the tax rules still favour home ownership by making gains on your only or main home free of capital gains tax. And if you use your home to make money – whether by taking in lodgers or letting it out – there are still ways to keep your tax bill down.

Tax when you buy a property

If you buy a property costing more than £60,000, you will face a tax bill in the form of stamp duty. And although there is nothing in the rules to say who should pay it, stamp duty is normally paid by the buyer.

Stamp duty is a tax on *documents* required for the change of ownership of property. Sales or exchanges of houses, flats, land and other property are subject to the tax, which is charged as a percentage of the purchase price.

- There is no stamp duty when the price of a property is £60,000 or less.
- When the price goes over £60,000, stamp duty of 1 per cent is charged on the *whole* price.
- When the price goes over £250,000, stamp duty of 3 per cent is charged on the *whole* price.
- When the price goes over £500,000, stamp duty of 4 per cent is charged on the *whole* price.

It is not possible to avoid stamp duty by splitting the purchase of a house or land into two or more parts, each part for £60,000 or less. To qualify for exemption from tax, you (or your solicitor) must submit a certificate which says: *'It is hereby certified that the transaction hereby effected does not form part of a larger transaction or of a series of transactions in respect of which the amount or value of the consideration exceeds £60,000 (or whichever of the higher thresholds is applicable).'*

Tenants buying their houses at a discounted price under the Right-to-Buy Scheme pay stamp duty on the discounted price.

Saving tax

If you're buying a home priced at a little more than £60,000 (or £250,000 or £500,000), it's going to pay you handsomely if you can get the price down to just below the nearest threshold. If bargaining won't do the trick, and if you are buying carpets, curtains and other fittings, try to get agreement to pay for these separately – duty is charged only on the price of the home. This could well save you around £610 (the difference between a home costing £60,000 and one costing £61,000); around £5,030 (the difference between homes costing £250,000 and £251,000); and around £5,040 (the difference between homes costing £500,000 and £501,000).

Exchanges of property

With an exchange of property there can be stamp duty to pay even if no money changes hands. For example, if two houses worth £250,000 each are exchanged, it counts as two property transfers and stamp duty of £5,000 is charged – 1 per cent for each property. If both houses were worth £50,000 there would be no stamp duty because each of the transfers is below £60,000.

If you are swapping one property plus cash for a more valuable property (for example you exchange your current property worth £80,000 for one worth £100,000 and hand over the extra £20,000 in cash) make sure that the contract makes clear the cash will be paid as *equality* money. If your contract does not make this clear, stamp duty will be charged on £100,000 for each of the two transfers. If you specify that the cash is equality money, duty will be charged only on £80,000 for the lower-value property.

The rules are different if you are buying a new property from a builder who accepts your old property (plus some cash). In this case, you would pay stamp duty only on what you pay for the new property (if it exceeds £60,000) – i.e. the value of your old house plus the cash. Handing over your old property as part payment for the sale would not be regarded as a separate sale, so there'll be no stamp duty on that part of the transaction. The rules for swapping can be complicated. To get advice contact a stamp office.*

Leases

What you pay for an *existing* lease on a flat or house is taxed in exactly the same way as transfers of houses and land. But *new* leases – such as a long lease on a new or refurbished flat – are treated differently, and often taxed twice over. The premium on a long lease (that is, the lump sum you are paying for the lease) is taxed in the same way as a transfer of a freehold house (except that you do not benefit from the £60,000 exemption if the yearly ground rent is over £600). But the yearly payments you have to make under the lease (excluding the service charges) are also taxed. The amount of tax depends on the length of the lease and is between 1 and 24 per cent of the average amount of the annual rent. Sometimes neither the lease nor the annual rent is expressed in actual cash amounts. In this case stamp duty will be based on the open-market value of the property, or the market rent in the case of a new lease.

Tax when you sell your home

Any gain you make when you sell your main home is normally exempt from capital gains tax. Exceptions are listed opposite. Gains on other homes or land you own will normally be liable to this tax.

A 'home' means a freehold or leasehold house, flat or maisonette. A caravan or a houseboat won't normally be liable to the tax. The land on which a caravan stands won't be exempt unless you can show that the caravan was your only or main home for the whole time you owned the land. For more on capital gains tax see Chapter 14.

More than one home

If you have two or more homes it's only your 'main' home which is exempt from capital gains tax. In certain cases, homes bought for relatives before 6 April 1988 can be exempt in addition to your main home. Talk to your tax office if you think this applies to you.

You can choose which home you want to be regarded as your main one – it doesn't have to be the one you spend the most time in, though in most cases you must live in it at some stage. It's best to nominate the one on which you think you'll make the largest *chargeable gain* (see Chapter 14 for what this means).

Make your choice by writing to the Revenue within two years of acquiring the second home. A married couple must both sign the letter, unless all the homes are owned by one of you. You can alter the choice at any time, simply by telling the Revenue, but this cannot affect the period more than two years before you make your new choice.

If you don't tell the Revenue within the two-year period which is your 'main' home, it will be decided for you. If the decision doesn't suit you, you can appeal within 30 days but you will have to prove that the home selected is *not* in fact your 'main' home.

If you live mainly in a rented home – or in one which goes with your job (for example as a caretaker or clergyman) – but also own a home where you spend some of your time or intend to live eventually, it is vital that you nominate the one you *own* as your main home. If this has applied for more than two years the Revenue may accept a late request.

When you might face a tax bill
You may not get full exemption from capital gains tax on your only or 'main' home in any of the following cases:

- the home wasn't your main one for purposes of capital gains tax for all the time you owned it
- you transferred the home to your ex-spouse
- you lived away from home
- you converted it into self-contained flats and then sold them
- you built a second home in your garden and then sold it
- you sold the house on its own, and the land around it afterwards
- the garden (including the house area) was bigger than half a hectare
- the home was one of a series of homes you bought, or spent money on, with the object of making a profit
- you let out all or part of the home
- you used part exclusively for work.

In many cases, only *part* of the gain you make when you sell your only or 'main' home will be taxable – see below.

If you have lived away from your only or 'main' home
The capital gain you are assumed to have made during periods when you were living away from your only or main home will normally not be exempt from tax. For example, if you have lived away from the home for 7 years out of the 15 you owned it, $\frac{7}{15}$ of the gain you made would not be exempt from tax. But the following absences may be ignored.

- **Before 6 April 1982** Generally, only gains made after 31 March 1982 are subject to tax, so any absence before this date becomes irrelevant. For the rules on when you might want to take account of the value of your house before this date, see Chapter 14.

- **The first year** If you can't move into your new home straight away because you're having a new home built on a plot you've bought, or because you're having the home altered or redecorated, or because you can't sell your old home, you will still get exemption from tax for up to a year (two years if there's a good reason). You must live in the home within the one- or two-year period.
- **If you live in job-related accommodation** A home which you (or your husband or wife) own and which you intend to live in one day can be exempt from tax while you are living in a home which goes with your job, or while you are self-employed and have to live in accommodation provided under the terms of your business.
- **Because of your work** You do not have to count absences if you are an employee carrying out all your duties outside the UK. And you can be away from home within the UK for up to four years if the location of your job means that you have to live away. Any excess over four years could also be exempt for one of the other reasons listed here. To get a work-related exemption you must have lived in the home as your only or main home at some time before the first absence and after the last absence unless your job prevents you from returning. A married couple can still get a work-related exemption even if the partner who owns the home is not the one whose job is causing the absence.
- **The last three years** Any absences in the last three years before you dispose of a home which has been your only or main home at some time are always exempt. It doesn't matter why you're away, or if you have another home which you've nominated as your main home during this period. If you're away for more than three years before you sell, the gain for the excess over three years won't be exempt unless one of the other exemptions applies.
- **Any other absences** for any reason totalling up to three years will not affect exemption, as long as you use the home as your main one for a time both before the first such period and after the last one.

Except in the first year or last three years, you can't get the exemptions above if any other home of yours is exempt. None of the exemptions above is lost if you let the home while you're away.

Transferring a home to your ex-spouse

You won't have to pay tax when you transfer a home to your ex-spouse provided the transfer takes place within three years of separation. But part of the gain you make on a transfer after three years is a chargeable gain unless your ex-spouse has lived in the home since you moved out *and* you haven't yet chosen another home as your main home for capital gains tax purposes.

If you stay in the old home and your ex-spouse moves out, you can later transfer it to your ex-spouse without paying capital gains tax so long as you haven't chosen another home as your main home for capital gains tax purposes.

EXAMPLE 1

In September 2000 Hamish was trying to sell his home in Edinburgh which he bought in December 1975. He didn't always live in his home, and when he was away he let it.

- The first absence: from August 1977 to May 1980 he lived in Wales.
- The second absence: from September 1983 to February 1984 he lived abroad where he was employed.
- The third absence: from March 1986 to February 1992 he was working in London.
- The fourth absence: in September 2000 he bought a new home in London where he now lives. He is trying to sell his empty Edinburgh home.

How do the absences affect his exemption from capital gains tax?

- The first absence is prior to 1 April 1982 and irrelevant to the calculation. Any tax bill would be based only on the rise in value after 31 March 1982, so Hamish would have to find out what the house was worth then. But if there is a tax bill, the time-apportionment method (see p. 190) will take account only of the period Hamish has owned his home since then. In fact, Hamish probably won't have to pay any tax.
- The second absence will be exempt because he was employed abroad.
- The third absence: the first four years will be exempt because Hamish had to live nearer his job in London; the last two years will be exempt because he is allowed to be absent for periods totalling three years for any reason, so long as he lived in the home after the absence (which he did, from March 1992 to August 2000).
- The fourth absence will be exempt provided he sells within three years of September 2000 (even though he has now nominated his London home as his main home).

If you divide the property or change its use

Exemption from capital gains tax for your only or main home is likely to be partly lost if:

- you divide up the property or use part of it for something other than living in
- you convert part of your home into self-contained flats, part of the gains you make when you sell the flats
- you build a second home in your garden
- you use part of the property exclusively for a trade or business or some other non-residential use

If you and your tax inspector cannot agree on what is taxable, the amount of the gain which is not exempt is whatever the commissioners (see p. 32) consider to be just and reasonable, but will normally be based on the proportion of the property affected.

For example, if you bought a home for £37,000 (after deducting buying costs) and spent £8,000 having part of it done up to sell, the cost of acquiring the whole home is taken to be £37,000 + £8,000 = £45,000. If you sell part for £40,000 when the whole home is worth £90,000, the cost of acquiring the part you sell is taken to be $\frac{4}{9}$ of £45,000 = £20,000. So the gain (before allowing for selling costs or indexation – see Chapter 14) on the part you sell would be £40,000 – £20,000 = £20,000.

Not all this gain is chargeable. The chargeable amount is the gain *less* what the commissioners reckon your gain would have been (on that part) if you hadn't spent money improving the property. So if, without the additional expense, the gain would have been £15,000, the chargeable part is £20,000 *less* £15,000 = £5,000.

If what you get for part of a property is no more than £20,000 and its market value is not more than 20 per cent of the value of the whole property, you can elect for the sale not to be treated as a disposal until you sell the rest of the property.

Your garden

The garden of your main home is not normally liable to capital gains tax even if you sell off part of it while you still own the home. But if it's over half a hectare, the gain on the excess will not be exempt unless the Revenue considers that a larger garden is appropriate for that house.

If you sell the home and retain some of the land, the gain you make on the land from the time when it stopped being part of your garden may be liable to tax.

The profit motive

If there is evidence that you bought your home wholly or partly with the object of selling it at a profit, you get no exemption from tax – even though it was your only or main home. Of course, it's not easy to prove what was in your mind when you bought it, but if you moved frequently from house to house – buying them in a derelict state and improving them, say – it would look as though your main aim was profit. The Revenue might even class you as a property-dealer, and tax your gain like income.

If you make major changes to your home (such as converting it into flats, buying the freehold if it's leasehold) in order to increase the price you get for it, the *extra* gain you make may not be exempt.

If you work at home

Use of part of your home *exclusively* for your business or employment (if you are an employee working from home) means that the part you use will not be exempt from capital gains tax for the period you use it. The exact *proportion* of the gain you make when you sell the house which will be liable to tax will have to be negotiated with your tax inspector.

However, if your business is on a modest scale, and if you've got an understanding tax inspector, you may be able to get the best of both worlds by using a room *almost* exclusively for business but not so exclusively as to risk a tax bill.

Even if there is a chargeable gain when you sell the home, you won't be liable for any tax at the time if you use the proceeds from selling the part of the home you used for your business to buy another property where you will carry on the same business or a similar one. The new building counts as replacement of a business asset, and the gain is *rolled over* (see Chapter 14). If you don't use all the proceeds in this way, only the part you use can qualify. If you eventually qualify for *retirement relief* (see Chapter 14), you may avoid a tax bill entirely.

Compulsory purchase

If part of your property is compulsorily purchased, special rules apply for working out any capital gains tax bill.

Working out the chargeable gain

In many cases, only *part* of the gain you make when you sell your home will be chargeable. For example, normally only gains made after 31 March 1982 are liable to tax. If you have let your home while you lived away for a few years (unless you lived away for one of the reasons listed on p. 185), or nominated another home as your main one for part of the period you owned this one, you will be liable for tax on the part of the gain you are assumed to have made in that period.

In general, the Revenue assumes the value of your home has increased by even, monthly steps from the price you paid for it to the price at which you sell. It then works out the gain using the *time apportionment* method. So it divides the gain you have made on the property by the total number of months you owned it to get an average monthly gain. It then multiplies the monthly gain by the number of months which are not exempt from tax. See Example 2 for how this works.

Broadly speaking, the gain is the amount you sold the home for *less* the amount you paid for it – but certain *allowable expenditure* may reduce your tax bill as may the *indexation* rule. Allowable expenditure normally includes:

- any costs of acquiring *and* disposing of the asset – for example estate agent's commission, conveyancing costs, stamp duty, valuation
- capital expenditure that's increased the value of the asset – for example improvements, but not ordinary maintenance.

For the general rules on capital gains tax, including indexation, see Chapter 14. There are special rules for limiting the chargeable gain arising from letting your only or 'main' home – see p. 195.

EXAMPLE 2

Sarah owned her home for exactly ten years. She made a total gain of £24,000 (after deducting buying and selling costs, and after indexation).

Because Sarah lived in another home which she had nominated as her main home for four of those years, the home she owned for ten years was not exempt for four years – i.e. 48 months. She owned the home for a total of 120 months. Her chargeable gain is £24,000 ÷ 120 = £200; £200 × 48 = £9,600.

Tax when you let property

If you let land or property, there are two main points to consider.

- How are rents you receive taxed, and what expenses and interest can you set against the income?
- Will you pay capital gains tax when you sell the property? If a property is not your only or main home, the gain you make will

be liable to tax. If you let part of your own home, the gain on the let part may be liable to tax, unless you were away from the home on a qualifying absence (see p. 185).

Income from property and land you let

Virtually all property income counts as Schedule A income, which is investment income, but tax is worked out in the same way as income from a business (i.e. Schedule D Case 1 – see Chapter 3). All your Schedule A income from property in the UK can be added together and treated as one pool. This includes rents you receive, ground rents, feu duties (in Scotland) and premiums on leases (though there are special rules for premiums on leases – check with your tax office). The rules also apply to immobile caravans and permanently moored houseboats. Rental income from abroad cannot be pooled with income from property in this country. It is taxed under Schedule D Case V.

The rules do *not* apply to:

- income from a hotel or guesthouse – it is taxed as a business under Schedule D Case 1, as is income you get from taking in lodgers if you provide services such as meals or laundry (see Chapter 6 for how businesses are taxed)
- mineral rents and mining royalties, which are taxed partially under Schedule D Case 1 and partially as capital gains.

You may not need to grapple with tax at all if you are letting a room in your home. Under the rent-a-room scheme (see p. 194), the first £4,250 of rent can be tax-free altogether.

When tax is due

You are taxed on the income you are entitled to receive in a tax year. This applies even if you haven't yet received the income, but not to debts you've tried unsuccessfully to recover.

When you work out your profits, you can deduct certain expenses and interest (see below) which you have actually paid during the tax year. If the expenses and interest come to more than your income, you will have made a loss – see p. 193.

The tax on property income you are entitled to is paid in two main instalments under the system of payments on account – see p. 27. If you pay tax through PAYE and your taxable rental income is under £1,000, your PAYE code may be adjusted to collect the tax you owe or you can pay in one lump sum on 31 January 2002 for income from property in the 2000–1 tax year.

If you are letting UK property while you live abroad, your tenants may have to deduct basic-rate tax from the rent if it is paid directly to you (see p. 134). If, however, it is paid to an agent, the collection of any tax will depend on your residence status in the UK. Check your position with your tax office.

Allowable expenses

You can deduct certain expenses from your letting income if they are 'wholly and exclusively' incurred for the letting. If you let only part of your home, or let it for only part of each year, you and the Revenue will have to agree on the proportion you can claim. You can't claim anything for your own time. For a list of business expenses which are normally allowable, see Chapter 6. The following expenses related to letting homes are allowable:

- interest you pay on a loan to buy or improve the property
- water rates, ground rent, feu duty (in Scotland)
- normal repairs and decoration, but not repairs necessary when you bought the property, nor improvements, additions or alterations to the property
- management expenses as a landlord (e.g. stationery, telephone bills, accountant's fees, cost of rent collection)
- cost of insurance and any necessary valuation for insurance
- legal fees for renewing a tenancy agreement (for leases of up to 50 years)
- estate agent's fees, accommodation agency fees, cost of advertising for tenants
- rent you pay for a property which you, in turn, sub-let
- cost of lighting common parts of property
- cost of services you provide, including wages of people who provide such services, e.g. cleaners, gardeners (it could be worth paying your husband or wife or other relative to provide the services if he or she is not fully using his or her tax-free allowances – see Example 3)
- cost of maintenance and repairs made necessary by improvements you've made, as long as you haven't changed the use of the property
- cost of maintaining roads, drains, ditches, etc. on an estate you own, if for the benefit of tenants
- the cost of statutory redundancy payments for staff and the cost of training or counselling staff.

In addition, you can deduct expenses incurred before you actually start letting, so long as they would have been allowable if incurred once the letting had begun.

You can also deduct interest you pay on a loan used to buy or improve property – see below. If you buy any machinery or equipment (e.g. a lawnmower or ladder) for upkeep or repair of property, you can claim *capital allowances* as if you were self-employed (see Chapter 6).

If you incur expenses while the home isn't actually occupied by a tenant, they should still qualify for tax relief as long as they were 'wholly and exclusively' incurred for the letting.

Note that if you let furnished accommodation to a tenant who pays you separately for any services you provide (for example meals, cleaning, laundry), what you get for these services counts as earnings from a business and is taxed under Schedule D Case 1.

EXAMPLE 3

Brian lets out three furnished flats and gets £12,000 a year in rent. His student son provides the tenants with an evening meal, cleans the flats twice a week and collects the rents. Brian pays his son £5,000 a year for this (but has to deduct some tax and National Insurance from what he pays). As his son has no other taxable income, £4,385 (the personal allowance) of this will be tax-free. Brian deducts the £5,000 wages from his letting income of £12,000, and will be taxed on £7,000, less the National Insurance he pays, and less any other allowable expenses.

Wear and tear

Capital allowances cannot be claimed for equipment let in a residential property. Instead, you can claim an allowance for wear and tear on fixtures, furniture and furnishings – such as chairs, cookers, lampshades, beds and sheets. You can claim *either* the actual cost of fixtures, furniture, etc. you replace during the year (called *renewals basis*), *or* a proportion (normally 10 per cent) of the rent *less*, if you pay them, service charges and water rates. Once you've chosen a basis, you must stick to it.

Losses

A loss on property in the UK can be set off against any income from other properties in the UK. If you haven't enough other property income to set it all against, you can carry what's left forward and set it against income from property in future years so long as you're still letting the property you made the loss on. Losses on property abroad cannot be set off against UK rental income.

Rent-a-room

If you let furnished accommodation in the home you live in you can receive a gross rental income of £4,250 (£81.73 a week) under the rent-a-room scheme. If your rental income exceeds £4,250, you can choose *either* to pay tax on the excess, without any relief for allowable expenses; *or* to pay tax on the whole lot but claim expenses in the normal way. If you choose to claim the £4,250, you must tell your tax inspector within one year of the end of the relevant tax year. Your choice will remain in force until you decide to change to the other method of assessing rent – i.e. by claiming expenses.

There is no need to make this choice if your rental income is £4,250 or less. If two or more people receive rental income, the tax-free limit is £2,125 for each person. So, for example, three joint owners could get £2,125 each, £6,375 between them.

Furnished holiday lettings

Income from letting property (including caravans) which is let as furnished holiday accommodation for part of the year is treated as earnings from a business.

The advantage is, for example, that you can claim roll-over relief and retirement relief from capital gains tax (see Chapter 14).

To qualify, both the following must apply.

- The property must be available for letting to the general public at a commercial rent for at least 140 days (which need not be consecutive) during each 12-month qualifying period (not necessarily a tax year).
- It must let out as holiday accommodation for at least 70 of those days, and during at least seven months of the 12-month period it isn't normally occupied by the same tenant for more than 31 days at a stretch.

If you let more than one unit of accommodation, you are allowed to average the days they're actually let to pass the 70-day rule.

If a furnished letting counts as holiday accommodation, all the income you get from it in the tax year counts as earned income. But if only part of the let accommodation counts as furnished holiday lettings, only a proportion of the income counts as earned income.

EXAMPLE 4

Winston started letting out a furnished bungalow in Skegness for holidays on 1 June 2000. It will count as a furnished holiday letting for the 2000–1 tax year, as long as it's available to the public at a commercial rent for 140 days during the 12 months from 1 June 2000 to 31 May 2001, and as long as he lets it out for 70 of those days, mainly for periods of 31 days or less.

Capital gains on let property

Your only home, or the home nominated as your main one for the whole time you've owned it, will be exempt from capital gains tax even if you let it out while you were away, as long as all your absences count as qualifying absences (see p. 185). But the gain attributable to any other period you let it while you were away (worked out by the time-apportionment method shown on p. 190) won't be exempt.

If you let part of your only or main home, you don't lose any exemption for having lodgers who share your living rooms and eat with you. In other cases it depends on whether you have occupied the part of the home you've let at any time. If you haven't, the gain on the part you let will not be exempt from tax.

The chargeable gain will normally be based on the number of rooms you let or the floor area of the part you let, but could alternatively be based on the rateable value of the part you let, or on its market value. It's up to you and the Revenue to agree which method to use; if you don't agree, you can appeal to the general or special commissioners (see p. 32).

If you have lived in the part of the home you've let out, the gain on the let part is apportioned according to the period you've let it.

The gain on the let part (after allowing for indexation – see Chapter 14) is exempt if:

- the let part is lived in by someone but is not a completely separate home (e.g. not a self-contained flat with its own access from the street)
- you have not had more than minor alterations made to the home
- the gain on the let part is no more than the exempt gain attributable to your occupation of the home
- the gain on the let part is no more than £40,000.

If the limits are exceeded, the excess is liable to tax. For example, the gain on the let part is £45,000 while your exempt gain is £35,000; £45,000 is £10,000 more than £35,000, and also £5,000 more than £40,000, so both limits are exceeded. You are taxed on the larger excess – £10,000 (see Example 5).

EXAMPLE 5

Elizabeth bought a house in May 1992 and sold it eight years later, in May 2000. Her gain, after deducting selling costs and her indexation allowance, was £200,000. Throughout this time the house was her main home for tax purposes. For the first two years she lived in the whole house, but then she let out two-thirds of the house as living accommodation.

The first two years of ownership (when she lived in the whole house) are exempt. The last three years of ownership are also exempt (see p. 185). Of the remaining three years, only one-third of the home is exempt (because she let out two-thirds). So the exempt part of the gain is 2 (first two years) + 3 (last three years) + 1 (one-third of three years) ÷ 8 = $\frac{6}{8}$. £200,000 × $\frac{6}{8}$ = £150,000. The non-exempt part of the gain is therefore £50,000. This is £10,000 more than £40,000, so £10,000 will be chargeable.

The first £7,200 of gains made in the 2000–1 tax year are exempt from tax. Elizabeth will have to pay tax on £10,000 – £7,200 = £2,800. She is a higher-rate taxpayer, so the tax bill will be £2,800 × 40 per cent = £1,120. She will also have to pay tax on any other chargeable gains in that tax year, as her annual exemption has been used up on her house sale.

If the letting counts as a business

If the let property counts as furnished holiday accommodation (see p. 194), or if income from the letting counts as earnings from a business because of services you provide, you may not have to pay tax when you sell the home even if a taxable gain arises. If you use the proceeds from selling the home (or from the part you let) to buy another property where you continue to provide similar accommodation and services, the new property can count as replacement of a business asset and the gain can be *rolled over* (see Chapter 14). If you don't use all the proceeds in this way, only the part you use can be rolled over.

Doing this only defers your tax bill, as you would normally have to pay tax on rolled-over gains when you finally sell up and cease letting. However, if you don't do this until you reach 50 (or retire earlier through ill health) you may qualify for *retirement relief*, which exempts part of the gains – see Chapter 14.

Useful Inland Revenue reading

You can ring the Inland Revenue Orderline* for helpsheets, leaflets and notes.

Leaflets and notes
IR87	Letting and your home
IR150	Taxation of rents – a guide to property income
IR223	Rent-a-room for traders
IR140	Non-resident landlords, their agents and tenants
SA105	Notes on land and property
SO199	Stamp duty on buying freehold house in England, Wales and Northern Ireland
SO199	Stamp duty on buying land or buildings in Scotland
SO799	Stamp duty and leases (England and Wales)
SO799	Stamp duty and leases in Scotland
SO89	Stamp duty on agreements securing short tenancies

Helpsheets
When you receive a helpsheet, make sure it relates to the tax year for which you want information.

IR250	Capital allowances and balancing charges in a rental business
IR251	Agricultural and land managed as one estate
IR283	Private residence relief (capital gains)
IR292	Land and leases – the valuation of land and capital gains tax

12

Investments

Two taxes affect savings and investments: income tax and capital gains tax. For how capital gains tax may affect your investment, see Chapter 14. This chapter shows which savings and investments:

- are tax-free
- are subject to income tax and capital gains tax
- have special tax privileges
- have particular features that affect tax.

Income tax is applied to interest and to dividend income in different ways. The three tax bands (see p. 6) have three rates of income tax for most income: 10 per cent, 22 per cent and 40 per cent. But income from savings and investments (and capital gains) adds two further rates of tax: 20 per cent and 32.5 per cent. Two of the tax bands have more than one rate of tax. For this reason, there is a strict order to determine what falls into which band. If you are not sure which band your interest or dividend income falls into, see p. 50.

Tax on interest

Sources of taxable interest income include:

- bank and building society deposit accounts and National Savings
- gilts
- corporate bonds, including loan stock and debentures
- local authority investments
- permanent income-bearing shares (PIBS)
- unit trusts and open-ended investment companies (OEICs) that invest predominantly in the above investments – check the tax

voucher that comes with any income payment or ask the fund's manager whether it's interest or dividend income, if you are not sure

- annuities you buy voluntarily (as opposed to those you have to buy with the proceeds of a pension fund).

Interest is usually paid with the savings rate of tax of 20 per cent deducted at source, but it can also be paid gross, i.e. without deduction of tax – see *Specific investments: tax points* on p. 204.

Non-taxpayers
Non-taxpayers and those whose interest is partially covered by their tax allowances can claim back the 20 per cent tax deducted at source. For example, a single, 64-year-old man with a part-time job paying £4,000 receives £800 net interest from a building society account. £200 tax has been deducted at source, making his gross interest £1,000. He has no other income.

His personal allowance of £4,385 covers all of his £4,000 pay and £385 of his interest. He can claim back the 20 per cent tax deducted on £385. This comes to £77. The remaining £615 of interest falls into the starting-rate band of 10 per cent tax. He can claim back another £61.50 (half of the 20 per cent tax of £123 deducted at source from £615). The total tax he can reclaim is £138.50.

10 per cent starting-rate taxpayers
Those who pay tax at the starting rate of 10 per cent can claim back half the tax deducted on interest to the extent that the starting-rate band of £1,520 covers the interest. For example, let's say the single, 64-year-old man (see above) earns £5,200 and receives gross interest of £1,200.

His personal allowance of £4,385 covers the first £4,385 of his pay. The other £815 of pay will be taxed at 10 per cent. That leaves £705 of the 10 per cent band (£1,520 – £815) to cover his interest. He can claim back tax of £70.50 (half of the 20 per cent tax of £141 deducted at source from £705). But the remaining £495 of his interest falls into the basic-rate band.

Basic-rate taxpayers
Interest that falls into the £26,880 basic-rate band (i.e. taxable income from £1,521 to £28,400) is taxed at 20 per cent – even though the main basic-rate of tax is 22 per cent. In other words, the 20 per cent tax deducted at source meets the basic-rate liability. If tax is not deducted at source, you owe 20 per cent tax on the interest.

Higher-rate taxpayers

Interest that takes you over £28,400 is taxed at 40 per cent. If 20 per cent has been deducted at source you'll owe a further 20 per cent. So if you get a statement showing that £200 tax has been deducted, you'll owe a further £200.

Reclaiming tax

If you need to reclaim tax you may well be sent a special tax claim form R40(SP) instead of the normal kind of tax return. You should fill it in and send it back to your tax office. You don't need to wait until the end of the tax year to do this and you can claim in instalments throughout the year. The Revenue will work out how much tax you are owed (if any) and send you a rebate. However, it will pay claims part way through the tax year only if they are for more than £50. If you reclaim less than £50, you won't be paid until the end of the tax year.

If you have to claim tax back regularly but aren't sent form R40(SP), ask your tax office for it. If you claim only occasionally, write to your tax office, giving details of why you are claiming and how much you are claiming (if you know).

Tax on dividends and equivalent income

Sources of dividend income include:

- shares, including investment trust shares and preference shares
- unit trusts and OEICs that invest predominantly in the above investments – check the tax voucher that comes with any income payment or ask the fund's manager whether it's interest or dividend income, if you are not sure.

Tax is paid with a 10 per cent tax credit. No one can claim back this tax credit, not even non-taxpayers. Basic-rate taxpayers have no further tax to pay. The 10 per cent tax credit meets the basic-rate income tax liability.

There is further tax to pay only if dividend income takes you over £28,800. In this case, you pay tax of 32.5 per cent of the gross dividend (i.e. the net dividend plus the tax credit), less the 10 per cent tax covered by the tax credit. Here's how it works.

- A dividend of £80 comes with a tax credit of £8.89 – making the gross dividend £88.90 (£8.89 is 10 per cent of £88.90).
- Tax at 32.5 per cent of £88.90 comes to £28.89.

- £28.89 less the £8.89 tax credit comes to £20.
- £20 is the higher-rate tax due.

In fact £20 is exactly one-quarter (25 per cent) of the net dividend of £80. So higher-rate taxpayers know that they'll owe in higher-rate tax £1 out of every £4 they receive in net dividend.

Your tax return

On your tax return, put the gross (before-tax) amount of the interest received, the tax deducted and (unless no tax was deducted) the interest after tax. With dividend income put the amount you received and the amount of the tax credit.

In each case, put the totals for each type of income – do not list each account, shareholding and so on. To find each total, add up the exact amounts for each account or investment, including both pounds and pence. Then round down income and round up tax deducted and tax credits to the nearest pound before putting the totals on your tax return. You do not need to send tax vouchers with your tax return, but keep them in a safe place. Investment income – whether interest or dividend income – is taxable even if it is re-invested rather than paid out. For example, you can arrange for many unit trusts automatically to re-invest income. Investment income still has to be taken into account when you work out your tax liabilities or fill in your tax return, just as interest left to compound in a building society is taxable in the tax year it is credited to an account.

Tax vouchers

You get a tax voucher from the company (or unit trust or OEIC) showing the amount of the dividend (or distribution) and the amount of the tax credit.

With other types of income taxed before you get it, including distributions from unit trusts which specialise in gilts, you normally get a tax voucher or other document from the payer. This tells you the gross (before-tax) amount of income, the tax deducted and the actual sum you get.

Keep any tax vouchers as proof that tax has been credited or deducted.

Paying the tax

The tax bill for your 2000–1 investment income will be based on the income you receive between 6 April 2000 and 5 April 2001. If you owe less than £1,000 and pay tax under Pay-As-You-Earn (PAYE), the tax will usually be collected along with other tax on your earnings or pensions, though you can opt instead to pay it as a lump sum on 31 January 2002.

In other cases, you will have to make direct payments. This means that you will normally make two equal payments on account on 31 January during the tax year and 31 July following the end of the tax year (i.e. 31 January 2001 and 31 July 2002 for 2000–1) based on your previous year's investment income. There will be a balancing charge or refund due on 31 January following the end of the tax year (i.e. 31 January 2002 for 2000–1) if your income for 2000–1 turns out to be more or less than the previous year.

Couples

Couples – married or not married (and including gay couples) are treated as individual taxpayers for both their investment income and investment (i.e. capital) gains.

If you own an investment jointly, each of you is taxed on half the income or gains – unless you have made a declaration that you actually own the investment in unequal proportions. You must notify your tax inspector using form 17 within 60 days of the declaration.

It may be worth changing the proportions in which you own investments if:

- one of you pays tax at a lower rate than the other
- one of you tends to use up the annual capital gains tax exemption while the other does not.

You could, for example, make an outright gift of shares to a partner who has no taxable income. There is no capital gains tax on gifts between husband and wife, but there may be tax in the case of unmarried couples. However, note that it must be a real gift. The donor can't keep control of the money.

A note of warning: you can't simply choose the proportions that are most convenient for you. You can make a declaration only according to your actual shares of the property and income. Of course, if you decide to split the investments into separate accounts in sole names and the other partner has no control or interest in either the investment or the income, then the income will belong to the partner whose account it is in, and will be taxed accordingly.

Interest from a bank or building society account is usually paid with 20 per cent tax already deducted. If you have a joint account and one of you is a non-taxpayer, you can usually arrange for part of the interest to be credited or paid out without tax deducted. However, some banks and building societies will deduct tax from the whole of the interest. In this case, the non-taxpayer will have to claim back tax on his or her share of the interest.

Children

Children are potentially taxpayers but have the personal allowance of £4,385 and the capital gains tax exemption of £7,200 in 2000–1 like everyone else. However, in practice most children are non-taxpayers because their income is much less than the personal allowance. This means, for example, that they can reclaim tax deducted on savings interest or have it paid without tax deducted (see p. 205). Note that people under 18 years of age cannot open ISAs or take advantage of some of the other schemes with special tax perks.

However, if a *parent* gives a child something which produces investment income – for example if the parent opens up a National Savings Investment Account for the child – the income is taxed as the parent's income, unless:

- the parent sets up an *accumulation trust* for the child and the interest is 'accumulated' (i.e. not spent) until the child reaches 18, or marries, or
- the investment is held in a bare trust for the child (i.e. the parent or someone else acts as nominee for the child), it was placed there before 9 March 1999, and the income is left to accumulate until the child reaches 18 or marries, or
- the income from investments given by the parent, including income from investments placed in a bare trust on or after 9 March 1999, is no more than £100 in a tax year (if it exceeds £100, all such income is taxed as the parent's, including the first £100), or
- the child is over 18 or married.

Income of up to £100 from investments from *each* parent can be taxed as the child's.

This rule applies only to income tax. Assets – for example a unit trust – given by a parent to a child count as the child's for capital gains tax purposes. The gift of an asset from parent to child would count as a disposal (see p. 230) by the parents. But when the child disposes of the asset (e.g. sells unit trusts) the disposal counts as the child's.

Tax-free investment income

Income or proceeds from the following investments are tax-free:

- Savings Certificates from National Savings (and, in most cases, Ulster Savings Certificates if you live in Northern Ireland) and National Savings Yearly Plans (withdrawn to new investors on 1 February 1995)
- National Savings Children's Bonus Bonds
- proceeds from some friendly society plans
- Premium Bond prizes and lottery winnings (which don't really count as income)
- first £70 interest each year from a National Savings Ordinary account (£140 in a joint account)
- interest on a tax rebate
- interest to do with delayed settlement of damages for personal injury or death
- return on investments held in an ISA
- return on qualifying venture-capital trusts
- the proceeds of a tax-exempt special savings account (TESSA) (from 6 April 1999, no longer available to new savers)
- investments held in a personal equity plan (PEP) (closed to new investment from 6 April 1999)
- Save-As-You-Earn (SAYE) schemes (from 29 November 1994, no longer available to new savers, except where linked to an employer's share-save scheme)
- proceeds from qualifying life insurance – see Chapter 13.

Specific investments: tax points

Alternative investments
If you invest in antiques, silver, gold coins or other tangible objects of this type, you will be hoping to make a capital gain. For how this is taxed, see Chapter 14.

Annuities
If you choose to buy an annuity voluntarily (as opposed to being obliged to buy an annuity with the fund you have built up in an employer's or personal pension) part of the income from it is treated for tax purposes as your initial outlay being returned to you, and is tax-free. The rest of the annuity income is taxable interest – see p. 198.

The insurance company normally deducts 20 per cent tax from the taxable part of your income before paying you. Non-taxpayers can apply to have annuity income paid without deduction of tax by completing form R89.

For each type of annuity the tax-free amount – the *capital* element set by the Revenue – is based on your age when you buy the annuity, the amount you pay for it, how often the income is paid and whether payments are guaranteed for a period after you die. A man gets a larger tax-free amount than a woman (his life expectancy is shorter).

With increasing annuities, the tax-free amount increases at the same rate as the income from the annuity increases. For example, for a 75-year-old woman buying an annuity that increases by 5 per cent a year, the tax-free amount in the first year would be £50.30 for each £1,000 spent on the annuity but increasing by 5 per cent each year.

By and large, if you buy an annuity out of your savings or investments which give a taxable income, you don't have to worry about the possible effect on age-related allowances (see p. 44). The chances are, in a case like this, that the *taxable* part of your annuity income will be less – or in any event not much higher – than the taxable income you were getting from your savings (a large part of the income from an annuity, remember, is tax-free).

But if you buy the annuity with savings or investments that were *not* earning you a taxable income, and if you are at present getting the benefit of age-related allowances, you might find that your allowance is reduced if you exceed the income limit (see p. 47). This would be the case, for example, if the annuity replaced an income being drawn from a PEP.

Bank and building society interest

Interest (see p. 198) from building societies, banks and other deposit-takers has tax of 20 per cent deducted before it is paid to you. Non-taxpayers can have their interest paid gross. Give each bank or building society with which you have an account a completed registration form (form R85 – available from post offices, banks, building societies and tax offices). Where a non-taxpayer and a taxpayer have a joint account, the bank or building society may agree to pay part of the interest gross and part net. There is no tax to pay on TESSA, ISA, or SAYE accounts.

Business expansion scheme

The business expansion scheme (BES), set up to encourage investment in new or small companies, ended on 31 December 1993. BES shares are free of capital gains tax on the first occasion they are sold (or given away) if they were issued after 18 March 1986 and if you hold them for at least five years. But losses won't count for tax purposes.

Corporate bonds

Interest (see p. 198) on company fixed-income loan stocks or debentures is paid with 20 per cent deducted. The rules of the *accrued income scheme* may apply to the taxation of your corporate bonds, depending on the total nominal value of certain types of securities you hold. See *Interest-bearing securities* on p. 211.

For company loans bought after 13 March 1984, the proceeds are free of capital gains tax, provided the stock is a 'qualifying corporate bond'. Broadly speaking, a qualifying bond is a debt security issued on commercial terms whose value does not reflect any foreign exchange element. So securities denominated in foreign currency, or linked to foreign-currency assets, do not qualify. Nor, for disposals on or after 29 November 1994, do securities linked to a UK share index. Sometimes a non-qualifying bond becomes a qualifying bond, and vice versa. Any gain attributable to the period when the bond was non-qualifying is liable to capital gains tax.

For bonds issued before 17 March 1998, if the loan is not repaid when it is due and not likely to be repaid in future, you can set the loss off against gains for capital gains tax purposes. This applies if the loan was a loan stock or a loan or guarantee made to a UK-resident trader for use in his or her business. Otherwise you can't set the loss off.

Commodities

Profits from buying and selling *physical* commodities are likely to be treated as trading profits, and so taxed as earned income. A loss might count as a trading loss and you could set it off against the total of your income from all sources, but not against capital gains.

Just one isolated venture into the commodity *futures* market is likely to be treated as giving rise to a capital gain (or loss). But if you make a profit from a series of transactions, or invest as a member of a syndicate run by brokers or by a professional manager, this is likely to be treated as investment income, which may mean that you don't benefit from your capital gains tax-free slice.

Enterprise investment scheme

The enterprise investment scheme (EIS) allows you to claim tax relief of 20 per cent on investments of up to £150,000 in 2000–1 in shares in unquoted companies issued after 1 January 1994. There is no capital gains tax when the shares are first disposed of, so long as the tax relief has not been withdrawn because the investment has ceased to qualify under the scheme. Losses on disposal can be offset against an income tax or capital gains tax bill.

If you make a chargeable capital gain when you dispose of *any* asset, you can defer the tax if you re-invest the money in EIS shares. There is *no* limit on the amount of chargeable gains you can defer in this way. But you cannot get income tax relief, or capital gains tax relief on the eventual disposal of the shares, on more than the £150,000 a year limit.

Where EIS shares have been issued since 6 April 1998 and are sold or otherwise disposed of, you may decide to re-invest the proceeds in new shares in another EIS scheme. In this case, you can (as described above) defer any capital gains tax bill. In addition, the two investments are treated as continuous for the purpose of working out taper relief (see Chapter 14). If the proceeds of the second EIS holding are re-invested in a further EIS, this is also linked to the earlier EIS investments for taper relief, and so on.

To get these tax advantages, shares must be held for at least three years if they were issued after 5 April 2000; five years if issued by that date. The capital gains tax exemption is restricted if you receive value from the company in some form – for example if it makes you a loan, provides a benefit or transfers an asset to you at less than its market value.

The scheme can apply to newly issued shares in unquoted companies trading in the UK and companies quoted on the alternative investment market (AIM). It is designed to encourage investors to back ventures which otherwise might seem too risky relative to the potential reward. But over the years, the rules have been progressively tightened to stop the exploitation of loopholes.

The list of excluded shares was expanded in 1998 to include shares with some form of arrangement or guarantee to ensure investors get their money back. This exclusion was backdated to 2 July 1997. And from 17 March 1998 companies involved in property-backed activities, such as farming, market gardening, property development and running hotels or care homes are excluded.

To some extent, the precise rules on what qualifies need not overly concern investors. They will be able to find out whether an investment qualifies by contacting the sponsor of the share issue and only qualifying issues should be marketed as enterprise investment schemes.

Half the amount of qualifying investments made in the first half of the tax year – i.e. by 5 October – can be carried back to the previous tax year, subject to a maximum of £25,000 from 1998–9 (but £15,000 in earlier tax years). You must not exceed the overall maximum for the previous tax year.

Friendly society policies
Some societies have tax advantages such as paying no income tax on a fund's income or capital gains tax on any gains made in the fund. You can invest £25 in monthly premiums, £270 in yearly premiums, in a friendly society policy of ten years or more without paying tax on what you get back at the end.

In line with the treatment of other tax-free investments, such as ISAS and PEPS, tax already paid on income from shares, unit trusts and so on held in a friendly society's tax-free fund can be reclaimed until 5 April 2004. After that date, it is likely that such income will be taxed.

Gilts (British government stocks)
Gilts bought by post (using forms from post offices) have interest (see p. 198) paid without tax deducted. Likewise, gilts bought through a broker (or other adviser) on or after 6 April 1998 have interest paid without tax deducted, unless you ask for tax to be deducted at source. Some taxpayers may prefer to pay tax at the time the interest is paid. You can ask to have interest from these gilts paid with 20 per cent tax deducted.

Before 6 April 1998, most gilts bought through brokers had tax at the 20 per cent savings rate deducted from the interest. This tax will continue to be deducted at source unless you apply to have the interest paid gross. You will still have to pay tax eventually if you are a taxpayer.

Interest from indexed-linked gilts and from 'strippable' gilts (i.e. where rights to the income payments and to the capital repayment can be sold separately) are also treated in this way.

The rules of the *accrued income scheme* may apply to the taxation of your gilts, depending on the total nominal value of certain types of securities you hold. See *Interest-bearing securities* on p. 211.

Buying gilts can be a useful way of investing for a capital gain. If you buy at a price which is lower than the price at which the gilt will eventually be redeemed or sold you'll make a capital gain which is free of capital gains tax. If you buy *low-coupon* gilts – i.e. gilts which pay relatively low amounts of yearly interest – you can invest for a return which is made up largely of a capital gain. But don't let tax considerations force you into investments which would otherwise be unsuitable.

Income and growth bonds
These bonds are set up in different ways, often consisting of one or more life insurance policies and one or more annuities. The tax treatment of any bond will depend on how it's set up. Bonds can include various life insurance products, such as deferred annuities

with a cash option, immediate temporary annuities, single-premium endowment policies or regular-premium endowment policies.

Very briefly, the tax treatment is as follows.

- **Deferred annuity with cash option** – proceeds are liable to tax at your highest rate on the profit you make but you may be able to get top-slicing relief – see Chapter 13.
- **Immediate temporary annuity** – the income you get is treated as income from a voluntarily purchased annuity. The company normally deducts 20 per cent tax before paying it out to you – see p. 204.
- **Endowment policies** – at the end of the term, proceeds are taxed as a gain on a life insurance policy if the policy is a non-qualifying one. Income from any bonuses cashed is treated as cashing-in part of a life insurance policy – see Chapter 13.

Individual saving accounts

On 6 April 1999, tax-free individual savings accounts (ISAS) replaced PEPS (see p. 212) and TESSAS (see p. 213). You must be aged 18 or over and resident in the UK to qualify for an ISA. An ISA is not itself an investment. It is a tax-free wrapper through which you can put money into a whole range of savings and investments. Like PEPS, ISAS must be taken out and run through an approved manager.

Income and gains on any of the savings and investments held in an ISA are tax-free and do not have to be entered on your tax return. This tax exemption applies to investments held directly in an ISA and to investments backing an insurance policy held in an ISA. Until 5 April 2004, the account manager can claim back the 10 per cent tax credit on share dividends and share-based investments and add this back to your account. However, other income – for example from cash deposits and corporate bonds – and all capital gains will continue to be tax-free.

An ISA can have up to three components:

- stocks and shares, corporate bonds, unit trusts, OEICs and so on
- investment-type life insurance
- cash, for example bank and building society deposits and National Savings.

There are two basic types of ISA – the maxi-ISA and the mini-ISA. In any one tax year, you can take out either one maxi-ISA with one account manager or up to three mini-ISAS with a different manager for each, if you choose.

Maxi-ISAs can include all three components. In 2000–1 you can invest up to £7,000. You can put all the money in the stocks and shares component or you can put up to £1,000 of the money in the life insurance component and up to £3,000 of the money in the cash component. Your choice may be restricted by what plan managers choose to offer within these rules. Some may offer only the stocks and shares component. If you want to invest all of your tax-free ISA allowance in stocks and shares, take out a maxi-ISA. From 2001–2, the overall investment limit for a maxi-ISA falls to £5,000, with the life insurance limit remaining at £1,000 but the cash limit falling to £1,000. This decrease in investment limits was due to take place from 2000–1; however the chancellor has since announced that the higher limits would apply for another year.

Mini-ISAs include just one component. In 2000–1, the investment limit is £3,000 for a stocks and shares mini-ISA, £1,000 for a life insurance mini-ISA, £3,000 for a cash mini-ISA. In subsequent tax years the limits remain at £3,000 for a stocks and shares mini-ISA and £1,000 for a life insurance mini-ISA. But the limit for a cash mini-ISA falls to £1,000. When added together, the limits for three mini-ISAs are the same as the limit for one maxi-ISA.

TESSA-only cash ISAs In addition to the limits for a maxi-ISA and a mini-ISA, you can transfer the capital (but not the interest) from a maturing TESSA into a special TESSA-only ISA. This must be invested in deposit-type investments from banks, building societies or National Savings.

In general, you must pay cash into an ISA. This means that if you have shares, say, which you would like to transfer to an ISA, you must sell them and then repurchase them within the ISA wrapper. Take care that gains on any shares you sell do not trigger a capital gains tax bill. However, you can transfer shares you have acquired under an approved profit-sharing scheme (see p. 97) or savings-related share option scheme (see p. 98) into an ISA without having to sell them first.

You can make withdrawals from any type of ISA at any time without any tax penalty. But ISA managers can set their own withdrawal terms.

Some ISAs are 'CAT-marked'. CAT stands for charges, access and terms. To earn the CAT-mark, the ISA must meet minimum standards or terms laid down by the government. For example, charges must come to no more than a given limit. In the case of a 'stocks and shares' ISA, the maximum annual charge is 1 per cent of the asset value. You must be allowed to invest low minimum amounts, for example as little as £10 in a cash ISA. You must be allowed to make withdrawals after no more than seven days' notice, and you must be given decent terms and conditions: for example, an insurance ISA should return at least the amount you have paid in premiums after three years.

Interest-bearing securities

You'll need to work out whether the *accrued income scheme* applies to you if you have bought or sold the sort of interest-bearing securities that are traded on the Stock Market. This includes things like gilts, local authority bonds, corporate bonds and PIBS (permanent interest-bearing shares issued by building societies and ex-building societies). It does not include shares which pay dividends (not interest) and which have a 10 per cent tax credit and where higher-rate taxpayers have to pay tax at a rate of 32.5 per cent – see p. 200. And it does not apply to certain discounted bonds (such as gilt strips).

The rules of the accrued income scheme do not apply if the *nominal* value of all the relevant securities you hold is £5,000 or less. You must have held securities of over £5,000 at some point during the tax year in which the next interest payment falls (after the purchase or sale) or during the previous tax year. The nominal value is the face value – often £100. With a conventional gilt, for example, this is what you get back when the gilt matures. So what you paid for your securities or what you sold them for is irrelevant.

An interest-bearing security usually pays-out interest at regular intervals. In between payments, the interest builds up day by day and the price will reflect the amount which has built up ('accrued') so far. This is the accrued interest and details are on the contract note for your purchase or sale. At most times, the person who buys the security is entitled to the next interest payment. But the buyer is not liable to tax on interest that accrued before the purchase *if* the accrued income scheme applies. So you can claim tax relief on the accrued interest when you *buy* a security. Conversely, when you *sell* a security you will be liable for tax on interest that accrued before you sold.

An exception to this rule applies to purchases and sales that take place during the *ex-dividend period*. In this case, the seller receives the next interest payment and will be liable for tax on most of the interest paid. But the seller won't be liable for tax on interest that covers the period after the sale and before the interest payment date. The seller can claim tax relief for this interest but the buyer will be liable for tax.

Investment trusts

Investment trust companies are companies quoted on the Stock Exchange. Their business is investing in the shares of other companies. You take a stake in the trust's investment fund by buying the shares of the trust itself. Investment trust shares are taxed in the same way as the shares of any other company (see p. 213).

Let property

In general, income from letting property is taxed as investment income. But the tax is worked out in the same way as for income from a business – see Chapter 11.

Life insurance policies

For details of how life insurance is taxed, see Chapter 13.

Local authority investments

Interest on local authority loans made after 18 November 1984 is paid with tax deducted. Interest (see p. 198) on local authority stock and yearling bonds is paid with 20 per cent tax deducted.

National Savings investments

With National Savings Investment and Ordinary accounts, and National Savings Capital Bonds, Income Bonds, Deposit Bonds and Pensioners Guaranteed Income Bonds, interest (see p. 198) is taxable but paid without deduction of tax. Fixed Rate Savings Bonds have 20 per cent tax deducted at source.

With Savings Certificates and the Yearly Plan (withdrawn to new investors on 1 February 1995), Children's Bonus Bonds and Premium Bonds, the proceeds are free of income tax. National Savings investments don't produce a capital gain and so are free of capital gains tax.

With a National Savings Ordinary account, the first £70 of interest is tax-free – for husband and wife, it's £70 each in separate accounts and £140 if in a joint account. Any one person is allowed only £70 free of tax, however many National Savings Ordinary accounts he or she has.

Open-ended investment companies (OEICs)

These are taxed in the same way as unit trusts – see p. 214.

Personal equity plans (PEPs)

Since 6 April 1999, PEPs have been replaced by ISAS – see p. 209. However, you can keep PEPs taken out before that date and switch from one PEP manager to another. PEPs are a way of investing in shares in UK and European Union (EU) companies, unit trusts, investment trusts and OEICs without having to pay tax on interest, dividend or distribution income or on any capital gains. They are run by plan managers, for example banks or investment companies, which take care of the administration.

You can invest in a range of investments in a *general* PEP, including:

• shares in UK or EU companies

- certain corporate bonds and convertibles and preference shares issued by UK or EU companies – the bonds must have a minimum of five years to maturity at the time of purchase, be denominated in sterling and carry a fixed rate of interest
- 'qualifying' unit trusts, investment trusts and OEICS, i.e. those with at least half their investments in UK or EU shares and corporate bonds, etc
- 'non-qualifying' unit trusts, investment trusts and OEICS but only up to a limited amount.

In addition to general PEPs, you might have one or more *single-company* PEPs. These must be invested in the ordinary shares of just one UK or EU company (investment trusts are excluded).

Income and gains from investments held in PEPs are treated the same way for tax as ISAS – see p. 209.

Shares

Dividends from UK companies come with a tax credit of 10 per cent – see p. 200. When you sell your shares, any increase in value counts as a capital gain – see Chapter 14 for more details.

If the company gives you more shares as a result of a *bonus* (or *scrip*) issue, you are not liable to income tax unless you've chosen to have the shares instead of a cash dividend (a few companies give you the choice). If this is the case, higher-rate taxpayers are liable to income tax on the cash equivalent of the shares.

Transfers of shares are currently liable for *ad valorem* duty of 0.5 per cent. This is rounded up to the nearest £5. The stockbroker adds the tax to the cost of the shares, and it's the buyer of the shares who normally pays the tax. There is no tax-free amount. However, if you give shares away – i.e. you transfer ownership and do not receive money or other 'consideration' in exchange – you pay a fixed rate of £5.

Stamp duty reserve tax is levied on transfers of shares for which no document is produced and which therefore escape stamp duty. Stamp duty reserve tax is payable on all 'paperless' transfers of share transactions at a rate of 0.5 per cent.

If you hold your shares in an ISA or a PEP, see pp. 209 and 212. If your shares qualify for the BES, see p. 205. For the EIS see p. 206. For details of special employee share schemes, see pp. 97–99.

TESSAs

Banks, building societies and other financial institutions offered tax-exempt special savings accounts (TESSAs) to anyone over 18 until 5 April 1999. You can no longer start a TESSA, but you can continue to save in a TESSA started by that date. Provided the savings are left in the account for five years, the interest earned on a TESSA is paid tax-free.

Most institutions will allow you to withdraw interest from your TESSA, but only an amount equivalent to the interest you'd receive after the deduction of 20 per cent tax. The remainder must stay in your account. If you withdraw too much interest (or any capital) the account will be closed. All the interest earned until then will be taxed as if it had been earned in the tax year the account is closed.

The most you can invest in a TESSA is £9,000 over the five years – up to £3,000 in the first year, and up to £1,800 in each later year, provided you don't exceed the £9,000 overall maximum.

Once you have held a TESSA for its full five-year life, it has to be closed. You can transfer the capital (but not the accumulated interest) from a maturing TESSA into a TESSA-only ISA. Capital transferred from a TESSA does not count towards the normal investment limits for ISAS – see p. 210.

Trust income

Trusts pay tax on most of their income, at 34 per cent if they are discretionary trusts, at the basic rate of 22 per cent otherwise. Since 6 April 1999, the rate of tax on income from shares and similar investments received by a discretionary trust has been reduced to 25 per cent to compensate for the reduction in the tax credit from 20 per cent to 10 per cent from that date. These rates apply whether the income is kept by the trust or paid out to beneficiaries. With income paid out by the trust, you get a tax credit of the amount of tax deducted.

If you are a beneficiary of a discretionary trust, and the highest rate of tax you pay is less than 34 per cent, consider asking the trustees to pay out to you as much of the trust's non-dividend income as possible. You'll be able to claim tax back from the Revenue. But with changes in the taxation of dividends from April 1999, the way a discretionary trust pays tax on dividend income will effectively prevent it from using tax credits, even where the beneficiaries of the trust are taxpayers. As a result, the trust may have to pay extra tax when dividend income is distributed to beneficiaries. The trust's investment and distribution policies will be crucial in determining its tax efficiency. Get advice from an accountant.

Trusts get only half the normal tax-free slice for capital gains tax – £3,600 in 2000–1 as opposed to the £7,200 individuals have. For more on trusts, see Chapter 15.

Unit trusts and OEICs

How distributions are taxed depends on the type of unit trust or OEIC. With a share-based fund, distributions come with a tax credit of 10 per cent – see p. 200.

With funds invested largely in corporate bonds, gilts, building society accounts and so on, the interest distributions are accompanied by a 20 per cent tax credit – see p. 198.

With the *first* distribution, you're likely to get an *equalisation* payment. This is a return of part of the money you first invested, so it doesn't count as income, has no tax credit and isn't taxable.

With an *accumulation* fund (where income is automatically re-invested for you) the amount re-invested – apart from any equalisation payment – counts as income and is taxable.

Where an existing unit trust converts to become an OEIC, the conversion is usually treated as if it were a share restructuring for capital gains tax purposes. This means that there is no gain (or loss) and so no tax to pay on conversion. When you dispose of the investment, you are treated as having acquired the shares in the OEIC on the date you invested in the unit trust and at the price you paid for the units.

If you buy unit trusts and OEICs within an ISA or a PEP, the income will be tax-free.

Venture capital trusts
Venture capital trusts (VCTs) operate like investment trusts, but invest in unquoted trading companies and companies on the alternative investment market (AIM). You can invest up to £100,000 a year in VCTs. They have four tax advantages.

- When you buy new ordinary shares in a venture capital trust you can get income tax relief at 20 per cent, provided that the shares are held for at least three years if issued after 5 April 2000, five years if issued by that date.
- Dividends from venture capital trusts are free of income tax.
- Gains you make when you dispose of your shares are free of capital gains tax.
- Tax on other chargeable gains can be deferred if those gains are re-invested in venture capital trusts.

You need to balance these tax advantages against the intrinsic risk of investing in small unquoted companies. And to get the tax advantages there are, of course, conditions to be met. For example, at least 70 per cent of a trust's investments must be in unquoted trading companies, with no more than 15 per cent in any one company or group of companies, and at least 30 per cent of a trust's qualifying investments must be in ordinary shares. The definition of an 'unquoted trading company' will be broadly the same as for the enterprise investment scheme.

Which Schedules?

Investment income comes under the following Schedules:

Schedule A – income from letting property in the UK
Schedule D, Case III – interest, annuities or other annual payments
Schedule D, Case IV – income from foreign securities
Schedule D, Case V – income from foreign possessions
Schedule D, Case VI – income not assessable under any other case or schedule
Schedule F – distributions and dividends of a UK resident company.

Income regarded as yours during the administration period of a will

Any income which is regarded as yours during the administration period of a will or intestacy (i.e. while the details of who gets what are being worked out), will be paid to you with either 20 per cent tax or basic-rate tax deducted, depending on whether the income represents savings income or income from other sources.

Tax on income from overseas investments

The tax treatment of income from abroad can be extraordinarily complicated, and if you have a substantial amount of such income you'll need to get specialist advice – and look at Inland Revenue leaflet IR20 – *Residents and non-residents*.

In general, if you're resident and ordinarily resident in the UK (see Chapter 7), all your income is liable to UK tax, whether or not it is brought into this country. However, income from overseas investments is often taxed in the country in which it originates – so two lots of tax could be charged on one lot of income. The UK government has made agreements with a wide range of countries to limit the extent to which income may be taxed twice. Under one of these *double-taxation agreements*, the amount of tax which a foreign government deducts from income before it reaches you is reduced. The tax which is actually deducted is allowable as a tax credit against the UK tax on the same income.

Suppose, for example, that you're entitled to £1,000 in dividends from the US. Tax at 30 per cent, say, would normally be held by the US before paying over the dividends to non-US residents. However, because of our double-taxation agreement with the US, only 15 per cent is withheld – i.e. you get £850. If, say, you're liable for tax in the UK at 40 per cent on your £1,000 gross dividends, there'd be £400 tax to pay. But the £150 you've paid in tax to the US would be allowed as credit against the £400 of UK tax you're liable for – so you'd have to hand over to the Revenue £250, not £400.

If you are liable for no UK tax (or less than has been deducted under a double-taxation agreement) there'll be no further UK tax to pay – but you can't claim back the extra foreign tax you've paid.

How to get your relief
If your foreign income is paid to you through an agent (for example a bank) in the UK, who passes it on to you after deducting basic-rate tax, the agent should allow for any double-taxation agreement when doing the sums. But if the income is paid direct to you from abroad, you have to apply for double-taxation relief yourself. To get the foreign tax reduced, get an application form from the Financial Intermediaries and Claims Office International (FICO).* To get a credit for the foreign tax withheld, apply to your tax inspector.

If the amount of foreign tax for which you are liable is altered so that your claim for UK tax relief becomes excessive, you have a duty (since 17 March 1998) to notify your tax office in writing of the change. This must be done within one year of the change to the foreign tax liability.

When UK tax is due
All foreign income you get is taxed for the year in which you are entitled to receive it.

Remittance basis
If this applies, you are taxed only on what income you bring into the UK. You can claim remittance basis if you are resident but not domiciled in the UK, or if you are a British subject or a citizen of Ireland *and* you are resident but not ordinarily resident in the UK.

Offshore funds
Any gain which you get when you sell an investment in an offshore fund is liable to income tax at your highest rate, unless the fund has *distributor status*. In this case only its income is liable to income tax

and any gain will be liable to capital gains tax. An offshore fund can get distributor status if, for example, it distributes all its income.

Useful Inland Revenue reading

You can ring the Inland Revenue Orderline* for helpsheets, leaflets and notes.

Leaflets and notes

IR110	A guide for people with savings
ISA/1	The answers on ISAs
IR89	Personal equity plans
IR114	Tessa
IR169	Venture capital trusts
IR137	The enterprise investment scheme
IR68	Accrued income scheme
IR20	Residents and non-residents

Helpsheets

When you receive a helpsheet, make sure it relates to the tax year for which you want information.

IR286	Income tax losses for shares you have subscribed for in unlisted trading companies
IR297	Enterprise investment scheme and capital gains tax
IR298	Venture capital trusts and capital gains tax

Concessions

Extra-statutory concessions let you off paying tax that is technically due. Booklet IR1 gives details of each concession.

A46	Variable purchased life annuities: carry forward of excess of capital element
A69	Building society conversions: declaration to society counts as declaration to successor company

13

Life insurance

Simple life insurance – called *term* insurance – is a way of providing for your dependants when you die. They pay no income or capital gains tax on the proceeds and can avoid inheritance tax if you write the policy in trust – see p. 227. The same applies to policies that are essentially investments, but these can have tax implications for you.

Qualifying policies

You won't have to pay income tax on the proceeds of *any* life insurance policy if (even with the policy gain added to your income) you pay tax at no more than the basic rate. And even if you're a higher-rate taxpayer, there'll be no tax to pay on the proceeds of a *qualifying policy* if you keep it for at least ten years (or three-quarters of the term if this is less than ten years). When a qualifying policy reaches the end of its term, or pays out on the death of the person insured, the proceeds are free of income tax.

Broadly speaking, a policy is a qualifying policy if you pay regular premiums on it (i.e. monthly or yearly). There are other conditions about the length of the policy and how much the premiums can vary from year to year, but the insurance company will take care of these to make the policy qualify. Note that all policies taken out on or before 19 March 1968 are qualifying policies, whether they are regular-premium policies or not – as long as they haven't been altered since that date. There is no tax to pay on the proceeds of qualifying policies.

You normally pay no capital gains tax on the proceeds of a life insurance policy – but see p. 225.

Tax the company pays

Though *you* pay no tax on the proceeds of a qualifying policy (and no basic-rate tax on the proceeds of a non-qualifying policy) it is wrong to think your return is tax-free. The insurance company has to pay tax on its profits, capital gains and income from investments. The company's tax bill is seen by the Inland Revenue as taking care of the basic-rate tax on what you get from the policy.

Note that some of the business done by friendly societies is *tax-exempt*. So they don't have to pay corporation tax, or tax on investment income or capital gains which come from this business.

Tax on non-qualifying policies

When a non-qualifying policy ends, the gain is normally the amount you get *less* the premiums paid (but see p. 222 if you've cashed in part of your policy earlier). A gain that arises on the death of someone is the cash-in value of the policy immediately before death (if this is less than the sum insured) *less* the premiums paid.

How the proceeds are taxed

The gain is added to your investment income for the year in which the policy comes to an end. You're liable for higher-rate income tax on the gain but *not* basic-rate (22 per cent) tax. So if you pay tax at the higher rate of 40 per cent, you'd have to pay tax at 40 – 22 = 18 per cent on the policy gain – see Example 1. But if you become a higher-rate tax payer only after adding the gain to your income, the Revenue should apply *top-slicing relief* to reduce your tax bill.

Top-slicing relief

Work out your *average yearly gain* by dividing the total gain by the number of *complete* years for which the policy ran. Then add this average yearly gain to your income for the tax year, and work out the higher-rate tax on the average yearly gain. To get your tax bill on the whole gain, multiply the tax bill on your average yearly gain by the number of complete years you have spread the gain over. See Example 1.

But note that cashing in *part* of a non-qualifying policy could create a *chargeable event* – see p. 223. If there has been a chargeable event before the policy came to an end, top-slicing relief uses only the number of years since the (last) chargeable event.

EXAMPLE 1

Tom bought a £20,000 single-premium bond in February 1996. He cashed it in for £30,000 in June 2000, making a gain of £10,000. He already has taxable income for the 2000–1 tax year of £26,000.

Without top-slicing relief, Tom would add £26,000 + £10,000 to get £36,000. This is £7,600 over the basic-rate limit of £28,400.

Tax would come to £1,368 – i.e. £7,600 × 18 per cent (40 per cent higher-rate tax less the 22 per cent already deducted at source).

But with top-slicing relief, the *average yearly gain* of £2,500 (i.e. the £10,000 total gain divided by the four complete years the policy ran for) is added to Tom's taxable income for the year.

The average yearly gain of £2,500 added to Tom's income of £26,000 comes to £28,500. This is £100 over the basic-rate limit.

Tax comes to £72:

£100 × 18 per cent = £18

£18 × 4 (for the four complete years the policy ran for) = £72

Top-slicing relief saves Tom £1,296 (i.e. £1,368 less £72).

Age-related allowances

Although when you cash in all or part of a non-qualifying policy any gain is free of basic-rate tax, the whole gain (i.e. without top-slicing relief) is counted as part of your income for the year. For most people this has no effect on their allowances. But if you're aged 65 or over during the tax year, increasing your income can reduce the *age-related allowances* you get (see Chapter 3).

Age-related allowances are reduced by half of the amount by which a person's *net statutory income* exceeds a certain limit – £17,000 for the 2000–1 tax year. So if the gain from an insurance policy (or the excess if you cash in part of a policy) means a reduction in your age-related allowances, you'll in effect pay more income tax whether or not you're liable for higher-rate tax.

Tax when you stop a policy early

Life insurance policies with an investment element may have some value – the *surrender value* – even before the policy comes to an end.

How much tax you have to pay (if any) depends on whether or not the policy is a qualifying one.

Making a policy paid-up

Making a policy paid-up means that you stop paying the premiums but don't take your money out. Making part of a policy paid-up means you can reduce your premiums.

If you make a policy paid-up, the same rules apply as if you were to cash it in. However, you won't have to pay any tax until the policy finally pays out.

Cashing in a qualifying policy

You'll have no tax to pay when you cash in a qualifying policy before the end of its term provided you've been paying regular premiums and the policy has run for at least ten years (or for three-quarters of the term of the policy if this is less than ten years). So with a 25-year term, there'd be no tax to pay if you surrendered after ten years; with a ten-year term, there'd be no tax after $7\frac{1}{2}$ years. But if you cash in the policy before this, you'll be taxed on the gain in the same way as when a non-qualifying policy pays out. So you'll be liable for higher-rate tax if it applies to you and will get top-slicing relief if this would cut your tax bill. You pay tax on the difference between the surrender value and the *gross* premiums paid (i.e. the premiums you've paid *plus* any premium subsidy – see p. 225).

Cashing in a non-qualifying policy

If you cash in a non-qualifying policy before the end of its term you pay tax on the surrender value in the same way as if it had run for its full term. So you may have to pay higher-rate tax (but not basic-rate tax) on the amount by which the cash-in value exceeds the premiums you've paid. You'll get top-slicing relief if this would reduce your tax bill.

EXAMPLE 2

Ernest has a ten-year unit-linked savings plan for which the premium is £50 a month. After five years he decides to cash in the policy. The total premiums to date are £3,000 and the surrender value is £3,500, so he's made a gain of £500. As he is a higher-rate taxpayer, he has to pay tax at $40 - 22 = 18$ per cent on the £500 gain – i.e. £90 in all.

Cashing in part of a policy

You may want to cash in part of your policy, rather than the whole of it. Or, if bonuses are added, you could surrender a bonus. This is treated in the same way as cashing in part of your policy.

Cashing in part of a qualifying policy

If you cash in part of a qualifying policy after ten years (or after three-quarters of its term if this is less), the gains you make are tax-free. But if you cash in part of the policy before this, you'll be taxed in the same way as for non-qualifying policies – see below.

Cashing in part of a non-qualifying policy

There's no basic-rate tax to pay when you cash in part of a non-qualifying policy. And higher-rate taxpayers can postpone a higher-rate tax bill, avoiding one altogether if they have become basic-rate taxpayers when the policy finally ends.

You get an allowance for each *complete* year that the policy has to run. Complete years are calculated from the date the policy is taken out – but you don't get an allowance until the first complete year starting after 13 March 1975. For each of the first 20 years of the term of a policy the allowance is $\frac{1}{20}$ (i.e. 5 per cent) of the premiums paid so far. For each year after the 20th year the allowance is $\frac{1}{20}$ of the premium paid in that year and the previous 19 years. So, if you pay £1,000 a year in premiums, your allowance after the first year will be £50, after the second £100, after the third £150, and so on. Allowances not used each year are carried forward.

EXAMPLE 3

Harvey pays tax at the higher rate of 40 per cent. He has bought a single-premium bond for £10,000 and wants to withdraw as much as he can without paying tax at the moment. For each of the first 20 years Harvey gets an allowance of $\frac{1}{20}$ of the total premiums paid so far – i.e. $\frac{1}{20}$ of £10,000 = £500. He can cash in £500 each year without paying tax in that year. For the 21st year onwards his allowance is $\frac{1}{20}$ of the premiums paid in that year and the previous 19 years. But the allowance is zero in Harvey's case as he paid for the policy all at once in the first year.

So if he uses up his allowances in the first 20 years he won't be able to cash in any more of his policy without paying tax at the time (unless he's a basic-rate taxpayer by then).

If you cash in more than your total allowances, this creates a *chargeable event*. The difference between your total allowances and what you've had from the policy (the *excess*) is counted as a gain. This gain is treated in the same way as if you cash in a whole policy and is therefore subject to higher-rate tax, but not basic-rate tax.

You'll get top-slicing relief if this reduces your tax bill, with the gain spread over the number of years you've had the policy, or the number of years since the last chargeable event, if there's been one already.

When an excess is added to your income, the allowances taken into account are cancelled, and you start building up allowances again.

EXAMPLE 4

When Harvey's single-premium bond comes to an end (see Example 3), he's still paying tax at 40 per cent and so he'll have to pay tax on his gain. If Harvey used up his £500 allowance for each of the first 20 years, he'd have had 20 × £500 = £10,000 from the policy. If he got another £10,000, say, when the policy ended, his total gain would be £20,000 *minus* the £10,000 premium = £10,000, which would be added to his income for the year. Harvey would pay higher-rate (but no basic-rate) tax on the proceeds – i.e. 40 – 22 = 18 per cent × £10,000 = £1,800.

When the policy comes to an end

If you've cashed in part of a policy before it finally comes to an end, the total gain on which you may have to pay tax is:

- the amount you get at the end *plus* any amounts you've taken in the past, *less*
- the total premiums paid, any excesses you've already had (see above) and any pre-14 March 1975 gains on the policy which the Inland Revenue was told about (either by you or the insurance company).

If after making these deductions you're left with a negative figure, you can subtract this from your 'total income' to reduce your higher-rate tax bill. But you can't subtract more than the total of the excesses you've made from partial surrenders and pre-14 March 1975 gains.

Capital gains tax and unit-linked policies

With a unit-linked policy, the insurance company invests your premiums in units in one or more investment funds. However, you don't own the units – the insurance company does. And so, while you can get a tax-free return, the company has to pay tax on its investment income and on the capital gains it makes (with the exception of life insurance held in an individual savings account (ISA) – see Chapter 12).

In practice, the company doesn't have to sell units every time a policy is cashed in. So, in effect, the rate at which it pays any tax on capital gains can be lower than the full percentage – say, 10 to 20 per cent. This is deducted either from the investment fund or from the proceeds of the policy when you cash it in. So if you see that a deduction has been made for tax on capital gains, it's not tax on *your* gains but on the company's.

You can't claim it back as being part of your annual capital gains tax exemption or by setting losses against it. If you're not likely to pay capital gains tax, consider investing in unit trusts and open-ended investment companies (OEICs) rather than life insurance.

Cluster policies

With some policies, your premiums can be used to buy several policies. For example, if your premium was £50 a month you might get a cluster of ten policies, each with a premium of £5 a month. The advantage of cluster policies is that you don't have to treat all the policies in the same way. If you're a higher-rate taxpayer and you cash in part of a non-qualifying policy, you will be taxed on any *excess* that arises (see p. 223). You could end up paying less tax at the time if you have a cluster of policies, and cash in one (or more) of them. But if you're paying tax at the same rate when you finally cash in the rest of the proceeds, you'll pay the same amount of tax in the long run.

Tax relief on premiums

If you took out a qualifying policy before 14 March 1984, you are probably getting a 12.5 per cent subsidy on the premiums whether you pay tax or not (so long as the premium falls within certain limits). You get the subsidy by paying lower premiums: if your premium is £100 a year (*gross*) you hand over £87.50 (*net*); the insurance company claims the extra £12.50 from the Revenue. But if you vary the terms of such a policy, and the benefits are increased or the term extended (whether or not this is by exercising an option already in the policy), you'll lose all your subsidy. However, benefits which increase automatically as part of the original contract will not affect the subsidy. If you're thinking of changing a policy, check with the insurance company to see if your planned change would affect the subsidy.

Life insurance with a personal pension
If you're self-employed or an employee not in an employer's pension scheme, you may be able to get tax relief at your highest rate of tax on premiums for special term insurance sold with personal pensions. You can claim full tax relief on premiums of up to 5 per cent of your *net relevant earnings* – i.e. your taxable profits from being self-employed or your earnings from a job where you're not in the employer's pension scheme. But what you pay in such premiums reduces the maximum amount you can pay into a personal pension.

Death and superannuation benefits
You can still get tax relief on certain combined sickness and life insurance policies issued by friendly societies. You'll get tax relief on the life part of your premium, at half your top rate of tax – so if you're paying tax at 40 per cent, you'll get tax relief at 20 per cent.

You can get tax relief at the same rate for the part of a trade union subscription which is for superannuation (i.e. pension), funeral or life insurance benefits.

Premium subsidy for deferred annuities
You get a 12.5 per cent subsidy on premiums used to buy a *deferred annuity*. You get this on gross premiums of up to £100 (i.e. premiums you pay of up to £87.50). These premiums count towards the limit on tax relief on premiums for a qualifying life policy – see p. 225. There's also tax relief at the basic rate on premiums for deferred annuities which will pay an income to your dependants after your death, providing you *have* to pay the premiums either under an Act of Parliament or under the rules of your job.

Buying or selling a policy

If you sell a non-qualifying policy, it's treated in the same way as though you had cashed it in – see p. 222. You may have to pay higher-rate tax on the amount that you sold the policy for *less* the premiums you've paid.

If you sell a qualifying policy you'll be taxed as above if you do so in the first ten years or within three-quarters of its term if this is shorter (this also applies if you made it paid-up in this period and then sold it later on).

If you buy a policy, there may be capital gains tax to pay if you eventually make a gain on it (as with other assets – see Chapter 15). Note that you can't avoid paying the income tax that's due by selling your policy and buying it back – in the hope that you'd be liable for capital gains tax instead. If you've had your own policy reassigned to you, you'll have to pay income tax, not capital gains tax, on the gain.

Security for a loan

You may be able to use your insurance policy as security for a loan either from the life insurance company or from somewhere else, for example a bank. A loan from the insurance company is treated as a partial surrender for the amount of the loan if the policy was taken out before 26 March 1974 and is non-qualifying, or if it's qualifying and the money is lent at less than a commercial rate of interest. Any repayment (other than interest) of the loan you make to the life insurance company is treated as a premium when working out the tax bill at the end. If you're still alive when the policy pays out, you'll be liable for any extra tax that's due.

Note that it won't be treated as a surrender if the loan is to a person over 64 borrowing the money to buy an annuity, nor if the loan is from somewhere else, for example a bank or building society, rather than the insurance company.

Preparing for a pay-out on death

A life insurance policy will usually pay out to your estate. But you may want the proceeds to go to someone else after your death. You could do this by simply leaving the money in your will. But in that case, the proceeds of the policy will be added to your estate, and there might be an inheritance tax to pay – see Chapter 15. You could instead *assign* the policy to someone else during your lifetime. You can do this by completing a *deed of assignment* and sending it to the life insurance company (ask the company or a solicitor for details). You may want to assign the policy for a number of reasons:

- to make a gift
- to avoid inheritance tax by writing the policy in trust
- to raise cash
- to get a loan.

Assignment and subsidy

If you get the premium subsidy and assign your policy, you can still get the subsidy while you continue to pay the premiums. But if the premiums are paid by someone else (other than your husband or wife) they won't qualify for the subsidy.

Gifts

If you give a policy away (by assigning it to somebody else) it counts as a gift for inheritance tax purposes. The value the Revenue puts on the gift is either the market value of the policy *plus* any amounts paid out earlier, or the total amount paid in premiums up to the time you give the policy away, whichever is higher. The market value will often be close to the cash-in value. But, for example, the market value of a policy on someone close to death will be almost as high as the amount the policy would pay out on death. If you continue to pay the premiums after you've given the policy away, the amount you pay also counts as a gift. But there shouldn't be any inheritance tax to pay as the payments will normally come into one of the tax-free categories – see Chapter 15. The proceeds won't form part of your estate.

Trusts

By getting the policy *written in trust*, you may be able to avoid inheritance tax as the proceeds are not added to your estate. The proceeds can then also be paid to the beneficiaries without waiting for probate.

If you want the policy to pay out to your wife (or husband) or children, the simplest way of setting it up in trust is to get a suitable trust wording from the insurance company involved. Most companies are happy to recommend the appropriate trust for your needs. As a gift, the proceeds of policies written in trust will not form part of your estate, but the premiums may count as gifts for inheritance tax purposes unless they come into one of the tax-free categories – see Chapter 15. If the policy pays out while you're still alive (for example a growth bond), you'll have to pay any income tax that's due, though you will be able to claim it back from the trustees. For more about trusts, see Chapter 15.

Useful Inland Revenue reading

You can ring the Inland Revenue Orderline* for helpsheets.

Helpsheets

When you receive a helpsheet, make sure it relates to the tax year for which you want information.

IR320   Gains on UK life insurance policies

Concessions

Extra-statutory concessions let you off paying tax that is technically due. Booklet IR1 gives details of each concession.

A41   Qualifying life insurance: ignoring minor infringements which would make them non-qualifying

A45   Life insurance: varying terms of policy

A96   Life insurance when collector stops collecting premiums

14 Capital gains tax

The simplest example of making a capital gain is *selling something you own at a profit*. For example, you buy a Victorian etching for £10,000, and sell it a couple of years later for £12,000. Your capital gain is £2,000, or a bit less if you can claim some expenses of buying and selling.

But you can make a capital gain even when no buying or selling is involved, for example if you give something away. Here are the basic rules.

- You can make a capital gain (or loss) whenever you *dispose of an asset,* no matter how you come to own it.
- Broadly, anything you own (whether in the UK or not) counts as an asset, e.g. houses, jewellery, shares, antiques.
- You dispose of an asset not only if you sell it, but also if you give it away, exchange it or lose it. You also dispose of an asset if you sell rights to it, e.g. grant a lease, or if it is destroyed or becomes worthless, or if you get compensation for damage to it, e.g. insurance money, and don't spend all the money on restoring it.
- Not every gain you make will be taxable, nor will every loss be recognised by the Inland Revenue.
- There are a number of reliefs which may reduce or defer your tax bill if you give assets away or have certain business assets (see *Capital gains tax and the family* on p. 244) or make certain investments (see *Deferring capital gains tax* on p. 250).

Tax-free gains

Gains on some assets are free from tax. The other side of the coin is that *losses* on these assets can't normally be used to reduce your taxable gains for tax purposes.

The main assets on which gains are tax-free are:

- your only or main home – see Chapter 11
- motor vehicles – if you sell, say, a vintage or classic car, bus or traction engine at a gain, that will be tax-free unless you make a habit of doing this, in which case you could be taxed as though you were trading in cars
- National Savings investments – none is liable to capital gains tax, though some are liable to income tax
- British money, including post-1837 gold sovereigns
- currency for personal use abroad – normally, foreign currency is an asset for tax purposes, but there is no tax to pay on gains on currency for the use of your family and yourself abroad, e.g. on holiday or to maintain a home abroad
- betting and lottery winnings
- gilts (or options in them), though income tax might be due on any accrued interest – this exemption extends to many types of corporate bond acquired after 13 March 1984
- shares, unit trusts, open-ended investment companies (OEICs), investment trusts and corporate bonds held in a personal equity plan (PEP) or individual savings account (ISA)
- shares in qualifying venture capital trusts (VCTs)
- shares issued after 18 March 1986 under the business expansion scheme (BES) on their first disposal only
- shares issued under the enterprise investment scheme (EIS)
- life insurance policies – the proceeds, whether on maturity, surrender or sale, are free of capital gains tax provided you didn't buy the policy from a previous holder, but note that the insurance company will have paid capital gains tax on gains before you get the proceeds
- damages for any wrong or injury suffered by you in your private or professional life, e.g. damages for assault or defamation
- compensation for mis-sold personal pensions you took out between 29 April 1988 and 30 June 1994
- settled property – if you have been given an interest under a UK settlement (but not the underlying property), the proceeds if you dispose of it are tax-free – but from 21 March 2000, new rules mean there may be tax to pay if you sell your interest

- timber – a gain on the disposal of timber, whether growing or felled, is tax-free provided that you're not taxed as carrying on a forestry trade, in which case the disposal will be liable for income tax as a trading transaction (the exemption does not apply to the land on which the timber was growing)
- decorations for valour – a gain on the disposal of an award for valour or gallant conduct is tax-free, e.g. your father's Victoria Cross or George Cross, provided that you did not buy the award
- gifts to charities or certain national institutions
- a gift of *heritage property* (see Chapter 15) is tax-free if it satisfies certain conditions
- 'wasting assets' – i.e. any chattel which had a predictable useful life of no more than 50 years when you first acquired it, provided that you have not used the asset in your business so that it qualified for capital allowances – this covers electronic equipment and racehorses, say, and also machinery (including antique clocks).

For chattels with a predictable life of more than 50 years, gains may be partly tax-free. If the *disposal proceeds* are less than £6,000, any gain is tax-free. So if you buy a watercolour for £1,500 and sell it for £5,750, the gain is tax-free.

If the *disposal proceeds* are more than £6,000, your taxable gain is *either* your actual gain *or* $\frac{5}{3}$ of the excess over £6,000, whichever is the lower.

If the disposal proceeds are less than £6,000, and you've made a loss, you're assumed to have received £6,000. So if you buy a picture for £7,000 and sell it for £5,000, your loss, for tax purposes, is £1,000.

If you sell a set of articles, for example a set of matching chairs, separately, but in effect to the same person, the Revenue is likely to treat the sales as a single sale. So if you sold six chairs for £2,000 each, you'd be taxed as though you'd made a single sale of £12,000, not six sales of £2,000.

Working out your gains or losses

The rules for calculating capital gains tax have changed several times over the years, with the most recent major change being the introduction of taper relief in April 1998. This means that if you have owned an asset for a number of years, you could be affected by several generations of capital gains tax rules. To calculate your taxable gain (or allowable loss) on assets which are not tax-free, work your way through the following six steps.

Step one   Take the *final value* of the asset. This will be:

- the *disposal proceeds* if you sold it
- its *market value* if you gave it away
- the *insurance proceeds* if it is destroyed – for damaged assets, see p. 259.

Step two   Subtract the *initial value* of the asset to get the *gross capital gain* (or loss). The initial value is:

- *what you paid for it* if you bought it
- its *market value at the time of the gift* if you were given it (though see p. 244 for special rules about gifts)
- its *probate value* if you inherited it.

However, if you acquired the asset before 31 March 1982, see p. 236).

Step three   Deduct any *allowable expenses* which you incurred in acquiring or disposing of the asset, or in increasing its value – this gives you the net capital gain (or loss). You can include:

- legal and valuation fees, stamp duty, commission, advertising
- the legal cost of defending your title to the asset
- money spent on the asset which has increased its value (but not maintenance or normal repairs).

Again, for assets acquired before 31 March 1982, see p. 236).

Step four   If you owned the asset before 1 April 1998, deduct *indexation allowance*; this is explained fully on p. 237. Indexation increases the amount of your initial value and allowable expenses in line with the retail prices index (RPI) between March 1982 and April 1998 and prevents you being taxed on gains made purely because of inflation during this period. Gains after indexation are called *chargeable gains*; losses after indexation are called *allowable losses*.

Step five   Deduct any *allowable losses* from your gains. You can also deduct any allowable losses from previous years that you have not already set against previous years' gains. Your losses must be set against each gain in a particular order, depending on when you made the losses and what taper relief you can claim. This is all explained on p. 237.

Step six   Finally, you may be able to claim *taper relief* on your asset. This reduces the taxable gain according to the length of time you have owned the asset after 5 April 1998 – see p. 239.

EXAMPLE 1

Larry bought a second home in January 1987 for £55,000. He paid legal fees of £450 and stamp duty of £550. In July 1988, he added an extension costing £10,000. In May 2000 he sells the home for £110,000, with agents' fees of £2,000 and legal fees of £300.

Larry works out his capital gain (before any indexation allowance or taper relief):

sale proceeds	£110,000
less **purchase price**	£55,000
less **allowable expenses:**	
costs of acquisition	£1,000
costs of improvement	£10,000
expenses of disposal	£2,300
net capital gain	**£41,700**

Working out the tax bill

The first step in calculating your tax bill is to add together all your *gains* (after indexation, losses and taper relief) for the tax year. The result is your *total taxable gains* for the tax year.

The tax-free slice
The first slice of your total taxable gains in any tax year is free of tax. The size of this tax-free slice is set for each tax year. For the 2000–1 tax year the tax-free slice is £7,200. A husband and wife get a £7,200 tax-free slice each, which they can set against only their own net gains.

If your total taxable gains are less than the amount of the tax-free slice, there will be no tax to pay. But you can't carry any unused part of the tax-free slice forward to future years.

Most trusts qualify for only half the tax-free slice – i.e. £3,600 for 2000–1. But if the trust is set up for the benefit of someone with a mental disability, or someone receiving attendance allowance or the middle or higher rate of disability living allowance, the full tax-free slice is available.

EXAMPLE 2

Nerys has made a chargeable gain on her holiday flat of £9,000 in the 2000–1 tax year. In the same year she sold shares, with a chargeable loss of £3,475.

Nerys has a total taxable gain for the tax year of £9,000 – £3,475 = £5,525. The tax-free slice for the year of £7,200 will wipe out this total taxable gain, and there will be no tax to pay.

Nerys needed only £1,800 of losses to reduce her total taxable gains to the level of the tax-free slice, and the extra £1,675 which brought the total below £7,200 can't be carried over to another year.

How much tax?

Taxable capital gains are now taxed as if they were investment income. This means that the amount of gains on which you have to pay tax is taxed at 10, 20 or 40 per cent depending on what tax band they fall into. The relevant tax band will depend on what (if any) taxable income you have. See pp. 50–51 for an explanation.

EXAMPLE 3

Lily has net chargeable gains of £14,200 in 2000–1, £7,000 after deducting the tax-free slice of £7,200. She has no unused losses from previous years. Her taxable income is £22,400, £6,000 below the basic-rate tax band of £28,400.

Here's the tax on Lily's capital gains.

- The first £6,000 of Lily's gains fall within the basic-rate tax band. Lily will pay tax of 20 per cent of £6,000 – i.e. £1,200.
- The remaining £1,000 is above the basic-rate tax band. Lily will have to pay tax of 40 per cent of £1,000 – i.e. £400.
- Lily's total capital gains tax bill is £1,200 + £400 = £1,600.

Assets acquired before 31 March 1982

Only gains made since 31 March 1982 are taxable.

So when working out the gain on an asset acquired before 31 March 1982, you use its market value on that date, not the cost when you originally acquired it. You also ignore any expenses incurred before 31 March 1982 in working out the net gain (or loss). Indexation allowance applies to the market value on 31 March 1982 and to any expenses incurred since that date.

In some cases, using the March 1982 value could mean a bigger tax bill, as Example 4 shows.

Where you've owned something before 31 March 1982 which fell in value up to that date, using the March 1982 value can artificially inflate your gain. The opposite is true if you bought something before 31 March 1982 which rose in price up to that date and then fell in value – the loss you make is artificially inflated.

Where either of these things would happen, the gain or loss will be worked out using the original cost. This means that the initial value is what you paid for the asset, and you can claim expenses incurred before 31 March 1982. In this case, both initial value and pre-31 March 1982 expenses are indexed from 31 March 1982.

If, in Example 4, Roger had sold the shares in June 1999 for £8,000, then using the March 1982 value there would have been an unindexed gain of £8,000 – £5,000 = £3,000; using the actual purchase price in January 1980, there would have been a loss of £10,000 – £8,000 = £2,000. If you make a gain under one set of rules and a loss under the other, it will be treated as though you had made neither a gain nor a loss on disposal.

EXAMPLE 4

Roger bought shares in XYZ Telecom plc in January 1980, at a cost of £10,000. By March 1982 their value had fallen to £5,000, though they then recovered. Roger sold them for £15,000 in June 1999. Ignoring indexation allowance, Roger had made a net gain of £15,000 – £10,000 = £5,000 on the shares.

But the gain is much bigger if Roger uses the March 1982 value for assets acquired before 31 March 1982:

sale proceeds	£15,000
less **value on 31 March 1982**	**£5,000**
net capital gain	**£10,000**

All seems too complicated?

You can elect for all assets acquired before 31 March 1982 to be treated as if you'd acquired them on that date, and only expenses incurred since then can be deducted from gains. You must make this *rebasing election* within two years of the end of the tax year in which you dispose of an asset bought before 31 March 1982. Once you make this election, you can't change your mind. You'll be no worse off if all or most of your assets were worth more on 31 March 1982 than when acquired.

Indexation allowance

Indexation allowance applies to assets acquired before 1 April 1998. It means that you are not taxed on gains in line with inflation between March 1982 and April 1998. The effect is that your taxable gain is reduced or eliminated (but you cannot use indexation to create or increase a loss). It works like this: your initial value and allowable expenses are linked to the retail price's index (RPI) and increased in line with the index.

Multiply the initial value and each allowable expense by the indexation factor (see below) for the month in which you acquired the asset or incurred the allowable expense. You deduct the indexed values from the final value when working out your net gain or loss.

Use the factor for the month in which you acquired the asset (or March 1982 if later). You cannot claim indexation allowance for periods after April 1998. These indexation factors cannot be used for disposals before April 1998. For disposals before April 1998, contact your tax office for the correct indexation factor to use.

Indexation factors

	Jan	Feb	Mar	Apr	May	Jun	Jul	Aug	Sept	Oct	Nov	Dec
1982	n/a	n/a	1.047	1.006	0.992	0.987	0.986	0.985	0.987	0.977	0.967	0.971
1983	0.968	0.960	0.956	0.929	0.921	0.917	0.906	0.898	0.889	0.883	0.876	0.871
1984	0.872	0.865	0.859	0.834	0.828	0.823	0.825	0.808	0.804	0.793	0.788	0.789
1985	0.783	0.769	0.752	0.716	0.708	0.704	0.707	0.703	0.704	0.701	0.695	0.693
1986	0.689	0.683	0.681	0.665	0.662	0.663	0.667	0.662	0.654	0.652	0.638	0.632
1987	0.626	0.620	0.616	0.597	0.596	0.596	0.597	0.593	0.588	0.580	0.573	0.574
1988	0.574	0.568	0.562	0.537	0.531	0.525	0.524	0.507	0.500	0.485	0.478	0.474

	Jan	Feb	Mar	Apr	May	Jun	Jul	Aug	Sept	Oct	Nov	Dec
1989	0.465	0.454	0.448	0.423	0.414	0.409	0.408	0.404	0.395	0.384	0.372	0.369
1990	0.361	0.353	0.339	0.300	0.288	0.283	0.282	0.269	0.258	0.248	0.251	0.252
1991	0.249	0.242	0.237	0.222	0.218	0.213	0.215	0.213	0.208	0.204	0.199	0.198
1992	0.199	0.193	0.189	0.171	0.167	0.167	0.171	0.171	0.166	0.162	0.164	0.168
1993	0.179	0.171	0.167	0.156	0.152	0.153	0.156	0.151	0.146	0.147	0.148	0.146
1994	0.151	0.144	0.141	0.128	0.124	0.124	0.129	0.124	0.121	0.120	0.119	0.114
1995	0.114	0.107	0.102	0.091	0.087	0.085	0.091	0.085	0.080	0.085	0.085	0.079
1996	0.083	0.078	0.073	0.066	0.063	0.063	0.067	0.062	0.057	0.057	0.057	0.053
1997	0.053	0.049	0.046	0.040	0.036	0.032	0.032	0.026	0.021	0.019	0.019	0.016
1998	0.019	0.014	0.011	n/a	n/a	n/a	n/a	n/a	n/a	n/a	n/a	n/a

EXAMPLE 5

Larry works out the indexation allowance due on the gain he made selling his holiday home in May 2000. The relevant indexation factors for indexation up to April 1998 are:

January 1987 (when he bought the home)	0.626
July 1988 (when he built the extension)	0.524

He can work out the indexation allowance on the initial value (£55,000) and costs of acquisition (£1,000) together, since they were incurred in the same month of January 1987:
£56,000 × 0.626 = £35,056

The indexation allowance on the cost of the extension is:
£10,000 × 0.524 = £5,240
Total indexation allowance = £35,056 + £5,240 = £40,296

Net chargeable gain on sale
of home   = £41,700* – £40,296 = £1,404**

*   See Example 1 on p. 234.

**For periods after April 1998, Larry can claim taper relief –
    see Example 7 on p. 241.

Losses

If you make an allowable loss on disposing of an asset, it is set against any chargeable gains you make in the same year. Losses not needed to reduce your gains (before taper relief) to zero can be carried forward to future years. This means that you 'waste' losses that reduce your gains below the tax-free slice (see Example 2 on p. 235).

By contrast, you need only use enough of your losses brought forward from previous years to reduce your gains to the level of the tax-free slice (again, before taking any taper relief into account, see *How losses and taper relief interact* on p. 242). Losses made in 1996–7 and later years must be used in priority to those made in earlier years. Any losses left over can be carried forward indefinitely, but losses made after 5 April 1996 must be formally 'claimed' by notifying the Inland Revenue.

You must notify the Revenue of a loss made in 1996–7 or later years within five years and ten months of the end of the tax year in which it was made. So the latest date for telling the Revenue about losses made in 2000–1 is 31 January 2007. Tell your tax inspector of the amounts involved either on your tax return (by completing the capital gains tax supplementary pages) or in a separate letter. Losses for 1995–6 or earlier do not need to be 'claimed', but if you are completing a tax return they should be shown on the capital gains tax supplementary pages of the tax return.

EXAMPLE 6

In the 1999–2000 tax year, Gregory lost £6,000 on some shares he had sold. He had no gains in that tax year to set the loss off against, so the loss was carried forward for future years.

In the 2000–1 tax year, Gregory made a net chargeable gain of £9,850 on selling some more shares (and no other gains or losses). His tax-free slice for 2000–1 is £7,200, so he would pay tax on £9,850 – £7,200 = £2,650. However, he can set off some of the £6,000 loss carried forward from the previous year to reduce this taxable gain to zero.

This leaves £6,000 – £2,650 = £3,350 in losses to be carried forward to future years.

Taper relief

Taper relief replaces indexation allowance for periods after 5 April 1998. For periods before this you can still claim indexation allowance. Taper relief reduces the chargeable gain according to the length of the time you hold an asset after 5 April 1998. It will apply to any net chargeable gains after deducting losses from the current year and losses brought forward from previous years. Taper relief distinguishes between business and non-business assets.

Non-business assets

The percentage of a gain chargeable to tax depends on the number of complete tax years for which you have held the asset after 5 April 1998:

- 3 years   95 per cent

- 4 years   90 per cent

- 5 years   85 per cent

- 6 years   80 per cent

- 7 years   75 per cent

- 8 years   70 per cent

- 9 years   65 per cent

- 10 years   60 per cent.

Non-business assets must be held for three complete tax years before you can claim taper relief. But all non-business assets held on 17 March 1998 have an extra year added to the period which qualifies for taper relief. This means 2000–1 is the first tax year in which you can dispose of non-business assets and claim taper relief, provided you held them on 17 March 1998. You will have held them for the whole of 1998–9 and 1999–2000 and you have a year added on, making three years in total – see Example 7.

EXAMPLE 7

Larry sells his holiday home in May 2000. He made a net gain of £41,700 (see Example 1, p. 234). This was reduced to £1,404 once he'd worked out his indexation allowance (see Example 5, p. 239). He can reduce the gain further with taper relief.

Net chargeable gains, including indexation allowance to April 1998	£1,404
Number of complete tax years asset held after 5 April 1998 plus one extra year because asset was held before 17 March 1998	3 years
Percentage of gain chargeable for non-business assets with qualifying period of 3 years	95 per cent
Net chargeable gain – 95 per cent of £1,404	£1,333.80

Business assets

The percentage of a gain on a business asset chargeable to tax depends on the number of complete tax years for which you have held the asset after 5 April 1998:

- 1 year   87.5 per cent
- 2 years   75 per cent
- 3 years   50 per cent
- 4 years   25 per cent

Business assets must be held for just one complete tax year before you can claim taper relief. The extra year added to non-business assets (see p. 240) does not apply, though it did apply for disposals before 2000–1. Also, the percentages above were also less generous for disposals before 2000–1 (92.5 per cent on first-year disposals).

A business asset is:

- an asset used wholly or partly in a trading business, owned either by you (alone or in partnership) or by an employer for whom you work more or less full-time, *or*
- shares or securities in a qualifying company – defined as either an unlisted trading company or a quoted trading company for

which you work full-time or part-time, or in which you have at least 5 per cent of the voting rights (a less restrictive definition of a qualifying company than before 6 April 2000).

Where an asset had been used partly as a business asset and partly as a non-business asset, the gain will be split pro-rata between business and non-business taper relief – see Example 8.

EXAMPLE 8

Beth buys shares in the company where she works full-time in March 1998. In May 2004, she will sell the entire holding at a gain of £30,000. The shares carry no voting rights.

But in April 2000 the definition of a business asset changes to include these shares.

The company will be a qualifying company for the last four years of the six years Beth owns the shares.

So $\frac{4}{6}$ of the gain – £20,000 – will qualify for six years' worth of business assets taper relief. Only 25 per cent of this part of the gain will be chargeable to tax; 25 per cent of £20,000 is £5,000.

The remaining $\frac{2}{6}$ of the gain – £10,000 – will qualify for six years' worth of non-business assets taper relief. Only 80 per cent of this part of the gain will be chargeable to tax; 80 per cent of £10,000 is £8,000.

The total taxable gain is £13,000 (i.e. £5,000 + £8,000).

How losses and taper relief interact

If you dispose of an asset that qualifies for taper relief, and you have losses, there are two things to bear in mind.

- You can allocate your losses to gains on which you would otherwise pay the largest amount of tax (those for which the least taper relief is available).
- If you have losses brought forward from previous years, you can use as much of them as you need to reduce your gains to the level of the tax-free slice *before* taking taper relief into account.

This means that if you have gains on more than one asset, you need first to work out how much taper relief you are entitled to on each. Then, taking each gain in turn and starting with the one with the least taper relief, deduct enough of your losses to reduce it (before taper relief) to the level of your unused tax-free slice. Keep a running total of how much loss and how much tax-free slice you have used so far, and then go on to the next gain – see Example 9.

Once you have used up all your losses – or once your total remaining gains are reduced to the £7,200 tax-free slice – apply the taper relief due to each remaining gain. Finally, total up all your gains still unrelieved and deduct £7,200 (the tax-free slice).

Any losses still unused can be carried forward to future years but, because taper relief is ignored in working out how much of your losses need to be used, you effectively 'waste' losses by setting them against gains which would be reduced by taper relief anyway. To put it another way, your losses are 'tapered' as well as your gains. There is not much you can do about this, but you can consider planning your disposals so that you make full use of any losses before much taper relief has built up.

EXAMPLE 9

Ammun has decided to become a full-time student and is selling her shop. The business is sold in August 2000, and Ammun's gain from the sale (after indexation) comes to £12,000. This is a business asset that has been owned for two complete tax years since 5 April 1998 so only 75 per cent of the gain will be chargeable.

Ammun also has a non-business gain of £5,000 and losses from previous years of £6,000. Because the non-business gain does not qualify for taper relief, she sets her first £5,000 of the loss against this gain, and the remaining £1,000 of the loss against the business gain.

	non-business gain	business gain
	£5,000	£12,000
less loss carried forward	£5,000	£1,000
chargeable gain after losses	£0	£11,000
percentage chargeable after taper relief	100%	75%
tapered chargeable gain	£0	£8,250

From her remaining gain of £8,250, Ammun deducts the tax-free slice of £7,200, leaving £1,050 taxable in 2000–1.

Gifts

When you give something away, you're usually treated as disposing of it for what it is worth, even though you get nothing for it. So if you buy a picture for £20,000 and give it away a few months later when it's worth £25,000, you'll make a gain of £5,000.

The person who receives the gift is treated as having paid what the property is worth. So, with the gift of the picture, if the person receiving the picture sells it later for £28,000, the gain is £28,000 – £25,000 = £3,000.

Capital gains tax and the family

If you dispose of an asset to a *connected person,* you are treated by the Revenue as disposing of the asset for its market value at the time of the gift. A *connected person* includes your wife or husband *and:*

- a relative – *relative* means brother, sister, parent, grand-parent and other ancestors or lineal descendants (but not uncle, aunt, cousin, nephew or niece)
- the wife or husband of a relative
- your wife or husband's relative
- the trustees of a settlement which you have set up
- a company which you control
- a person with whom you are in partnership or their wife or husband or relative.

So if you don't sell for the proper commercial price, you'll be taxed as if you had, even if you didn't intend to make a gift.

More important still is that if you make a loss on a disposal to a connected person, you can set that loss off only against a gain from another disposal by you to that person. This is the case even though your loss is a proper commercial one – i.e. based on the market value. So if you sell shares at a loss to your son, the loss cannot be used to reduce your general taxable gains for the year. Losses which can be set against only certain types of gain are called *clogged* losses. The restrictions are designed to prevent tax avoidance and they may also apply if losses are transferred to you from a trust.

Gifts between husband and wife
The following applies to gifts between a husband and wife who are not separated.

- Whether or not any money changes hands, there is no tax to pay at the time of the disposal, and there is no gain or loss for tax purposes.
- The recipient gets the giver's initial value plus the giver's allowable expenses, plus any indexation allowance the giver could have claimed.
- Where there has been a transfer between husband and wife and taper relief applies when the asset is finally disposed of, the taper relief will be based on the total period the asset was held by both spouses.

Capital gains tax vs. inheritance tax

There is no capital gains tax to pay on death. This has profound impli-cations on whether you should make gifts in your lifetime, or wait until you die.

- Rates of inheritance tax for gifts made on death are higher than for gifts made more than three years prior to death – see Chapter 15.
- For capital gains tax, there is often a tax liability on gifts made during life.

There is, therefore, often a 'trade-off' between the two taxes. If your estate is likely to be liable for a lot of inheritance tax on death, it may be worth giving now – paying capital gains tax and cutting down inher-itance tax on your death. The alternative is to hang on, avoiding capital gains tax altogether, but risking a higher inheritance tax bill.

- In general, the less well off you are, the better it is to hang on to things until you die.
- Remember that you can pass property gradually from your estate without tax, by making use of the annual tax-free slice for capital gains tax, and by using the exemptions for inheritance tax.
- If you can claim a large indexation allowance and/or taper relief, lots of allowable expenses and, in the case of homes, various periods where the gain is ignored (see Chapter 11), the capital gains tax bill may be little or nothing. It may be worth giving something away before you die.

Capital gains tax and executors
On death, your estate passes to your personal representatives. The Revenue regards them as acquiring the property at its *market value at the date of your death*. The effect is that the value of everything you

own is given a 'free uplift' to its value at the date of death. The beneficiaries of your estate acquire the assets at the market value as from the date of death (this is the probate value).

Allowable losses in the tax year of your death (made before your death) are set off first against your taxable gains for that period. If there are still losses left over they can be set against your taxable gains for the three tax years before the tax year of death, taking later years first (but the losses are needed only to reduce the chargeable gains to the level of the tax-free slice – see Example 6, p. 240). This is the only time when allowable losses can be carried back.

Capital gains tax and your business

Replacing business assets
If you dispose of a *qualifying business asset* and invest an amount equal to the disposal proceeds in another qualifying business asset during the period of one year *before* the disposal or within three years *after* the disposal, you can claim *roll-over relief* on your taxable gain on the disposal of the old asset.

Qualifying assets include:

- land and buildings occupied and used for the purpose of your trade
- plant or machinery which is fixed but which does not actually form part of a building, e.g. heavy engineering equipment bolted to the floor of the workshop
- ships, aircraft and hovercraft – but not vehicles
- goodwill.

How it works
The gain is usually rolled over by reducing (for tax purposes) your acquisition cost for the new asset by the amount of the chargeable gain. So when you dispose of the new asset, its initial value (in working out your gain) is reduced. You can roll over your tax liability again by investing in another qualifying asset.

If you re-invest in a *wasting asset* – i.e. in an asset with a predictable life not exceeding 60 years when you acquire it – your gain is deferred until the earliest of the following:

- you cease to use the new asset for the purposes of the trade
- the tenth anniversary of your acquisition of the new asset
- you dispose of the new asset without re-investing the proceeds

in a new qualifying asset – if you *do* re-invest in a non-wasting asset before selling the old asset, the original gain is rolled over into the new asset, and the deferred gain is cancelled.

Other points
- Any indexation allowance available on the old asset is taken into account in determining the size of the gain rolled over.
- If you have more than one business, the re-investment need not be in the same business as the one in which the old asset was used.
- If the asset you disposed of was used for private purposes as well as business purposes, or if you do not spend an amount equal to the whole of the disposal proceeds on the new asset, only a proportionate part of your taxable gain is deferred.
- You may even be able to claim roll-over relief if you dispose of an asset which you own personally but which is used for the purposes of the trade carried on by your *personal* company if you then purchase a new qualifying asset which is used for the purposes of the trade carried on by the same personal company. A personal company is one in which you own at least 5 per cent of the voting rights. Roll-over relief is available in this situation even if you charge the company a full market rent for the asset.
- The qualifying period for taper relief will be the period that the new asset is owned after 5 April 1998.

Retirement relief
If you are aged 50 or over or have to retire before then due to ill-health, and you dispose of a business (or shares in it), part or all of your gain may be tax-free. This relief is available for any kind of disposal including sale, gift and selling off assets after the business has ceased. You don't actually have to retire to get the relief. You will be able to claim the relief if:

- you are 50 or over, *or*
- you are retiring due to ill-health – in this case, you'll need to satisfy the Revenue that you are incapable of carrying on your work and that your incapacity is likely to be permanent.

The disposal requirements are as follows.

- You must be disposing of the whole or part of a business which you have owned for at least one year in most cases (but see p. 249).

- Alternatively, you must be disposing of shares which you have owned for at least one year (but see p. 249) in a company or a holding company for the business you worked in. To satisfy this condition, you must be entitled to at least 5 per cent of the voting rights *and* you must be a *full-time* working officer or employee of the company or a subsidiary. 'Full-time' generally means that you spend substantially the whole of your working hours in the job.

Relief is also available where trustees dispose of shares or assets in which you have an interest (though not if your interest is only for a fixed period of time).

How much tax relief?

Retirement relief is being phased out. For disposals in the tax year 2003–4 and subsequent years there will be no retirement relief. Instead, business assets taper relief will be applied against gains.

Until 2003–4 you'll be able to get 100 per cent relief on part of your gain and 50 per cent on another chunk as follows:

Year	100% relief on gains up to:	50% relief on the next:
2000–1	£150,000	£450,000
2001–2	£100,000	£300,000
2002–3	£50,000	£150,000

There is no relief on gains in excess of these amounts but taper relief will be available on any qualifying gains which remain after retirement relief has been given. You get the maximum retirement relief if you have owned the business for ten years.

If you have owned the business for less than ten years, you get 10 per cent of the maximum relief for every complete year of ownership. So, in the 2000–1 tax year, if you have owned the business for just one year, gains up to 10 per cent of £150,000 are tax-free, i.e. gains of up to £15,000. And 10 per cent of half the excess up to £450,000 is tax-free, a maximum of 10 per cent of £225,000, ie £22,500. You must have at least one complete year of ownership (but see below) for the period of ownership. After that, you're entitled to relief in proportion to the period. So if you have owned the business for 8 years and 3 months, your relief is 82.5 per cent.

The relief applies to the permanent capital assets of the business – it doesn't apply to the value of trading stock. Similarly, if you dispose of shares, the relief will apply only to the value of the shares that represents chargeable business assets. You don't have to have owned every asset for the whole time that you have owned the business – you can still get the full relief on assets owned for less than ten years if you have owned the business for more than ten years.

You get only one lot of retirement relief, but you need not use it on one disposal – you can claim it bit by bit as you divest yourself of the business. A husband and wife can each claim it, in effect doubling the amount of relief if they each qualify.

Owned several businesses? The last one for under a year?

The period that qualifies for retirement relief can be extended if you have carried on two or more qualifying businesses in succession, provided that the gap between businesses is two years or less. The different periods of business in the ten years before the date for which you want to claim relief can be added together. In this case you can include the last period of business even if it was for less than one year.

EXAMPLE 10

Bill bought a newsagent's shop in March 1995 when he took early retirement. In July 2000, at the age of 65, he sold the shop as a going concern – his chargeable gain was £45,000.

Bill had owned the business for five years and four months (5.3 years), so is entitled to 5.3×10 per cent = 53 per cent of the maximum retirement relief. This means that 53 per cent of the first £150,000 (in 2000–1) of gain can be tax-free – a total of £79,500 tax-free. So Bill's whole gain is tax-free.

Gifts of business assets

You may be able to defer a chargeable gain if you are giving away business assets, agricultural land and gifts which count as chargeable transfers for inheritance tax purposes (see pp. 278, 279 and 263). This is known as gifts hold-over relief.

If you give business assets (or sell them at an undervalue) to an individual, company or trust you can claim hold-over relief as long as the recipient (or shareholder in the case of a company) isn't resident overseas. Shares count as business assets, but since 9 November

1999 you have not been able to claim hold-over relief on gifts of shares to a company.

The relief works in a similar way to roll-over relief (see p. 246). The the gain you make on the disposal is held over and deducted from the acquisition cost of the asset for the recipient. Note that your gain is not adjusted for taper relief and the recipient's taper relief runs only from the date of the gift. If you charged a special low price for the asset but still made some gain, that gain is chargeable. But the rest of the gain is rolled over.

Retirement relief or hold-over relief?

Ideally, you should go for retirement relief, rather than for hold-over relief, because hold-over is only a deferral of tax, not exemption from tax.

If retirement relief is not available, or is insufficient, the general hold-over relief for gifts or the special relief for gifts of business assets can be very useful in passing on your business in your lifetime. But holding over your gain is likely to reduce the other person's acquisition cost and increase his or her gain.

Deferring capital gains tax

Deferral relief allows you to postpone tax on a chargeable gain if you re-invest the gain in venture capital trusts (see p. 215) or shares qualifying under the enterprise investment scheme (see p. 206). You must make the re-investment within one year before or after the disposal of the chargeable gain which you want to defer if re-investing in venture capital trusts: if re-investing in enterprise investment scheme shares, between one year before and three years after. The gain becomes taxable when you finally dispose of the shares (or the venture capital trusts), if they cease to meet the conditions for venture capital trusts or the enterprise investment scheme, or if you cease to be resident in the UK within five years.

When the deferred gain eventually becomes taxable, you get the taper relief applying for the period you owned the original asset. But from 6 April 1999, if you dispose of enterprise investment scheme shares issued after 5 April 1998 and re-invest them in another company within the scheme, the taper relief runs from the time you acquired the first set of shares.

Deferral relief replaces re-investment relief, which could be claimed on some investments made before 6 April 1998.

Shares, unit trusts and open-ended investment companies

The capital gains tax rules for shares and similar investments are straightforward if all the shares you own of a particular type were acquired by you at the same time, and disposed of all together. In this case, you calculate tax in the same way as for any other asset – see Example 11.

Problems begin if you have acquired shares of the same description at different times. When you come to dispose of the shares, special rules decide how much the shares cost you; which shares you've disposed of; and your indexation allowance or taper relief (if any). The rules are explained below. For shares and unit trusts bought through a regular savings plan, see p. 257.

Which shares do you sell?

If you have acquired shares of *the same class in the same company* at different times, the Revenue has special rules for deciding which shares you've disposed of. The rules determine:

- the price you paid for the shares (or their *market value* if you didn't buy them – see below)
- when you acquired the shares
- how much indexation allowance you have, if any.

See p. 254 for how the rules work in practice.

If you did not buy the shares, the market value of the shares listed on the Stock Exchange is the *lower* of:

- the lower of the two quoted prices shown in the Stock Exchange Daily Official List for that day, plus *one-quarter* of the difference between the lower and the higher price
- the average of the highest and lowest recorded prices for normal bargains on the day of valuation.

If you dispose of shares in stages, the Revenue looks at an earlier disposal before a later disposal in seeing which shares you have disposed of.

EXAMPLE 11

Don has a holding of 2,500 £1 ordinary shares and 500 7 per cent £1 preference shares in European Plastics plc. He acquired the ordinary shares for £2,100 in August 1992 and he acquired the preference shares for £250 in May 1981.

In the 2000–1 tax year he disposes of all the ordinary shares for £5,250 and all the preference shares for £360. The gross gain on each disposal, ignoring incidental costs, is:

Ordinary shares	£	Preference shares	£
proceeds	5,250	proceeds	360
less cost	2,100	less cost	250
gross gain	3,150	gross gain	110

In each case, Don is entitled to an indexation allowance to April 1998. The indexation factor for March 1982 (the date from which indexation begins for assets acquired before that date, in this case the shares bought in 1981) is 1.047. For August 1992 it is 0.171.

The indexation allowance is:

Ordinary shares	Preference shares
$0.171 \times £2,100 = £359$	$1.047 \times £250 = £262$
The chargeable gain on the ordinary shares $£3,150 - £359 = £2,791$	The chargeable gain on the preference shares $£110 - £262 = $ minus £152, i.e. there is no chargeable gain

If Don had sold only half of his holdings, his allowable costs for each disposal would have been half the allowable costs shown.

The Revenue will say that you have disposed of the shares in the following order:

Batch 1: acquired on the same day as disposal
If you acquire and dispose of (or vice versa) shares of the same type on the same day, the disposal will be matched to the acquisition made on that day.

Batch 2: acquired within 30 days of disposal
A sale is matched to a purchase if you sell shares and later purchase shares of the same class in the same company within 30 days. The acquisition cost of the later purchase will count as the initial value of the shares you have just sold.

Batch 3: acquired after 5 April 1998
Disposals will be matched with previous acquisitions made after 5 April 1998, taking shares acquired at a later time first (a last-in, first-out basis).

Batch 4: acquired after 5 April 1982 and before 6 April 1998
Shares in this batch are pooled. The cost of each share is the average cost of acquiring the shares in the pool. So if you bought 2,000 shares for £5,000, 2,000 for £6,000 and 2,000 for £7,000, the average is £18,000 ÷ 6,000 = £3 a share. You have a separate pool for each type of share you hold in a company. The total acquisition costs of pooled shares are treated as expenditure on a single asset.

Batch 5: acquired after 5 April 1965 and before 6 April 1982
If you bought several lots of the same share at different times they are put into the 1982 pool. The cost of each share is its market value on 31 March 1982 (or the original cost if this is to your advantage and you have not made the rebasing election – see p. 237). Indexation runs from March 1982 until April 1998.

Batch 6: acquired before 6 April 1965
The Revenue will match the shares you dispose of with shares bought later rather than earlier – see p. 259 for how they are valued. However, you can elect for all such shares to be treated as if they had been acquired on 6 April 1965 and pooled with your Batch 5 shares instead. In most cases, this will not only greatly simplify the calculations, but will also mean you pay less tax – tell your tax inspector within two years of the end of the first tax year after 5 April 1985 in which you dispose of such shares.

Rights and bonus issues

Shares you get under a rights or bonus issue are not treated as an acquisition. They belong to the same batch as the original shares to which they relate.

Rights issues give you the right to buy new shares in proportion to your existing shareholding. When you come to sell shares, you take the cost of the original shareholding *plus* the cost of the rights issue, apply the index-linking rules to them separately, divide by the number of shares in the whole shareholding and multiply by the number of shares you've sold. This is your acquisition cost for the shares you've sold.

Bonus issues give you free shares to tack on to existing shares. Your acquisition cost (or your pool cost) will be affected – for example if you buy 2,500 shares for £5,000, and get a bonus of 1,500 shares, your cost per share falls from £2 to £1.25. This adjusted cost is indexed from the same day as the original shareholding was indexed.

A company may give you shares in the form of a *scrip* or *stock dividend*. They are treated in the same way as a rights issue if they were issued before 6 April 1998. Indexation runs from the month the dividend was payable. Scrip dividends issued on or after 6 April 1998 are treated as a separate acquisition. In both cases, the initial value of the shares is the cash amount shown in your dividend voucher.

An example of shareholding

Sue built up a holding of Worldwide Pharmaceuticals 50p ordinary shares between 1972 and 1998, and they can be batched as follows.

date	number of shares	cost
Shares acquired after 5 April 1965 and before 6 April 1982		
4 September 1972	1,000	£850

Shares acquired after 5 April 1982 and before 6 April 1998

26 November 1982	2,500	£2,350
16 July 1985	3,250	£5,000
total number of shares	5,750	

Shares acquired after 5 April 1998

30 May 1998	1,000	£925

Sue sold some of her shares – one lot in June 1987, one lot in May 2000:

date	number of shares	sold for
25 June 1987	2,000	£4,500
19 May 2000	5,000	£15,400

The June 1987 sale

The shares sold in 1987 came from Sue's batch of shares acquired after 5 April 1982 and before 6 April 1998, acquired in two lots. The cost price was increased by indexation to the date of the sale in June 1987.

Indexing shares costing £2,350 on 26 November 1982 (indexation factor = 0.233)

$$0.233 \times £2,350 = £548 \quad £548 + £2,350 = \textbf{£2,898}$$

Indexing shares costing £5,000 on 16 July 1985 (indexation factor = 0.070)

$$0.070 \times £5,000 = £350 \quad £350 + £5,000 = \textbf{£5,350}$$

The cost price including indexation to June 1987 of these two lots of shares was

$$£2,898 + £5,350 = \textbf{£8,248}$$

There were 5,750 shares in this post-April 1982 batch. 2,000 shares were sold in June 1987. The remaining 3,750 had a cost price in June 1987 of

$$£8,248 \times \frac{3,750}{5,750} = £5,380$$

The May 2000 sale

5,000 shares were sold for £15,400 in May 1999. The shares are first matched with the 1,000 bought after 5 April 1998 for £925. These do not qualify for indexation allowance nor, since they are personal assets held for less than three years, is there any taper relief. The initial value is therefore just £925, and the sale proceeds are:

$$£15,400 \times \frac{1,000}{5,000} = £3,080$$

The chargeable gain, after deducting the cost, is £3,080 – £925 = **£2,155**.

The next 3,750 shares came from what remained of the post-April 1982 batch. The cost price of these shares was £5,380 in June 1987. This figure can be indexed to April 1998. The indexation factor is 0.596

$$0.596 \times £5,380 = £3,207 \qquad £3,207 + £5,380 = \textbf{£8,587}$$

So £8,587 is the cost price in May 2000.

The sale proceeds of those shares is a proportion of £15,400:

$$£15,400 \times \frac{3,750}{5,000} = \textbf{£11,550}$$

So the chargeable gain on 3,750 shares is £11,550 – £8,587 = **£2,963**. However, the shares were owned before 17 March 1998. Three years' taper relief applies and only 95 per cent of the gain is taxable:

$$£2,963 \times 95 \text{ per cent} = \textbf{£2,814}.$$

The remaining 250 shares sold in May 2000 come from the 'shares acquired after 5 April 1965 and before 6 April 1982' batch.

There were 1,000 shares in this batch. Their initial value was £850 if the actual cost is used. But Sue has the option of using the market value on 31 March 1982. Worldwide Pharmaceuticals shares were then valued at 92p, so 1,000 shares were worth £920. Sue decides to use the 1982 value. A higher initial value means a lower capital gain.

£920 can be indexed from March 1982 to April 1998 (there is no indexation before March 1982). The indexation factor is 1.047.

$$1.047 \times £920 = £964 \qquad £920 + £964 = \textbf{£1,884}$$

The indexed cost of the 250 shares sold is

$$£1,884 \times \frac{250}{1,000} = \textbf{£471}$$

The sale proceeds of those 250 shares is a proportion of £15,400:

$$£15,400 \times \frac{250}{5,000} = \textbf{£770}$$

So the chargeable gain on those 250 shares is £770 – £471 = **£299**. Again, three years' taper relief applies and only 95 per cent of the gain is taxable:

$$£299 \times 95 \text{ per cent} = \textbf{£284}.$$

The total chargeable gain on the May 2000 sale is £2,155 + £2,814 + £284 = **£5,253**

For Sue's records, she still has 1,000 – 250 = 750 shares in her 1982 batch. Their indexed cost is:

$$£1,884 + \frac{750}{1,000} = £1,413$$

Because there is no further indexation to take account of, this figure can be used when calculating the cost of subsequent disposals from this pool.

Regular savings plans

With monthly savings plans of unit and investment trusts and open-ended investment companies (OEICs), working out your gains and losses could be very complicated. You would have to work out the gain and indexation allowance for each instalment when making a disposal.

The calculations are simpler with taper relief, since this works on the basis of whole years. To work out the relief, you can treat all the shares or units of one type bought in one year as a single purchase. But if you started to invest regular monthly sums in a unit trust, investment trust or OEIC before 6 April 1998, you can opt for a simplified way of working out the initial costs and indexation allowance. This simplified method applies only to monthly sums invested during the accounting year of the fund which ended before 6 April 1999: after that period you work out the taper relief in the normal way.

The simplified method assumes that all 12 monthly instalments plus small one-off investments or re-invested income, less small with-drawals, are made in the seventh month of the accounting year of the fund. Indexation will run from the seventh month.

Special rules will apply if:

* you added a one-off lump sum of more than twice the monthly instalment in any month (this is treated as a separate investment)

- you increased the monthly instalments after the seventh month (the extra is added to next year's fund)
- you withdrew more than a quarter of the amount invested in the year by regular instalments (you will have to calculate the gain and indexation allowance on each investment).

To opt for this simplified method, you must write to your tax office within two years of 31 January in the first tax year in which you are legally required to complete the capital gains tax supplementary pages of the self-assessment tax return.

Payment by instalments

Newly issued shares are often paid for by instalments. With a privatisation issue, indexation allowance on the total paid runs from the date you acquire the shares. With other share issues, indexation allowance depends on when the instalments are paid:

- if paid within 12 months of when the shares were acquired, indexation allowance on the instalments runs from when the shares were acquired
- if paid more than 12 months after the shares were acquired, indexation allowance runs from when the payments were made.

Takeovers, mergers and reconstructions

If you exchange your existing shares for new shares on a takeover or merger, or if the company is being reconstructed, the exchange will not normally give rise to a disposal. As far as *time of acquisition* and *cost* are concerned, the new shares will be in the position of the old.

But if you exchange your old shares for new shares and cash, you are taken to have disposed of a proportion of your old shares. The gain or loss which you make on the disposal is a proportion of the gain or loss you would have made if you had disposed of the shares entirely for cash. That proportion is the percentage of the exchange represented by cash. So if the exchange is one-quarter cash, three-quarters new shares, your gain or loss will be one-quarter what it would have been if you had taken all cash.

However, you need do this only if the cash you receive is £3,000 or more or if it is more than 5 per cent of the value of the shares in the original company. If the cash is below these limits you simply reduce the allowable cost of the shares by the amount of cash.

Quoted shares acquired before 6 April 1965

The Revenue assumes that these shares were disposed of by you on 6 April 1965 and immediately re-acquired by you for what they were worth on that date. The normal rule for calculating the market value of quoted shares (see p. 237) is *not* used. Instead, the Revenue uses the greater of:

- the average of the highest and lowest prices shown in the Stock Exchange Daily Official list that day (excluding bargains at special prices)
- the price halfway between the highest and lowest prices at which bargains were recorded on that day.

These shares are *not* pooled with shares of the same type which you acquired after 5 April 1965 unless you have chosen this option. Instead, your chargeable gain (or loss) on a disposal of the shares is the difference between market value at 6 April 1965 and the disposal proceeds (less any indexation allowance).

This calculation is then compared with the 'truth' – i.e. the Revenue sees whether you would have made a gain, or a loss, using the initial value of the shares when you first acquired them (in most cases, what you actually paid for them).

If the first calculation would have the effect of increasing a real loss (or gain), the Revenue takes the actual loss (or gain) instead.

If one calculation shows a gain, and the other shows a loss, you are treated as having made neither a gain nor a loss for tax purposes.

Note that if you have made the 'rebasing election' for assets owned before 31 March 1982 (see p. 237) this will also apply to any shares held in April 1965.

Insurance proceeds

If you receive insurance proceeds for damage to, or the loss of, an asset, you may have to pay capital gains tax, unless the proceeds of disposal of that asset are tax-free. So if you receive insurance money in compensation for theft of your jewellery, you may have a tax liability – but not if you get insurance money when your main home burns down.

However, the proceeds are not taxable if they are £3,000 or less, or if no more than 5 per cent of the value of the asset. The proceeds are deducted from your allowable costs for the asset when you finally dispose of it. There is also no liability on the proceeds if you spend them in restoring or (generally within one year of the loss) replacing the asset. The rules work like this.

For restorations:

- the proceeds are deducted from your allowable costs for the asset
- if you spend the money on restoring or replacing the asset, and if this is an allowable expense for capital gains tax (it normally is), the figures balance – i.e. what you spend is added back to your allowable expenses.

For replacements:

- the proceeds are deemed to be equal to your allowable costs for the original asset including any indexation allowance
- any excess of the proceeds (plus any remaining value in the original asset) is deducted from the allowable cost of the replacement asset.

There may be difficulty where insurance proceeds are spent restoring a damaged item which was badly in need of repair at the time of the damage, since part of the expense will be for repair (not allowable) rather than for restoration (allowable). You also have to be a little careful about what constitutes replacement: if you 'replace' your stolen necklace with a watercolour, the Revenue is unlikely to be co-operative.

Overseas

If you are domiciled in the UK (see Chapter 7), capital gains tax applies to gains you make anywhere in the world – i.e. overseas as well as in the UK. If the gains cannot be remitted to the UK (because of exchange or currency controls operated by the country the gain is made in), you can ask the Revenue to defer bringing them into the tax net until they can be remitted.

If you are living abroad, the tax still applies to you for any tax year in which you are *resident* or *ordinarily resident* in the UK (see Chapter 7) – even if only for part of that tax year and even if you are temporarily non-resident. If you are not domiciled in the UK, gains made abroad are liable to tax only if remitted to the UK.

Useful Inland Revenue reading

You can ring the Inland Revenue Orderline* for helpsheets, leaflets and notes.

Leaflets and notes

CGT1	Capital gains tax – an introduction
IR45	What to do when someone dies
SA152	Tax calculation guide – capital gains
SVD1	Shares Valuation Division. An introduction

Helpsheets

When you receive a helpsheet, make sure it relates to the tax year for which you want information.

IR284	Shares and capital gains tax
IR287	Employee share schemes and capital gains tax
IR291	Reinvestment relief
IR297	Enterprise investment scheme and capital gains tax
IR298	Venture capital trusts and capital gains tax
IR285	Share re-organisations, company take-overs and capital gains tax
IR286	Income tax losses for shares you have subscribed for in unlisted trading companies
IR283	Private residence relief (capital gains)
IR289	Retirement relief and capital gains tax
IR290	Business asset roll-over relief
IR280	Rebasing – assets held at 31 March 1982
IR281	Husband and wife, divorce and separation
IR282	Death personal representatives and legatees
IR288	Partnerships and capital gains tax
IR292	Land and leases – the valuation of land and capital gains tax
IR293	Chattels and capital gains tax
IR294	Trusts and capital gains tax
IR295	Relief for gifts and similar transactions
IR296	Debts and capital gains tax
IR301	Capital gains on benefits from non-resident and dual resident trusts
IR278	Temporary non-residents and capital gains tax

Inheritance tax

When you come to pass your money on – whether as a gift in your lifetime or as a legacy when you die – there could be an inheritance tax bill. And this can be the case even if you don't think of yourself as being rich. This chapter explains the basic rules, and tells you how to work out an inheritance tax bill. It explains the straightforward ways of saving tax and gives an introduction to more complex schemes, including the use of trusts.

Inheritance tax is levied on what you leave on death (your estate) and on some gifts you make in your lifetime, especially if you die within seven years of making them.

Gifts in your lifetime

There are three types of gifts you can make during your lifetime.

- **Tax-free gifts** (also known as *exempt transfers*). This includes gifts between husband and wife, gifts to charity and small gifts of up to £250 a year to anyone else – see p. 271 for a full list of tax-free gifts.
- **Gifts which may become taxable** (also known as *potentially exempt transfers*). These are tax-free at the time you make them but become chargeable if you die within seven years of making them. The tax is collected after your death. This includes gifts to people (such as gifts to children) and gifts to some types of trust.
- **Chargeable gifts** (also known as *chargeable transfers*) are gifts on which tax may be due at the time of the gift – i.e. while you are still alive. Chargeable transfers are largely gifts to companies and certain types of discretionary trust.

It's only with a very narrow range of gifts that you might have to pay tax in your lifetime. If you're not involved with trusts or companies, you can miss out the next section and go straight to *What happens when you die* (see below).

Tax on chargeable lifetime gifts

If you make a gift which is liable to inheritance tax in your lifetime, you begin to clock up a *running total* of chargeable gifts. The tax bill depends on the amount of your running total of chargeable gifts over the most recent seven years. The rates for the 2000–1 tax year are as follows:

Running total	Rate of tax
£0–£234,000	nil
over £234,000	20 per cent of the excess over £234,000

When you make your first chargeable gift, there will be no tax to pay if it falls in the nil-rate band. If it is more than the amount of the nil-rate band, then tax is due on the excess at 20 per cent. When you make your next chargeable gift, it is added to the first, and if the running total is more than the nil-rate band, tax is due on the excess.

Further chargeable gifts will be added to your running total to see if tax is due on them. But any chargeable gifts made more than seven years before drop off the running total.

A voluntary tax?
Don't be misled. Careful planning can greatly reduce – or even wipe out – any liability to the tax. No planning at all can mean a heavy bill. But if you don't plan, you will be no worse off yourself. It just means that there's less for your heirs. So don't gamble with your own financial security just to save tax for others.

Domicile
We're assuming that everyone who reads this is domiciled in the UK. Your domicile is, broadly, the country where you've chosen to end your days. It can be quite different from the country where you're living – though if you've been resident in the UK for 17 out of the last 20 tax years you'll have UK domicile (as far as inheritance tax goes). If you're not domiciled in the UK, rules are different. For example, if you *are* domiciled in the UK, gifts to a non-UK-domiciled spouse are exempt only up to £55,000.

How large is the gift?

Tax is charged on the *loss to the giver,* not on the gain to the recipient of a gift. With chargeable gifts, it's normally the giver who pays the tax at the time of the gift, so the tax paid is part of the gift. This means that the tax bill is worked out on the *grossed-up* value: the amount which after deduction of tax would leave you with the amount you actually hand over.

Suppose, for example, you gave £80,000 in a chargeable gift, and your running total meant that the whole gift was liable to tax at 20 per cent. To give £80,000 after deduction of 20 per cent inheritance tax, you'd have to give a grossed-up gift of £100,000 – making a tax bill of £20,000 (20 per cent of the £100,000 grossed-up value).

If the receiver of the gift agrees to pay the tax, then the gift does not have to be grossed up. The gross gift would be £80,000 and 20 per cent tax would be £16,000.

EXAMPLE 1

Marion regularly uses up her £3,000 tax-free gift each year (see p. 274). In addition, she gave £100,000 to a discretionary trust in March 1997, with a further £175,000 in June 2000. The gifts were not tax-free and count as chargeable gifts. The trustees agreed to pay the tax, so there is no need to gross-up the value of the gifts. Marion had made no chargeable gifts in the seven years before March 1997.

Until the March 1997 gift, Marion's running total was nil: the £100,000 gift in March 1997 gave her a running total of £100,000. However, this was within the nil-rate band for the 1996–7 tax year and so no tax was due on this gift.

When Marion made the second gift of £175,000 in June 2000, her running total rose to £100,000 + £175,000 = £275,000. This is over the top of the nil-rate band for the 2000–1 tax year of £234,000, so tax is paid on the excess:

$$£275,000 - £234,000 = £41,000$$
$$\text{tax at 20 per cent of £41,000} = £8,200$$

Any further gifts Marion makes to the trust in the next few years would be added to the £275,000 running total, and taxed at the rates in force at the time of the gift. Seven years after the March 1997 gift – in March 2004 – the £100,000 would drop out of the running total.

What happens when you die

On your death, the whole of your estate – roughly speaking, what you own when you die – is treated as your final gift. It is added to a running total of gifts (other than tax-free ones) you have made over the previous seven years. Inheritance tax will be due if the total exceeds your nil-rate band. In addition, there may be extra tax to pay on chargeable gifts (see p. 266) and on other gifts you made during the seven years before your death. Your running total at death comprises:

- all property you owned at the time of death
- the proceeds of any insurance policies paid into your estate (but not policies *in trust* to your dependants)
- any potentially exempt gifts made in the seven years before death (they are reassessed as chargeable gifts)
- any chargeable gifts made in the seven years before death
  less
- debts (e.g. an outstanding mortgage), though the amount deducted may be restricted if the debts arise from gifts you made previously
- reasonable funeral expenses (including the cost of a headstone).

Tax on death
Some of the bequests in your will may be tax-free, for example those to your spouse or to charity (see p. 271 for a list). If there is no will, what you have left will be distributed according to the rules of intestacy, and again some of the resulting transfers may be tax-free.

The value of the tax-free gifts is deducted from your estate to give its chargeable value. The tax depends on the total chargeable value – the rates for the 2000–1 tax year are as follows:

Running total	Rate of tax
£0–£234,000	nil
over £234,000	40 per cent of the excess over £234,000

So if your running total including the value of the estate is less than the amount of the nil-rate band (£234,000 in 2000–1), there is no tax to pay. If the total is more than the nil-rate band, tax is due at 40 per cent of the excess only.

Tax due on the estate may be paid either by the estate or by your heirs depending on the types of bequest which you make. You can specify that a bequest is *subject to tax*, in which case it is treated as a gross gift out of which the recipient must pay the tax due. More commonly, bequests will be *free-of-tax* (not to be confused with tax-free gifts). In this case the recipient gets the amount you specify and tax on its grossed-up value is paid from the remaining estate. The apportioning of the overall tax bill on the whole estate to the various bequests can be complicated.

EXAMPLE 2

Gerald dies leaving an estate worth £300,000. His will donates £5,000 to charity, makes bequests of £5,000 each to his son and daughter, and leaves the rest to his wife. He has made no other gifts while alive.

Bequests to charity and spouses are tax-free gifts. Only the two gifts to his children are chargeable, and at £10,000 they are well within the nil-rate band. No tax is due on his estate.

Is tax now due on lifetime gifts?

Chargeable gifts and potentially exempt gifts made during the seven years before death are reassessed when you die, and there may be tax to pay on them. In the first instance, any tax due is payable by the person who received the gift, but your estate will be billed if they are unwilling or unable to pay. You can specify in your will that tax which becomes payable on lifetime gifts will be paid by your estate.

To work out how much tax is due from each person, you must work out the tax on each gift as it is added to the running seven-year total at the time the gift was originally made (i.e. possibly taking into account gifts made up to 14 years before your death but only if you made gifts more than seven years before your death which were chargeable while you were alive – see p. 263). But you use the tax bands and rates which apply at the time of death. Any tax which was paid on chargeable lifetime gifts when they were made is deducted from the recipient's new tax bill; but there's no refund if the new bill comes to less.

Gifts which become chargeable on your death will use up part of your nil-rate band (if it has not already been used up by gifts chargeable while you are alive). There will be no tax on gifts that become chargeable on death if they are covered by the nil-rate band, but they may push more of your estate over the nil-rate band.

EXAMPLE 3

Alison dies in September 2000 leaving her whole estate of £200,000 to charity. In December 1998 she made a large gift of £400,000 to her son. No tax was payable at the time. The gift became chargeable only if Alison died within seven years of making it – and she did. It is reassessed as a chargeable gift on her death.

She made no gifts in the seven years before December 1998 except small amounts which used up her £3,000 annual exemption each year, so her running total after making the gift was £400,000. This is more than the nil-rate band at death of £234,000. Tax is worked out as follows.

- There is no tax on the part of the gift which falls within the nil-rate band, in other words the first £234,000.
- The taxable part of the gift is the excess over the nil-rate band, which is £400,000 – £234,000 = £166,000.
- Tax is due on £166,000 at 40 per cent. This comes to £66,400. Alison's son agrees to pay the tax.

Alison is leaving her estate to charity. This is a tax-free gift, so there is no tax on her estate.

Gifts more than three years before death

If tax becomes payable on gifts made more than three years before death, it is reduced on the sliding scale below. If there is no tax on the gift – for example because it falls within the nil-rate band – the question of reducing the tax does not arise. And there is never any reduction in the tax on the estate itself. The fact that an estate

Years between gift and death	Percentage of the 40 per cent rate payable	Bill for each taxable £1,000
Up to 3 years	100	£400
More than 3 but not more than 4	80	£320
More than 4 but not more than 5	60	£240
More than 5 but not more than 6	40	£160
More than 6 but not more than 7	20	£80
More than 7	tax-free	tax-free

becomes taxable solely as a result of the running total of gifts made in the seven years before death is irrelevant.

EXAMPLE 4

When Susan, a widow, died in July 2000 she left £10,000 to charity and the remaining £290,000 of her estate to be divided between her two children.

Susan had made one gift of £179,000 in February 1994. It was not chargeable at the time she made it. That gift is now reassessed as a chargeable gift. Susan had not used her £3,000 annual exemption (see p. 274) in 1993–4, so the chargeable amount now is £176,000.

This uses up part of the nil-rate band of £234,000 but £58,000 (£234,000 − £176,000) remains to be set against the estate on death.

Turning to the estate, the £10,000 bequest to charity is tax-free, but the £290,000 left to Susan's children is not. Tax is worked out as follows:

- the first £58,000 falls within the nil-rate band and is not taxed
- £232,000 (£290,000 − £58,000) is taxed at 40 per cent: 40 per cent of £232,000 is £92,800.

After deducting the £92,800 tax from £290,000, the children are left with £197,200. This is divided equally between them. They each get £98,600.

EXAMPLE 5

Roger gave his son John £120,000 in June 1997, his daughter Margaret £120,000 in July 1997, and his youngest child Brian £120,000 in March 1998. He died in May 2000, leaving £180,000 to be divided between the three children.

The gifts made in 1997 and 1998 were initially exempt from the tax, but Roger died within seven years of making them. They are reassessed as chargeable gifts and so count towards the running total of gifts in the seven years up to death. Roger had already used his £3,000 annual exemption for gifts in 1997 and 1998, so the full amount of all three gifts is chargeable.

The whole of the estate, £180,000, represents Roger's final gift. The running total of gifts is £540,000, i.e. £120,000 + £120,000 + £120,000 + £180,000. The first two gifts in 1997 together come to £240,000 – i.e. more than the nil-rate band of £234,000 available in the tax year in which Roger dies. Anything over £234,000 is taxable. So the whole of the £180,000 estate is taxable at the death rate of 40 per cent. The tax bill on the £180,000 is £72,000 (40 per cent of £180,000).

After paying the tax, the estate is worth £108,000 (£180,000 – £72,000). The children each get one-third of this – i.e. £36,000.

Some tax will be due on the earlier gifts – see Example 6.

EXAMPLE 6

The gifts to Roger's children (see Example 5) during his lifetime were reassessed as chargeable gifts when he died.This has two effects: it increases the running total affecting the tax due on the estate, and tax becomes due on the gifts themselves, as follows:

1 The first gift was £120,000 to John. Since there were no previous gifts, this creates a running total of £120,000. This is within the nil-rate band of £234,000, so no tax is due.

2 The next gift was £120,000 to Margaret. This is added to the running total of £120,000 to give a new cumulative total of £240,000. That is £6,000 over the nil-rate band: 40 per cent tax on £6,000 is £2,400. So Margaret will have to pay £2,400 tax.

3 The next gift was £120,000 to Brian. This is added to the running total of £240,000 to give a cumulative total of £360,000, £126,000 over the nil-rate band. The whole of the gift to Brian is therefore taxable. His tax is £48,000 (40 per cent of £120,000).

The gifts of £120,000 to each of the three children end up being worth very different amounts:

- John paid no tax on his, so it's worth the full £120,000
- Margaret paid £2,400 on hers, so it ends up worth £117,600
- Brian paid £48,000, so his gift is worth just £72,000.

The children could have taken out a special life insurance policy to pay out enough to cover the tax if Roger died within seven years of making the gifts. Alternatively, Roger could have made provision in his will for tax on the lifetime gifts to come from his estate.

EXAMPLE 7

Harry gave his son a gift of £250,000 four-and-a-half years before he died (having already used up his £3,000 annual tax-free allowance). Harry left all of his estate to his wife, so there was no tax to pay on it. But the gift to his son became chargeable because Harry died within seven years of making it.

Harry had made no other gifts in the seven years before the gift of £250,000 – i.e. there was no running total of gifts. The tax on the £250,000 was (at 2000–1 rates) worked out as follows:

- the first £234,000 isn't taxed
- £16,000 (£250,000 – £234,000) is taxed at 40 per cent: 40 per cent of £16,000 = £6,400.

However, the gift was made more than three years before Harry died, so the tax bill of £6,400 is reduced on the sliding scale. Only 60 per cent of the tax is payable, as the gift was made more than four but not more than than five years before Harry's death. So the tax is 60 per cent of £6,400, i.e. £3,840.

When is a gift made?

It's usually easy to decide when a gift is made. For example, if you give your son £100,000 by cheque, it will be the date on which the cheque is cleared by your bank and your account is debited.

If you make a gift with some strings attached (known as a *gift with reservation*) the gift will not be made for tax purposes until it becomes a completely free gift (i.e. the benefit ceases to be reserved). For example, if you gave your home to your son but continued to live there, you would have made a gift with *reservation of benefit*. If you were still living there on your death the house would be counted as part of your estate, even though it would actually belong to your son. You could avoid the problem if you paid your son a full market rent for the property, but this might not be sensible if your son had to pay tax on the rent.

In a tax-case (Ingram v. Inland Revenue Commissioners) completed in 1998, the courts ruled that a scheme that enabled someone to give away the freehold of their home but to continue living there rent-free under a lease (called a 'lease carve out' scheme) did not count as a gift with reservation. However, the government subsequently closed this loophole in the law.

Where you give away land on or after 9 March 1999, it will count as a gift with reservation if you or your husband or wife have a significant right or interest, or are party to an arrangement, relating to that land and as a result can occupy the land or have some other rights over it.

The rules for gifts with reservation of benefit apply only to gifts made after 17 March 1986, so a gift made before then is unaffected. The rules are complicated: if you are considering a gift with a possible reservation of benefit, get professional advice.

Tax-free gifts

Tax-free gifts are ignored by the Revenue. If a gift is tax-free:

- there's no tax to pay on it, by you or by anyone else
- the gift isn't added to your running total, so it doesn't eat up your nil-rate band.

If you're going to make gifts, it's clearly sensible to use the opportunities you have to make tax-free gifts. They fall into three categories:

- gifts which are tax-free whenever they are made – i.e. regardless of whether they're made during life or on death
- gifts which are tax-free only if made on death
- gifts which are tax-free only if made during life.

Gifts tax-free whenever they are made
- Gifts between husband and wife of any amount. These can be in cash, property, or anything else. There's no limit at all – even if you're separated. Once you're divorced, only maintenance for your ex-spouse or children, transfers made under the divorce settlement and, in some cases, money transferred following a change to an agreement you made on or before your divorce are tax-free – get advice. (But you can still make gifts which would in any case be tax-free – see p. 272.) If the person who receives the gift isn't domiciled in the UK but the donor is, a gift above a total of £55,000 will count as a potentially exempt gift – i.e. it could become chargeable if you die within seven years of making the gift.
- Gifts to UK charities of any amount. Special anti-avoidance rules can apply if you give part of a property (e.g. a share in land or a business) to a charity and keep the rest yourself.
- Gifts of any amount to British political parties.

- Gifts of any amount to certain public institutions, e.g. the National Gallery, the British Museum, the Victoria and Albert Museum, local authorities and universities.
- Gifts of *heritage property* – provided the Treasury agrees, the property is kept permanently within the UK, and an agreement is reached giving the public reasonable access to the property. Heritage property is outstanding land or buildings, and books, manuscripts or works of art of special interest. For transfers on or after 17 March 1998 a claim to have a gift treated as heritage property must be made within two years of the gift being made (or death, if the gift was originally potentially tax-free but has been reassessed as a chargeable gift).
- Gifts of land in the UK made to registered housing associations after 13 March 1989.
- Gifts of shares or securities to a trust for the benefit of all or most of the employees of a company, provided that the trustees hold more than half of the ordinary shares in the company and have voting control.

Gifts tax-free on death only
- The estate of a person whose death was caused or hastened by active military service in war or of a warlike nature. This would include the estates of servicemen killed in Northern Ireland. It can also include people wounded in earlier conflicts who die earlier than they otherwise would have done.
- A lump sum paid under an employer's pension to your dependants if you die before reaching retirement age, provided the trustees have discretion as to who gets the money (they usually do). Because they have discretion, the lump sum never forms part of your estate, so there's no gift for tax purposes. Within set limits you can say who you want to get the money, and your wishes will normally be respected. The total lump sum can be up to four times your salary at the time of your death together with a return of your contributions to the pension.
- A lump sum paid to your dependants on your death at the discretion of the trustees of your personal pension.

Gifts tax-free in life only
The following gifts are tax-free in your lifetime. But if you exceed the limits (for example give more as a wedding gift than the tax-free limit – see below), that doesn't mean you have to pay any tax when you make the gift. It will become chargeable only if you die within seven years.

- Wedding gifts. Each parent of the bride or groom can give up to £5,000 tax-free (it doesn't have to be to their own child). A gift by either the bride or the groom to the other in anticipation of the marriage is tax-free up to £2,500, though once they are married they can normally make tax-free gifts of any amount to each other. A grandparent or more distant ancestor can give up to £2,500 tax-free. Anyone else can give up to £1,000. Gifts don't need to be in cash. Strictly speaking, wedding gifts have to be made *in consideration of the marriage,* and *conditionally on the marriage taking place.*
- Gifts up to any amount made as normal expenditure out of income. This allows you to give money away year after year without a tax liability. The gifts must be part of a pattern, though not necessarily to the same person each time. If your giving has just begun, the first gift will be covered by the exemption if it's clear a pattern of gifts will follow, e.g. you start to pay regular premiums on a life insurance policy for someone's benefit. Gifts must come out of income, so anything other than cash won't usually be covered. (Note that part of some annuity payments is return of capital, and does not count as income.) Your gifts must leave you with sufficient income to maintain your normal standard of living. If you resort to capital, e.g. sell shares, in order to live in your usual way, you will lose the exemption unless you make up the lost capital out of income in a later year. In practice, the Revenue will usually accept without question that cash gifts up to £3,000 a year qualify for this exemption.
- After divorce, transfers of property to an ex-husband (or ex-wife) will usually be exempt from tax. This is because there won't usually be any *donative intent* – i.e. any intention to make a gift. In other words, the transfer is made as part of the divorce settlement.
- Gifts for the maintenance of your family. A gift for the maintenance of your spouse or ex-spouse is tax-free. So is a gift for the maintenance of a child of one or both of you (including an adopted child) if the child is under 18 or is still in full-time education or training. The exemption also covers gifts for the maintenance of a child you have been taking care of for some time in place of either of his or her parents.
- Gifts to meet the regular needs of a relative of either you or your spouse are tax-free if the relative is unable to support himself or herself owing to age or infirmity. Gifts to your mother or mother-in-law are covered even if she is able to support herself, provided she is widowed, separated or divorced.

- Small gifts. You can give an unlimited number of people gifts of up to £250 (each) a year. You won't need to use this exemption if the gift is tax-free for another reason. If you give more than £250 to anyone, the exemption (for that person) is lost *even for the first £250*.
- Any gifts of up to £3,000 in a single tax year which aren't tax-free for any other reason. These gifts don't have to be in cash. If you don't use up the exemption in one year, you can use the rest of it in the following year, provided you've used up that year's exemption first. Any part of the £3,000 still unused at the end of the following year is lost – i.e. it can't be carried any further forward.

EXAMPLE 8

In the 1999–2000 tax year, Simon used up £1,000 of his £3,000 exemption. In the 2000–1 tax year, he makes gifts of £4,500 which aren't tax-free for any other reason. The Revenue will say that the first £3,000 (of the £4,500) came out of the 2000–1 allowance. The other £1,500 of the gift comes out of the unused 1999–2000 allowance. But the remaining £500 unused allowance from 1999–2000 can't be carried forward to 2001–2.

Valuing a gift

The next few pages deal with how to value (for inheritance tax purposes) something which is given away. This is the first step in working out the tax on a gift. Remember that it's the loss to the giver, not the gain to the recipient, which counts. Also bear in mind that it's the value of the gift at the date it's made on which tax will be charged if you do not survive seven years. If you are going to make a gift of land, antiques, paintings, a business, or unquoted shares or securities, get a professional valuation first. It's useful evidence when you're negotiating a value with the Revenue and you're less likely to get an unexpectedly high tax bill.

If property counts as *business property* or *agricultural property* there are special rules for valuing it which can reduce the tax – see p. 278.

'Market value'
In the normal case, *value* equals *open market value*. This means that the value of an asset is taken to be the price that it would fetch if it were sold in the open market at the time of the gift.

For gifts of money, there's no problem. The value of the asset is the amount of money. For a gift of a car or furniture, the value is what you could expect to have sold it for. (So when you're valuing an estate on death, you should use the *second-hand* value of furniture, fridges, etc.)

The rest of this section deals with exceptions to the normal rule.

Value of property on death
The Revenue assumes that any piece of property, for example land, or a holding of shares, is sold in one lump. So it won't speculate as to whether your property could have been broken up for sale in parts to get a higher or a lower price, unless the division would have been a natural and easy thing to do.

No account is taken of the difficulty (or impossibility) of putting the property on the market at one time. The Revenue will assume that there's a ready market, and that the sale itself would not affect the market value. This can cause severe problems where shares in a private company are involved: the value, for tax purposes, can be higher than the price you could get.

Joint interest in land
If you have a joint interest in land, for example you're a co-owner of a house, the starting point is to take the open market value of the land as a whole, and allocate to you your share of that value. Your share is then discounted (i.e. reduced in value for inheritance tax valuation purposes – by 15 per cent, say, to reflect the lack of demand for property without vacant possession).

Unit trusts
Units in a unit trust scheme authorised under the financial services regulations are valued at the manager's buying ('bid') price on the day concerned, or the most recent day before that on which prices were published.

Quoted shares and securities
The market value of quoted shares and securities is the lower of *either:*

- the lower closing price on the day of the gift plus a quarter of the difference between the lower and higher closing prices for those shares for the day (known as the *quarter up* rule), *or*
- half-way between the highest and lowest recorded bargains in those shares for the day.

EXAMPLE 9

You hold £1 ordinary shares in XYZ Plc, whose ordinary shares are listed on the Stock Exchange. You need to know their market value on 1 June 2000. The Stock Exchange Official Daily List, which is published after that day but which records prices on that day, shows that a £1 ordinary share in XYZ Plc was quoted at 175–181p with bargains marked at 176p, $176\frac{1}{2}$p and 179p. The quarter up valuation gives $176\frac{1}{2}$p and the mid-way valuation gives $177\frac{1}{2}$p. So the market value is taken to be $176\frac{1}{2}$p a share.

Unquoted shares and securities

Valuing these can get you into murky waters. It's very much a matter for negotiation with the Revenue.

- If the Revenue has recently decided for someone else what your particular type of shares are worth, that value will probably apply to your holding.
- The fictional 'purchaser' of the shares will be assumed to possess information about the company confidential to the directors at the time of the gift. This could put the value up or down.
- The Revenue will probably try to compare your unquoted shares with quoted shares in a company of equivalent size in the same line of business (if there is one).
- If you own 75 per cent of the ordinary shares you will usually have the power to put the company into liquidation. This could mean your holding is worth 75 per cent of the underlying assets of the company.
- If you have a bare majority of the ordinary shares, you will be able to decide what dividends are paid, so the after-tax earnings of the company must be a better guide to the value of your shares. The value of the assets will probably still be the starting point – *less* a discount, because you can't put the company into liquidation.
- If you are a minority shareholder (and not a director), the dividends paid will be a good guide to the value of your shares.
- For securities other than shares, e.g. loan stock, the rate of interest and the likelihood of its being paid are important. If you have a right to repayment of your capital at any time and the company is in a position to repay you, the value of your securities should be increased.

Life interests and reversions

If you give someone, for example your spouse, the right for life to all the income from particular property or the exclusive right to occupy or enjoy certain property, for inheritance tax you will put him or her in the same position as if he or she owned the property – see p. 283. So there is no tax advantage in giving your spouse just a *life interest*. However, from a practical point of view, you may wish to give a person no more than a life interest so that you can be sure that your capital will find its way to your children or grandchildren, for example, once the *life tenant* has died.

But make sure that your trustees have a wide power to apply capital for the benefit of the life tenant in case of emergencies.

Because the person with the life interest is treated as owning the whole property, a gift of the *reversion* (i.e. rights to the property when the life interest ends) is normally valued at *nil* – provided it's never been bought or sold.

Related property

Property is *related*, for tax purposes, if it is owned by your spouse (either directly or through trustees), or if it is now, or has been in the previous five years, owned by a charity to which you or your spouse gave it.

Where property is related to other property, and its value as part of the combined properties is greater than its value on its own, the higher value may be taken as the actual value.

EXAMPLE 10

Suppose you own 55 per cent of the ordinary shares in ABC Ltd and your wife owns 45 per cent. The value of your holding on its own is £70,000 and the value of your spouse's is £40,000. Suppose the value of a 100 per cent holding is £160,000. The value of your holding for inheritance tax is 55 per cent of £160,000, i.e. £88,000 – and not £70,000.

Related property disposed of after your death

Suppose that on your death you own 45 per cent of the ordinary shares of a family company, your wife owns 35 per cent and your son 20 per cent. Your 45 per cent will be valued as $\frac{45}{80}$ of an 80 per cent holding (i.e. your share of your and your spouse's combined holding).

However, if your executors make an actual sale of your 45 per cent and your spouse does not sell at the same time, and if the sale is to a complete outsider – at a price which is less than the holding's related value – within three years of your death, your executors can claim that the valuation on your death should be readjusted to a valuation on an unrelated basis.

Other sales after death: quoted shares or securities; interests in land

- If quoted shares or securities, shares in an open-ended investment company (OEIC) or units in an authorised unit trust are part of your estate on death, and the person who is liable to pay the inheritance tax on them sells them within a year of your death for less than their value immediately before your death, the later (lower) value may be substituted to re-calculate the tax liability.
- If your estate on death includes an interest in land which is later sold – by the person liable to pay the inheritance tax on the property – within four years of your death, and the sale price is less than the value at the date of your death (*less* by at least 5 per cent or £1,000), that later value may be substituted for the value on your death and the tax recalculated.

Business property

If certain conditions are met, business property is valued at less than its market value. This *business property relief* cuts the tax bill on a gift or bequest.

- An unincorporated business (e.g. a solicitor's practice or a corner shop) receives 100 per cent relief, i.e. tax on a gift is nil.
- From 6 April 1996, 100 per cent business relief is extended to all unquoted shares in qualifying companies regardless of the size of holding or voting entitlement. Prior to this, if you held 25 per cent or less of the voting rights, you would receive only 50 per cent relief if you transferred your shares. Shares dealt on the Alternative Investment Market are treated as unquoted.
- Quoted shares with a controlling interest receive 50 per cent relief.
- Land, buildings or equipment you own that are mainly or wholly used by a business you control, or a partnership of which you are a member (the rules are complicated), receive 50 per cent relief.

In all these cases, to get the relief, you must have owned the property for at least two years immediately before the gift or your death. If you've owned it for less than this, you may still qualify if the property replaces other property which you acquired more than two years before.

You won't, in any case, get the discount if the business consists wholly, or mainly, of:

- dealing (but not acting as a market-maker) in securities, stocks or shares, land or buildings
- the making or holding of investments (but holding cash on deposit for later use in the business does not count as an investment).

Property for personal use doesn't qualify for the discount. So if, for example, you control a company which owns cars used mainly for private purposes, the relief won't apply to the cars.

If the person giving the property dies within seven years, business relief may be lost if, for example, the property has been sold or unquoted shares have been floated on the Stock Exchange. Get professional advice before handing on your business.

Agricultural property

If you own agricultural land or buildings (which, from 6 April 1996, includes land used for short-rotation coppice), they can be valued at less than their market value for inheritance tax if certain conditions are met. You can get *agricultural property relief* at:

- 100 per cent if you have vacant possession or can get it within 24 months
- 50 per cent if the land is tenanted and you haven't the right to vacant possession within two years – but relief is increased to 100 per cent for land which is let after 31 August 1996, i.e. the rule requiring vacant possession within 24 months will not apply to new lets.

You need to have either owned the land for seven years while someone else has used it for agriculture, or to have farmed it yourself for two years.

Basic tax planning

Inheritance tax is not only a tax on the rich. On the other hand, many people who are no more than comfortably off – worth up to £350,000, for example – worry too much.

If you don't plan for inheritance tax, it's no skin off your nose. It simply means that there's less for your heirs. So don't dive into complicated schemes just to give your children slightly more than they would otherwise get. Above all, don't risk your own – or your spouse's – financial security by giving away more than you can afford while you're still alive.

All that apart, it does of course make a lot of sense to take account of the tax rules when you're planning your gifts. You may not necessarily go for the biggest tax-saving: tax planning is a mixture of knowing the rules and applying common sense.

First principles

- Make use of your exemptions – in particular, the annual exemption of £3,000 and the *normal expenditure out of income* exemption.
- Watch out for capital gains tax on lifetime gifts. Gifts of cash and certain other assets are not liable to the tax, but gifts of things like shares, holiday homes and valuables to anyone other than your spouse may mean a tax bill – see Chapter 14.
- If you can afford to make substantial gifts – more than the nil-rate band – make them sooner rather than later. If you survive for three years after making the gift, the tax is reduced on a sliding scale, and if you survive seven years there is no tax at all.
- If you have a stable marriage, make gifts to your spouse so that he or she can make tax-free gifts to other people. The gifts to your spouse must be genuine. If he or she *must* hand it on, the husband and wife exemption won't apply and the whole gift may become chargeable if you die within seven years.

In its pre-election manifesto, the Labour Party indicated that it would reform inheritance tax. However, major changes have so far failed to materialise since it entered government. It is impossible to say whether or not the inheritance tax regime will be tightened up in future. But, given the possibility that it might be, you might consider taking any planning measures sooner rather than later. But beware of making hasty decisions or entering into ill-thought-out schemes which could later prove to be costly mistakes.

Estate spreading

Estate spreading means giving away wealth now. The idea is to reduce the amount you're worth, so that there will be less tax to pay when you die. Estate spreading can make sense if:

- it doesn't destroy your financial independence *and*
- tax on death would be substantial, *or*
- the person receiving the gift needs it now.

For a married couple the first step in estate spreading is often said to be the equalisation of their estates – i.e. their total wealth is divided equally between them. Because gifts between husband and wife are normally exempt, this can usually be done tax-free.

This can have a number of advantages, particularly if one spouse had little personal wealth before. For example, both may be able to make use of the annual exemption, the small gifts exemption, and the nil-rate band. If the family wealth remains largely in the hands of one spouse, only that spouse may be able to make use of these exemptions. If the joint wealth is fairly substantial, it may be possible for each spouse to make gifts of more than the exemptions available. These will be totally tax-free after seven years.

The other major advantage is in the amount of tax payable on death. If each spouse now has wealth in his or her own right, each can leave at least part of their estate to the children or grandchildren. Without equalisation, there might be no tax at all to pay on the first death, but a very high bill on the second.

Estate freezing

You can use various techniques for 'freezing' the value of some of your wealth now by allowing the increase in value to go to someone else. There are various ways of doing this for a family business, for example, so that future growth goes to your children – you should take professional advice if you think you could benefit.

You could put investments into trust for your children or grandchildren. This reduces the value of your estate, though it may involve a tax bill at the time of the gift – see p. 262. But the gift can be set up to take advantage of the nil-rate band (i.e. up to £234,000 in 2000–1). Any growth in the investments accumulates in the trust and is no longer part of your estate. There's more about trusts on p. 283.

A simple way of setting up a trust for your children or grandchildren is to use life insurance policies. Provided the premiums can be paid out of your *normal expenditure,* they will be tax-free gifts. But you must make sure that the proceeds don't form part of your estate – see p. 228.

Unit trusts can also be put into trust for your children or grandchildren in this way, using a regular savings plan. Some unit trust managers can help set up the trust.

The family home

This is most people's largest single asset and can, on its own, push you over the nil-rate band. If you give it away and continue to live in it, this may count as a *gift with reservation* (see p. 268) and may not save any inheritance tax. If the person you give it to lives in the property with you and pays a fair share of the expenses, you might save tax – get advice.

A couple may be able to save some tax if they jointly own the home, depending on the form of ownership (in England and Wales). *Joint tenants* share ownership of the home. But they both (or all if there are several owners) own the whole home and have identical interests in it. If one dies, their share automatically goes to the other, and can't be given to anyone else.

It still forms part of the estate for tax purposes, so there could be tax to pay if the other joint tenant is not the wife or husband. If the joint tenants are married, there'll be no tax on the first death, but the whole value of the house would be in the estate when the second partner died.

With a *tenancy in common,* each owns a completely separate share of the home which can be left to whomever they wish. So you could leave your share to your children rather than to your spouse: there would be a possible tax liability on the value of your share, but the size of your partner's estate would be reduced.

If it's important to you to pass on the family home intact, take professional advice on the best way to organise it.

Make a will

Your will can be a very important step in planning to reduce inheritance tax (though it is currently possible to rearrange things after your death to reduce the bill – see p. 287). Drawing up your will may also alert you to steps you need to take to minimise your tax bill, for example by making lifetime gifts.

Apart from any tax-saving, a will is also the best way to make sure that your worldly goods end up where you want after your death. If you don't leave a valid will, the intestacy rules distribute them in ways that might not be what you intended. For example, if you live with someone without being married to him or her, he or she might get nothing.

Here are some points to bear in mind.

- If you're married, make sure that you leave your spouse enough to live on. Remember that old age can be expensive and prolonged – so, if you can, leave a large safety margin. It's only when you've done this that you should look at ways of cutting the inheritance tax bill.

- Consider making enough taxable gifts on death to use up your nil-rate band. You can do this by making gifts direct to your children or grandchildren.
- Unless you say that gifts are *subject to tax,* the tax on them will normally come out of the residue of your estate. If you've left the residue to your spouse, much (or all) of it could be swallowed up in paying the tax on other gifts you've made in your will.
- If you are uncertain about what to do with the whole or part of your estate, you can set up a discretionary trust (see p. 285) in your will, giving the trustees two years to give away the property. You can discuss your wishes with the trustees so that they know what sorts of priorities you would set; and if they make the gifts within the two years, the tax is the same as if you had made the gifts yourself.

If there's a large asset you're hoping to pass on, such as a family home, business or farm, take professional advice about drawing up the will – there are various subtle tax points to be watched.

Trusts

Trusts are not only for the rich. Even if you're no more than comfortably off, one type of trust – the *accumulation and maintenance trust* – can be worth considering for your children, grandchildren or other younger people for whom you've got a soft spot. And many people who are not rich at all set up trusts in their wills. Most trusts have a settlor, trustees and beneficiaries.

- **The settlor** sets up the trust and puts money (or property) into it.
- **The trustees** 'own' the trust property. But, unlike a normal owner, they can't do what they like with it. They have to follow the instructions of the *instrument* – often a deed or a will – which sets up the trust. There are also legal rules about what they must (and must not) do.
- **The beneficiaries** are the lucky people who will – or, in some cases, may – be given money, or property, or the use of property, from the trust. See Example 11.

Trusts with an interest in possession

The simplest type of trust is one with a life interest, for example a gift 'to Gladys for life, and then to my children in equal shares'. Gladys has an *interest in possession*, while the children have a *reversionary*

EXAMPLE 11

Ned sets up a trust in his will. He wants his wife Gladys to have all his money, but he wants the house to go to the children after her death. So he leaves the money direct to Gladys, but he leaves the house to trustees 'in trust for my wife Gladys for her life and afterwards to my children in equal shares'. Gladys and the children are the beneficiaries.

Note: Ned is careful to take competent legal advice. As a result, the trust is worded so that if Gladys is short of money, the trustees can 'advance' money to her – i.e. they can raise capital on the security of the house and give it to Gladys. (If they do advance money in this way, the children will get less.) If Gladys wants to move, she can sell the house and buy another.

---

interest – i.e. they are entitled to the trust property when the interest in possession comes to an end.

With gifts to an interest-in-possession trust made during your lifetime, there will be a possible tax bill only if you die within seven years of making the gift. If you make the gift on death, the property forms part of your estate.

The property covered by the interest in possession is treated as being owned by the person who has the interest. If he or she dies or gives it away, tax is charged as if it were his or her own property:

- if the person dies, the value is added to his or her estate
- if the person gives it away, tax is due only if he or she dies within seven years of the gift.

The only difference between an interest in possession and ordinary property is that the tax is paid by the trustees, not by the person with the interest in possession.

If you have an interest in possession and the property becomes yours, you become 'absolutely entitled' to it – there is no tax at this stage. There could, of course, be tax when you die or give it away. There's also no tax if the property goes back to the settlor (or to the settlor's widow or widower, if the settlor has died, provided fewer than two years have passed since the death).

If you have the reversionary interest in a trust, the interest has no value for inheritance tax purposes, so you can give it away without incurring any tax problems. For example, if Gladys' children grow up and become comfortably off in their own right, they might decide to pass their reversionary interest on to their own children, a process sometimes referred to as *generation skipping*.

Discretionary trusts

These are trusts where the trustees can decide who gets the money. For example, you could set up a trust under which the trustees could pay income (or capital) 'in such proportions as they in their absolute discretion shall decide, to all or any of my children, David, Maureen, Alison, any of their children, grandchildren or remoter issue, with any income or capital remaining on 1 August 2080 to be given to charitable purposes'.

Gifts to discretionary trusts on death, for example if you set one up in your will, count as part of your estate. In your lifetime, they count as chargeable transfers (see p. 262). But with gifts to the following types of discretionary trusts there will be no inheritance tax unless you die within seven years of the gift (when there may be a tax bill):

- a trust for disabled people
- an accumulation-and-maintenance trust (see below).

Gifts from a discretionary trust of its capital are liable to inheritance tax at a rate which depends on the amount given away. And the money or property in the trust may be liable to inheritance tax even if it is not given to anyone else. Once every ten years, there will be a *periodic charge* on the trust, which has the effect of collecting about the same amount of tax as if the trust's property belonged to an individual and were passed on at death once every 30 years.

Accumulation-and-maintenance trusts

This is a special type of discretionary trust. If you stick to the rules, there is no tax to pay when the capital from the trust is paid to the beneficiaries, and there is no periodic charge.

Accumulation-and-maintenance trusts are commonly used to put money into trust for children. While your children are still young, you set up the trust and put some capital in it. Income made by the trust is accumulated (i.e. kept in the trust). Any income which isn't accumulated must be used for the 'maintenance, education or benefit' of your children.

Some time after your children reach 18, and by the time they reach 25, the trust may come to an end and the property may be shared among them. If you don't want the trust to hand out the capital, you can give the children the right to the income instead. You can give the capital later (see Rule 2 opposite).

If you set up a trust for your children, you'll be taxed at your top rate of tax on any income paid out for them while they're under 18 (unless they're married) – see below for rules. The money will count as *your* income, not your children's.

If the trust *isn't* for your children, or they're over 18 or married, income paid out for them will count as *their* income. Any child, no matter how young, is entitled to the full personal allowance of £4,385 in 2000–1. In 2000–1, income received by an accumulation-and-maintenance trust is taxed at either 34 per cent or, if it is income from shares, unit trusts and so on, at 25 per cent. If income, which is taxed at 34 per cent when distributed, is paid out to the child, he or she can claim back the tax deducted. So, for example, the trustees might pay a gross income of £3,000 from which they deduct tax at 34 per cent (£1,020). They hand over a net amount of £1,980 to the child, who can then claim back the £1,020 tax already deducted.

Income paid to your children

Income paid from a trust set up by you to children of yours who are under 18 and unmarried is taxed as your income and at your top rate of tax (unless the total comes to no more than £100 – see p. 203). You get a tax credit equal to the tax which the trustees have to deduct before they pay out the income.

Normally, the trustees have to deduct tax at the 22 per cent basic rate, *plus* an additional rate of 12 per cent – making 34 per cent in all. If you pay tax at the starting rate of 10 per cent or the basic rate of 22 per cent only, you can claim the extra 24 or 12 per cent back from the Revenue – but you must pay this to the trustees or your child.

If you have to pay tax at the higher rate of 40 per cent on the income, you will have to hand over an extra 40 – 34 = 6 per cent to the Revenue. You can claim back this extra tax from the trustees (or – though you probably wouldn't want to – from the child who receives the income).

The rules in detail

Rule 1   At least one of the beneficiaries must be alive when the trust is set up. So a trust 'for my son Alan's children' is no good unless Alan already has a child. Any children of Alan's born later are added to the list of beneficiaries. If all the beneficiaries die, but others could be born, the trust still keeps going.

Rule 2   At least one of the beneficiaries must get an *interest in possession* in at least part of the trust property by the time he or she reaches the age of 25. A right to the income of part (or all) of the property is an interest in possession. So is the right to a share of the trust capital.

Rule 3   There can be no entitlement to trust property until a beneficiary has acquired an interest in possession. (This doesn't contradict Rule 2: to get an interest in possession you must have a *right* to income or capital. If trustees decide merely to hand out income or capital to you there's no right to it, and no interest in possession.)

Rule 4   The trust must come to an end within 25 years, unless all the beneficiaries have one grandparent in common. Illegitimate and adopted children count in the same way as legitimate children. If one of the beneficiaries dies before getting an interest in possession, his or her share can go (if the trust deed says so) to his or her widow, widower, or children.

After your death

Re-arrangement of your estate by agreement

After your death the gifts you made on death can currently be re-arranged – the revised gifts take effect for inheritance tax just as if they had actually been made by you. (The same is true of arrangements made between your relatives if you die without leaving a will.) Various rules apply:

- the new arrangements must take effect within two years of your death
- the arrangements must have the consent of all beneficiaries under your will who are affected by them
- the parties to the arrangement must give their consent in return for what they get under the arrangements (or for no return at all) – not in return for anything else.

Bare trusts

As an alternative to setting up a formal trust, you can simply hold property as nominee for someone else – e.g. as a parent you could act as nominee for your child. This type of arrangement is called a bare trust. A bare trust does not have to be restricted to one person – it can cover a group of people but, once set up, the individuals in the group and the shares they have in the property cannot be changed.

Unlike the other trusts described in this chapter, the ultimate beneficiary of a bare trust continues to be treated as the owner of the trust property, so there are no inheritance tax implications either when a bare trust is set up or when it ceases. The nominee must carry out any instructions from the owner. Since a child under the age of 18 and unmarried cannot give legally valid instructions, a bare trust can be a useful way of accumulating property until a child reaches his or her majority. However, once the child is 18 (or marries if earlier), he or she can decide to take full possession of the trust property.

If you hold property you've given to your child on bare trust for him or her, any income paid out to the child or used for his or her benefit may count as yours (see p. 203). Until 5 April 1999 any income left to accumulate within a bare trust was taxed as that of the child. However, where on or after 9 March 1999, a gift from a parent is paid into or added to a bare trust, after 5 April 1999 income paid may be taxed as that of the parent even if it is not paid out. Capital gains on investments held in the trust continue to count as those of the child, so bare trusts can still be useful.

To reclaim any inheritance tax paid, you must do so generally within six months of re-arrangement. The relief can be claimed even if:

- the effect is to make someone a beneficiary of your estate who was not one under your will
- the people concerned have already received their gifts.

If someone refuses a gift (or disclaims it within two years) your estate is taxed as if the gift to that person was never made. No claim needs to be made in this case.

Re-arrangement – is it worth it?

A re-arrangement of your gifts is a good idea if you haven't left enough for your surviving spouse and have given more than enough to other members of your family. They can redirect their gifts without a further tax charge. (Such a re-arrangement could mean a *refund* of tax because more of the revised gift would be tax-free.)

Alternatively, if your surviving spouse has far more than will be needed, he or she can direct gifts to other members of your family. And if, for example, you have given property to your wife for life and after her death to your son, they could (if your son is over 18) agree to split the property between them now. This might reduce the tax when your wife dies. However:

* the arrangements can't alter retrospectively the income tax position. Someone who has been entitled to receive income from a gift which is subsequently given up is taxed on the income he or she was entitled to receive
* if a parent redirects a legacy producing income of more than £100 a year (see p. 203) to his or her unmarried child under 18, the parent will be taxed on that income until the child reaches 18 or marries
* there is a similar rule for capital gains tax. Variations and disclaimers within two years of your death can be treated as if you had made the revised gifts yourself and as if the original gifts had not been made. Without this rule, one of your heirs who gave away inherited assets could face a capital gains tax bill, because there can be capital gains tax to pay on assets that are given away.

Paying inheritance tax

Who has to pay

The Revenue looks first to the giver for tax on a chargeable gift. So if you want the other person to pay the tax, get a promise that he or she will pay. If you don't pay the tax, the Revenue can get it from the other person anyway. If the person receiving the gift has given it away to someone else, the Revenue can recover the tax from that person.

If you die within seven years of making a potentially tax-free gift, the tax, if any, is due from the person you made the gift to. The same is true if you die within seven years of making a chargeable transfer on which further tax becomes due. If the recipient of the gift does not pay up, the tax can instead be collected from your estate.

For tax on your death, your personal representatives – or the trustees of settled property if you died having an *interest in possession* in settled property – are liable for the tax. So are the beneficiaries if they have received the property. In general, neither the estate nor individuals can be asked to pay more inheritance tax than the value of the assets they have received. But where a beneficiary has an interest in part of an asset, he or she can be liable to pay tax on the whole asset.

When to tell the Revenue
When you make a chargeable gift you have to tell the Revenue if:

- your total of taxable gifts for the current tax year exceeds £10,000, or if
- your running total, including the current gift, exceeds £40,000.

You tell the Revenue about lifetime gifts on form IHT-100 which you get from the Capital Taxes Offices.*

Always keep accurate records of the gifts you've made, and the tax, if any, you've paid on them.

For tax on your death, your personal representatives usually have to prepare an *Inland Revenue account* and submit it to the Probate Registry as part of seeking probate. This lists the value of every asset in your estate (shares, homes, valuables, etc.), including those which are jointly owned. They'll also have to give details of:

- gifts made in the seven years before death which aren't tax-free, including transfers of value (e.g. where you sold something for less than its market value)
- interests you had in trusts.

You give these details on form IHT200 available from the Capital Taxes Offices. If your estate counts as a *small estate*, meaning that its gross value is no more than twice the nil-rate band – i.e. twice £234,000 = £468,000 in 2000–1 – your representatives can instead send in simplified accounts using form IHT202. And if your estate is valued at no more than £210,000 (and various other rules are met), your representatives do not have to submit accounts at all unless the Revenue requests them (which it does in a sample of cases).

When to pay the tax
Tax on lifetime gifts is normally due six months after the end of the month in which you make the gift. But if you make the gift after 5 April and before 1 October, tax is due on 30 April in the following year.

Tax on your death is payable six months after the end of the month in which you die, but your personal representatives will usually want to get probate (or letters of administration) before then. To do so they will have to deliver the accounts and pay the tax first.

Interest is charged on unpaid tax from the time it was payable. The rate for inheritance tax was 5 per cent when we went to press.

Payment by instalments

Sometimes inheritance tax can be paid in instalments and in some cases the instalments do not attract interest. The instalment option is available for lifetime gifts (if the other person pays the tax) and for gifts on death of:

- land and buildings, wherever situated
- a business or an interest in a business
- timber, where a lifetime gift has triggered tax deferred from a previous owner's death
- a controlling holding of shares or securities – whether quoted or unquoted – in a company
- a non-controlling holding of unquoted shares or securities in a company, if certain conditions are specified.

If you want to pay by instalments you should tell the Revenue in writing by the normal due date for paying tax (see above). The tax has to be paid in ten equal yearly instalments. The first instalment is due on the normal due date for paying the tax. Normally interest is due on the outstanding tax. However, in the case of agricultural land, a business or an interest in a business, or many holdings of unquoted shares or securities, interest is due only if instalments are not paid on time. Bear in mind that these types of assets might, in any case, qualify for business property relief or agricultural property relief, in which case inheritance tax might not be payable at all – see p. 278.

If you are paying by instalments, you do not have to spread payments over the full ten years – you can pay off the remaining balance at any time.

Giving property in place of tax

If the Treasury and relevant government ministers agree, you may be able to give property to the nation as an alternative to paying some or all of an inheritance tax bill.

The property must be exceptional enough to count as heritage property (see p. 272) and is usually valued at the date on which you make the offer. The property may be handed over to an appropriate public body. Alternatively, it may remain in your hands, provided the property stays permanently within the UK and the public has reasonable access to it.

Quick succession relief

If you die within five years of receiving a gift on which tax has been paid, some of that tax can be subtracted from the tax due on your estate. The amount subtracted is worked out by two simple calculations:

- divide the net value of the gift to you by the gross value of the gift, and multiply the result by the tax paid on the gift
- deduct 20 per cent of the answer for each *complete* year since the gift.

The tax credit is given whether or not you still own the gift at your death.

There is a similar relief for inheritance tax on the termination of your interest in settled property, whether or not the termination takes place on your death.

EXAMPLE 12

Joe left Bruce £30,000 free of tax in January 1999. Joe's estate paid the tax on the gift, which came to £20,000. Bruce died 18 months later. His estate is given a tax credit of:

$$\frac{30,000}{50,000} \times £20,000 \times 80 \text{ per cent} = £9,600$$

Life insurance

Life insurance policies provide a way of paying inheritance tax (in addition to offering a simple way of setting up trusts – see Chapter 13):

- *term* insurance can provide money to pay tax if you die within seven years of making a potentially tax-free gift (this would have helped Margaret and Brian pay the tax on their gifts in Example 6)
- *whole life* insurance can pay out to cover the tax when you die on an asset you don't want to sell, such as a family home or business.

For how to keep the proceeds out of your estate (and avoid paying inheritance tax on them), see Chapter 13.

Inheritance tax rates since 1986

From 15 March 1988, tax above the nil-rate band is 40 per cent (except that the rate on gifts which are chargeable while you are still alive is 20 per cent, i.e. half the death rate).

Before 15 March 1988, there were several tax bands. The bands and tax rates are given below. The first percentage is the tax rate on death; the second (in brackets) is the tax rate on gifts chargeable while you are still alive.

Date		nil-rate band
6 April 2000 to 5 April 2001		£234,000
6 April 1999 to 5 April 2000		£231,000
6 April 1998 to 5 April 1999		£223,000
6 April 1997 to 5 April 1998		£215,000
6 April 1996 to 5 April 1997		£200,000
6 April 1995 to 5 April 1996		£154,000
10 March 1992 to 5 April 1995		£150,000
6 April 1991 to 9 March 1992		£140,000
6 April 1990 to 5 April 1991		£128,000
6 April 1989 to 5 April 1990		£118,000
15 March 1988 to 5 April 1989		£110,000
17 March 1987 to 14 March 1988		£90,000
£90,001 to £140,000	30% (15%)	
£140,001 to £220,000	40% (20%)	
£220,001 to £330,000	50% (25%)	
£330,001 and over	60% (30%)	
18 March 1986 to 16 March 1987		£71,000
£71,001 to £95,000	30% (15%)	
£95,001 to £129,000	35% ($17\frac{1}{2}$%)	
£129,001 to £164,000	40% (20%)	
£164,001 to £206,000	45% ($22\frac{1}{2}$%)	
£206,001 to £257,000	50% (25%)	
£257,001 to £317,000	55% ($27\frac{1}{2}$%)	
£317,001 and over	60% (30%)	

Useful Inland Revenue reading

You can ring the Inland Revenue Orderline* for helpsheets, leaflets and notes.

Leaflets and notes

IHT2	Inheritance tax on lifetime gifts
IHT3	Inheritance tax – an introduction
IHT8	Alterations to an inheritance following a death – inheritance tax
IHT11	Inheritance tax and penalties
IHT14	Inheritance tax – the personal representatives responsibilities
IHT15	Inheritance tax – how to calculate the liability
IHT16	Inheritance tax – settled property
IHT17	Inheritance tax – business, farms and woodlands
IHT18	Inheritance tax – foreign aspects
IR45	What to do when someone dies
IR67	Capital taxation and the national heritage
IR88	Capital tax relief for national heritage property – how to make a claim
IR152	Trusts – an introduction
IR152	Our heritage – your right to see tax exempt works of art
SA107	Notes on trust etc.
SA154	Tax calculation guide for trusts and estates
SA901	Notes on trust and estates
SA901L	Notes on trust and estate Lloyds underwriters
SA902	Notes on trust and estate partnerships
SA903	Notes on trust and estate property
SA904	Notes on trust and estate foreign
SA905	Notes on trust and estate capital gains
SA906	Notes on trust and estate non-residence
SA950	Trust and estate tax return guide

Helpsheets

When you receive a helpsheet, make sure it relates to the tax year for which you want information.

IR270	Trusts and settlements – income treated as the settlor's
IR294	Trusts and capital gains tax
IR390	Trusts and estate of deceased persons – tax credit relief for capital gains

Addresses

Inland Revenue contacts

General web site:
www.inlandrevenue.gov.uk

Orderline
Tel: (0845) 9000 404
for tax returns, helpsheets, leaflets and notes

Self-assessment helpline
Tel: (0845) 9000 444
Fax: (0845) 9000 604
Email:
saorderline.ir@gtnet.gov.uk
Web site: www.ir-efile.gov.uk

Electronic version of the tax return
Helpline: (01952) 294005

Payment of tax by debit card
Helpline: (0845) 305 1000

Individual Savings Accounts (ISAs)
Helpline: (0845) 604 1701

Working families tax credit
Helpline: (0845) 609 5000
Northern Ireland:
(0845) 609 7000

Disabled person's tax credit
Helpline: (0845) 605 5858
Northern Ireland:
(0845) 609 7000

New employers
Helpline: (0845) 607 0143
Minicom: (08457) 419402

Established employers
Helpline: (08457) 143143
Minicom: (08457) 419402

Construction industry scheme
Orderline: (0845) 300 0551
Contractors' helpline: (0345) 335588
Subcontractors' helpline: (0845) 300 0581

Inland Revenue IR35 Service
Penhaligon House
Trinity Street
St Austell
Cornwall PL25 5BA
Fax: (0845) 302 3535
*Copies of contracts must be
supplied together with relevant
information (such as recent
history of work engagements),
National Insurance number,
Inland Revenue reference
numbers and the intermediary
company's postcode*

Inland Revenue Tax Bulletin
Subscription from:
Miss S Williams
Room 530
22 Kingsway
London
WC2B 6NR
Tel: 020-7438 7700
Web site:
www.inlandrevenue.gov.uk

**National Insurance
Contributions Office (NICO)**
(Refunds Group)
Longbenton
Newcastle upon Tyne NE98 1ZZ

Other contacts

Adjudicator's Office
3rd Floor
Haymarket House
28 Haymarket
London SW1Y 4SP
Tel: 020-7930 2292
Fax: 020-7930 2298
Email:
adjudicators@gtnet.gov.uk
Web site:
www.open.gov.uk/adjoff

Capital Taxes Office
Ferrers House
PO Box 38
Castle Meadow Road
Nottingham NG2 1BB
Tel: 0115-974 2400
Fax: 0115-974 2432
Web site:
www.inlandrevenue.gov.uk/cto

Capital Taxes Office
16 Picardy Place
Edinburgh EH1 3NB
Tel: 0131-524 3000
Fax: 0131-524 3096
Web site:
www.inlandrevenue.gov.uk/cto

Capital Taxes Office
52–58 Great Victoria Street
Belfast
BT2 7QL
Tel: 028-9050 5353
Fax: 028-9050 5305
Web site:
www.inlandrevenue.gov.uk/cto

Financial Intermediaries and Claims Office (FICO)
Customer Support Team
St John's House
Merton Road
Bootle
Merseyside L69 9BB
Tel: 0151-472 6106
Fax: 0151-472 6142

Financial Intermediaries and Claims Office International
Fitz Roy House
PO Box 46
Nottingham NG2 1BD
Tel: 0115-974 2000
Fax: 0115-974 1863

Shares Valuation Division
Fitz Roy House
PO Box 46
Nottingham NG2 1BD
Tel: 0115-974 2222
Fax: 0115-974 2197

Stamp Offices
Belfast 028-9050 5124/5/6
  Fax: 028-9050 5130
Birmingham 0121-633 3313
  Fax: 0121-643 8381
Bristol 0117-927 2022
  Fax: 0117-925 3599
Edinburgh 0131-556 8998
  Fax: 0131-557 2886
Manchester 0161-476 1741
  Fax: 0161-834 2752
Newcastle 0191-261 1199
  Fax: 0191-230 4258
Worthing (01903) 508962
  Fax: (01903) 508953

Stamp Allowance Claims Section
Manchester Stamp Office
Alexandra House
Parsonage
Manchester M60 9BT

Index

Which? Way to Save and Invest

With an estimated 30,000 financial products now on the market, among them many based on the performance of the ever-proliferating 'dot.coms', what chance do you have of making an informed choice which will ensure that your money works for you?

Fully revised and updated, *Which? Way to Save and Invest* helps you to choose a reliable home for your money, whether it is £50 or £50,000.

This no-nonsense, accessible guide shows you how to formulate a strategy that suits your financial circumstances and how to put it into effect, with or without an adviser, via traditional routes or the Internet. It assesses the vast range of financial products, including bank and building society accounts, National Savings, Individual Savings Accounts (ISAs), Venture Capital Trusts, other tax-efficient investments, annuities, pensions, shares, and ethical and 'alternative' investments.

Paperback   210 x 120mm   448 pages   £14.99

Available from bookshops, and by post from
Which?, Dept TAZM, Castlemead,
Gascoyne Way, Hertford X, SG14 1LH
or phone FREE on (0800) 252100
quoting Dept TAZM and your credit card details

Be Your Own Financial Adviser

Financial advice, like any other advice, can be good, bad or indifferent. But armed with the right facts, and some basic techniques, you can be your own financial adviser. This guide shows you how to clarify your financial needs and create a financial plan to meet them, just as a personal adviser would do for you.

Be Your Own Financial Adviser profiles the different products (investments, savings, insurance, loans) available, shows you how they can fit into your financial plan, how to choose the type best suited to you and where to get current information about them. It alerts you to any areas where you could be losing out, such as having savings in uncompetitive accounts, or where you are taking unnecessary risks with investments.

The book also lists the points to check out when you're talking to providers of financial products or financial advisers and how to interpret the information you're given. Simply written and full of useful tips and warnings, the book puts you in charge of your financial destiny.

Paperback   216 x 135mm   432 pages   £9.99

Available from bookshops, and by post from
Which?, Dept TAZM, Castlemead,
Gascoyne Way, Hertford X, SG14 1LH
or phone FREE on (0800) 252100
quoting Dept TAZM and your credit card details

The Which? Guide to Shares

In Britain, one in four adults has become a share-owner, having responded to privatisation issues and, more recently, windfall shares from building society conversions. If you already have one or two shareholdings, or you are considering shares for the first time, this book will show you how these fascinating and versatile investments can help you achieve your financial ambitions.

It covers the role of shares in financial planning; how to buy and sell shares in the high street, through a traditional broker, or over the Internet; the range of shares available; risk – and how to turn it to your advantage; how shares are taxed, and how, legitimately, to avoid tax; portfolios for every pocket; the perks that accompany some shares; mastering rights issues, takeover bids, and so on; and how to play the stock market without even buying any shares. Other topics covered include private share transfers, the taxation of capital gains, share buybacks and special types of share such as 'zeros'.

The Which? Guide to Shares is a detailed introduction to the intriguing, fun and potentially rewarding world of share ownership, complete with extensive glossary and a useful address section.

Paperback   216 x 135mm   288 pages   £9.99

Available from bookshops, and by post from
Which?, Dept TAZM, Castlemead,
Gascoyne Way, Hertford X, SG14 1LH
or phone FREE on (0800) 252100
quoting Dept TAZM and your credit card details